THE ASTROLOGY BOOK OF SURPRISING DISCOVERIES

THE ASTROLOGY BOOK OF SURPRISING DISCOVERIES

DREW SLATER

iUniverse®

THE ASTROLOGY BOOK OF SURPRISING DISCOVERIES

iUniverse books may be ordered through booksellers or by contacting:

iUniverse
1663 Liberty Drive
Bloomington, IN 47403
www.iuniverse.com
1-800-Authors (1-800-288-4677)

ISBN: 978-1-5320-6880-5 (sc)
ISBN: 978-1-5320-6881-2 (e)

Library of Congress Control Number: 2019901861

Print information available on the last page.

iUniverse rev. date: 07/16/2019

PREFACE

The purpose of this book is to clarify the fundamental tenets of astrology through the use of research. What we will emerge with is a new kind of astrology that is faithful to what the ancients believed, but also compatible with the research. All that is required of the reader is a logical mind. You are about to embark upon an exciting intellectual adventure! Enjoy the ride!

Readers should know that astrologers have their own special way of speaking. For example, it is very common for us to refer to the Sun, Moon and planets as simply "the planets." It is just easier to speak in this shorthand fashion. Astrologers know perfectly well that the Sun and Moon are not numbered among the planets, although the rocky Moon seems more like a planet than the fiery Sun.

It is also common for astrologers to anthropomorphize the planets. Venus is often called "she," while such planets as Mars, Jupiter or Saturn may be called "he." Astrologers know perfectly well that planets are inanimate objects and therefore without gender, but sometimes what the planets symbolize can have gender connotations. Astrologers, in their shorthand style, will also confer qualities on the planets, when we actually mean that persons symbolized by the heavenly bodies possess those qualities. We may say that Venus is "artistic" or that Jupiter is "optimistic."

A quaint term that is still very fashionable in astrological circles is the word "ruler." Since Mercury is associated with thought and mental pursuits, we may say that Mercury "rules" intellectuals. Each of the twelve zodiac signs has a planetary ruler, but the type of person that you are gives you another ruler as well that describes that kind of person. This other ruler is apt to be a planet that is placed in a powerful position in your chart. Researchers have found that the zones of your horoscope known as "cadent" are the most powerful, which is contrary to what astrologers previously had believed. Just like other disciplines, astrology needs to evolve and advance when new facts come to light, such as those in this book.

PART ONE

RESEARCH ON THE TWELVE SIGNS

THREE ZODIACS

As we push forth through the twenty-first century, we find astrology, that venerable old study of the heavens, in a state of considerable chaos and confusion. Did you know that there are two different zodiacs currently in use? The tropical zodiac, popular in the western world, is based on the four seasons. The sidereal zodiac, popular in the eastern world, is based on the twelve constellations. When a Tropicalist speaks of Aries, he refers to a person born between March 21 and April 20. When a Siderealist speaks of Aries, he means a person born between April 14 and May 15. Obviously, when you have different astrologers referring to separate groups of people by the same name, you've got a problem! Since the twelve familiar names rightfully belong to the sidereal zodiac, it would have helped if Tropicalists had chosen new names for their twelve signs, but that did not happen. Here are the twelve signs and some basic information about them:

	Sign	Ruler	Element	Action
1.	Aries	Mars	fire	cardinal
2.	Taurus	Venus	earth	fixed
3.	Gemini	Mercury	air	mutable
4.	Cancer	Moon	water	cardinal
5.	Leo	Sun (?)	fire	fixed
6.	Virgo	Mercury	earth	mutable
7.	Libra	Venus	air	cardinal
8.	Scorpio	Mars	water	fixed
9.	Sagittarius	Jupiter	fire	mutable
10.	Capricorn	Saturn	earth	cardinal
11.	Aquarius	Saturn	air	fixed
12.	Pisces	Jupiter	water	mutable

If the reader is not already familiar with this information, he will need to memorize it. Otherwise, he will not be able to understand the rest of this book. That would be a shame because these pages are filled with facts and concepts that you won't find anywhere else.

We have placed a question mark after the Sun because we do not consider it the true ruler of Leo. The reason for this will be explained later. You'd think that, if astrology had been properly researched, there would be no argument between Tropicalists and Siderealists. Everyone would know whether the traits of Aries were possessed by a person born April 8 or a person born May 8, or perhaps neither one. In this book, we hope to learn once and for all what is true. Our goal is to construct an astrology based entirely on research as its foundation. We will break down each month into keywords that will tell us the basic traits of that month. From there, it should be easy to determine which sign possesses those traits. We also will discover, from time to time, new traits that have never been considered before. We will list the names of persons in numerous occupations, along with their birthdays. What a person does ought to tell us who he is. Is it not better to base our conclusions on facts rather than unsubstantiated folklore? Our 7,000 birthdays can't be wrong.

Opposite signs are important in astrology. There are six pairs of opposites: Aries and Libra, Taurus and Scorpio, Gemini and Sagittarius, Cancer and Capricorn, Leo and Aquarius, and Virgo and Pisces. The twelve signs are twelve directions from the Earth. If I am standing north of you, then you must be standing south of me, since north and south are opposite directions. Similarly, if the Sun is in the direction from the Earth known as Scorpio, then the Earth must be in the direction from the Sun known as Taurus, since Scorpio and Taurus are opposite directions. For every Sun sign, there is a corresponding Earth sign that is opposite it. Therefore, we can construct an Earth sign zodiac and show the dates for each sign. The dates fall midway between the tropical dates and the sidereal dates. For example, Tropicalists have a sign (Leo) that starts July 23, while Siderealists have a sign (Cancer) that starts July 17. We will have an Earth sign that begins July 20. We will use our own names for our signs, so as not to add further confusion to the already existing chaos.

Here are the Earth signs:

Sign	Precise Dates	Extended Dates
Patterns	July 20 - Aug. 20	July 14 - Aug. 26
Towers	Aug. 20 - Sept. 20	Aug. 14 - Sept. 26

Fences	Sept. 20 - Oct. 20	Sept. 14 - Oct. 26
Rocks	Oct. 20 - Nov. 19	Oct. 14 - Nov. 25
Rapiers	Nov. 19 - Dec. 19	Nov. 13 - Dec. 25
Antennas	Dec. 19 - Jan. 17	Dec. 13 - Jan. 23
Lights	Jan. 17 - Feb. 16	Jan. 11 - Feb. 22
Slingshots	Feb. 16 - Mar. 18	Feb. 10 - Mar. 24
Bridges	Mar. 18 - Apr. 17	Mar. 12 - Apr. 23
Drills	Apr. 17 - May 18	Apr. 11 - May 24
Trumpets	May 18 - June 18	May 12 - June 24
Hammers	June 18 - July 20	June 12 - July 26

The reason for the extended dates is that the change from one sign to the next is believed to be gradual. This is known as the "cusp effect." We will explain later why each name was thought appropriate for each sign. Our research samples are not large enough to convince some who don't believe in astrology that they should believe in it — but we think the samples are big enough so that a person who does believe would expect to see some kind of a trend that suggests a particular kind of person who is apt to be born in a particular month. Also, we should remember that the greater the quantity of a sample, the lesser the quality. If we were to study the fifty greatest tennis players, that would be a very impressive group. But if we studied the top 500, we would be including a great many players that nobody has ever heard of. And the lesser the talent, the less likely that the person will have the right astrological significators.

CREATIVE WRITERS

3/12 Edward Albee
3/18 Ovid
3/20 Henrik Ibsen
3/21 Phyllis McGinley
3/26 Tennessee Williams
3/26 Maxim Gorky
3/26 Robert Frost

3/26 A. E. Housman
3/27 Louis Simpson
3/30 Paul Verlaine
3/30 Sean O'Casey
3/31 Nikolai Gogol
4/01 Edmond Rostand
4/02 Emile Zola
4/04 Robert Sherwood
4/04 Maya Angelou
4/05 Algernon Swinburne
4/05 Richard Eberhart
4/07 William Wordsworth
4/09 Charles Baudelaire
4/13 Samuel Beckett
4/15 Henry James
4/16 Anatole France
4/17 Thornton Wilder
4/23 Edwin Markham

ARTISTS

3/15 Michelangelo
3/22 Anthony Van Dyck
3/25 Gutzon Borglum
3/30 Vincent van Gogh
3/30 Francisco de Goya
4/16 Raphael
4/17 El Greco
4/20 Joan Miro
4/23 Leonardo Da Vinci
4/23 J. M. W. Turner

UNUSUAL IDEAS, MYSTICISM

3/18 Manly Palmer Hall
4/02 John Blofeld
4/04 Edwin Steinbrecher
4/05 F. T. Brooks
4/05 Marilyn Ferguson
4/06 Richard Alpert
4/12 Joan Grant
4/13 William Quan Judge
4/14 Erich Von Daniker
4/15 Bessie Leo
4/17 George Adamski

TOP FILM ACTORS

3/14 Michael Caine
3/18 Robert Donat
3/20 William Hurt
3/20 Michael Redgrave
3/22 Joseph Schildkraut
3/22 Karl Malden
3/22 Haing S. Ngor
3/25 Ed Begley
3/28 Dirk Bogarde
3/29 Warner Baxter
3/31 Christopher Walken
4/02 Alec Guinness
4/03 Marlon Brando
4/04 Heath Ledger
4/05 Spencer Tracy
4/05 Gregory Peck
4/05 Melvyn Douglas

4/06 Walter Huston
4/07 Russell Crowe
4/10 George Arliss
4/14 Rod Steiger
4/14 Adrien Brody
4/14 John Gielgud
4/17 William Holden
4/21 Anthony Quinn
4/22 Jack Nicholson

WERE JUVENILE ACTORS

3/26 Johnny Crawford
3/28 Freddie Bartholomew
4/04 Nancy McKeon
4/06 Candace Cameron
4/09 Brandon de Wilde
4/09 Keshia Knight Pulliam
4/10 Haley Joel Osment
4/12 Jane Withers
4/12 Claire Danes
4/13 Rick Schroder
4/13 Tony Dow
4/14 Gloria Jean
4/18 Hayley Mills
4/19 Elinor Donahue
4/23 Shirley Temple
4/23 Valerie Bertinelli

CONCERT PIANISTS

3/20 Sviatoslav Richter
3/24 Byron Janis
3/25 Bela Bartok
3/26 Wilhelm Backhaus
3/28 Rudolf Serkin
4/01 Eddy Duchin
4/01 Sergei Rachmaninoff
4/03 Garrick Ohlsson
4/07 Robert Casadesus
4/17 Artur Schnabel
4/19 Murray Parahia
4/19 Dudley Moore

ORCHESTRA CONDUCTORS

3/25 Arturo Toscanini
3/26 Pierre Boulez
3/28 Willem Mengelberg
4/02 Kurt Adler
4/04 Pierre Monteux
4/05 Herbert von Karajan
4/05 George Schick
4/06 Andre Previn
4/08 Adrian Boult
4/08 Josef Krips
4/09 Antal Dorati
4/15 Neville Marriner
4/18 Leopold Stokowski
4/20 John Eliot Gardiner
4/20 Reginald Stewart

BLUES, JAZZ, SOUL

3/15 Lightnin' Hopkins
3/15 Sly Stone
3/22 George Benson
3/25 Aretha Franklin
3/26 Diana Ross
3/27 Sarah Vaughan
3/28 Irene Cara
3/30 Tracy Chapman
4/02 Marvin Gaye
4/04 Muddy Waters
4/07 Billie Holiday
4/13 Peabo Bryson
4/13 Al Green
4/15 Bessie Smith
4/20 Luther Vandross

BOTANY, HORTICULTURE

3/15 Liberty Bailey
3/21 Thomas Meehan
3/25 Norman E. Borlaug
3/27 Karl Nageli
4/03 John Bartram
4/05 W. Atlee Burpee
4/05 David Burpee
4/07 David Fairchild
4/08 Maria Hall
4/13 Thomas Jefferson

BELIEVED IN MARXISM

3/26 Palmiro Togliatti
3/27 Francis Ponge
4/01 Whittaker Chambers
4/09 Paul Robeson
4/11 Ferdinand Lassalle
4/11 Morton Sobel
4/15 Ernst Torgler
4/15 Kim Il-Sung
4/16 Tristan Samueli
4/16 Ernst Thaelmann
4/17 Nikita Khrushchev

DIPLOMATS, NEGOTIATORS

3/16 James Madison
3/18 John C. Calhoun
3/18 Neville Chamberlain
3/19 Wm. Jennings Bryan
3/23 Ludwig Quidde
3/24 Rufus King
3/27 Cyrus Vance
3/27 James Callaghan
3/27 Eisako Sato
3/28 Christian Herter
3/28 Edmund Muskie
3/28 Aristide Briand
3/28 William M. Rountree
4/01 Otto von Bismarck
4/05 Colin Powell
4/05 Chester Bowles
4/10 Clare Boothe Luce

4/10	Matthew C. Perry
4/11	Dean Acheson
4/11	Edward Everett
4/11	Charles Evans Hughes
4/12	Henry Clay
4/13	Thomas Jefferson
4/16	Earl of Halifax
4/19	Roger Sherman

THE BRIDGES(MARCH–APRIL)

The Earth was passing through ***Libra*** when the Bridges were born. Their Sun sign is Aries. If you know your astrology, you can see right away that the activities favored by the Bridges are absolutely nothing like Aries! Where are all the leaders? The military men? They're seldom found in this month. On the other hand, this batch of birthdays looks like a very good fit for Libra! We've got widespread participation in the arts. We've got diplomats. We've got flowers (ruled by Venus). And lest we forget romance, Casanova was born April 2, and "Bluebeard" was born April 12.

Our three keywords for the Bridges are Culture, Accord, and Flowers. There is more culture in the Bridges' data than in that of any other sign. Venus harmonizes and civilizes. Negotiators produce accord between people and nations. Flowers bloom mostly in spring, the season ruled by the goddess Venus. We call these people the Bridges because a bridge unites two opposite points. This is obviously the function of the negotiator, but it's also the artist's function. The artist seeks common ground with the spectator. He wants you to feel what he feels.

Venus is like a green traffic light, signaling that all is well and you may proceed forward. In the spring, much greenery appears. Now what about the First House? (There are twelve astrological "houses," whose locations are determined by your hour of birth.) This house is about the first impression you make. You try to put your best foot forward by showing the world a pleasing appearance and an amiable personality (Venus traits). The Venus person gets along well in the world, like Clare Boothe Luce. He doesn't encounter much opposition (Mars) against which to balance himself (Seventh House). However, Venus does rule balance in the sense of the grace of a dancer.

ZEALOUS PATRIOTS

9/19 Lajos Kossuth
9/20 Robert Emmet
9/27 Samuel Adams
9/27 Louis Botha
9/29 Lech Walesa
10/02 Mohandas Gandhi
10/02 Paul von Hindenburg
10/06 Gerry Adams
10/07 Oliver North
10/09 E. Howard Hunt
10/13 Molly Pitcher
10/13 Virgil
10/14 Eamon de Valera
10/18 Vytautas Landsbergis

FOR PEACE

9/29 Paul McCloskey
10/01 Jimmy Carter
10/02 Sting
10/02 Cordell Hull
10/02 Mohandas Gandhi
10/03 Gore Vidal
10/03 Karl von Ossietzky
10/04 Susan Sarandon
10/05 Philip Berrigan
10/07 Henry Wallace
10/07 Desmond Tutu
10/08 Dennis Kucinich
10/08 Jesse Jackson
10/09 Jody Williams

10/09 John Lennon
10/10 Harold Pinter
10/10 Fridtjof Nansen
10/14 Natalie Maines
10/15 Barry McGuire
10/15 Arthur Schleshinger Jr.
10/16 Tim Robbins
10/16 Austen Chamberlain
10/17 Margot Kidder
10/18 Melina Mercouri
10/20 Wayne Morse
10/21 Alfred Nobel
10/21 Frances Fitzgerald
10/24 William Penn

FOR CIVIL RIGHTS

9/23 Mary Church Terrell
9/26 Winnie Mandella
10/02 Nat Turner
10/03 Al Sharpton
10/04 H. Rap Brown
10/07 Elijah Muhammad
10/07 Desmond Tutu
10/08 Jesse Jackson
10/10 Frederick D. Patterson
10/12 Dick Gregory
10/20 Wayne Collett
10/22 Bobby Seale

"ALIENS," THEIR CO-STARS

9/17 Roddy McDowall
9/19 Paul Williams
9/20 Kristen Johnston
9/25 Mark Hamill
9/26 Linda Hamilton
10/01 James Whitmore
10/04 Charlton Heston
10/05 Karen Allen
10/18 Pam Dawber
10/19 John Lithgow
10/21 Carrie Fisher
10/23 James Daly

BRITISH CHARMERS

9/17 Roddy McDowall
9/19 Jeremy Irons
9/19 David McCallum
9/19 Twiggy
9/24 Anthony Newley
9/26 Edmund Gwenn
9/30 Deborah Kerr
10/01 Julie Andrews
10/01 Stanley Holloway
10/05 Glynis Johns
10/05 Robert Kee
10/06 Melvyn Bragg
10/07 Clive James
10/12 Magnus Magnusson
10/14 Roger Moore
10/15 Sarah Ferguson

10/16 Angela Lansbury
10/23 Una O'Connor

ETHNIC ROLE

9/16 George Chakiris
9/22 Paul Muni
9/30 Philip Dorn
10/03 Warner Oland
10/05 Bill Dana

FOREIGN-BORN BEAUTIES

9/18 Greta Garbo
9/19 Twiggy
9/20 Sophia Loren
9/23 Romy Schneider
9/25 Juliet Prowse
9/26 Olivia Newton-John
9/28 Brigitte Bardot
9/29 Anita Ekberg
9/29 Greer Garson
9/30 Deborah Kerr
10/06 Britt Ekland
10/13 Lily Langtry
10/18 Melina Mercouri
10/22 Catherine Deneuve
10/23 Sarah Bernhardt
10/23 Diana Dors

CARTOONISTS

9/17 Jeffrey MacNally
9/21 Harold T. Webster
9/21 Frank Willard
9/24 Ham Fisher
9/26 Bill Perry
9/27 George Cruikshank
9/27 Tom Little
9/27 Thomas Nast
9/28 Al Capp
10/02 Alex Raymond
10/05 Bil Keane
10/07 Reg Smythe
10/09 Russell Myers
10/13 Herb Block
10/17 Virgil Partch
10/21 Jay N. Darling
10/23 Bob Montana

PUPPETEERS

9/21 David Coulier
9/24 Jim Henson
9/30 Fran Brill
10/13 Burr Tillstrom

FOR ANIMAL RIGHTS

9/19 Alison Sweeney
9/21 Ricki Lake
9/24 Linda McCartney

9/24 Justin Bruening
9/25 Robert Walden
9/27 Jayne Meadows
9/28 Brigitte Bardot
9/30 Angie Dickinson
10/04 Tony La Russa
10/18 Jean-Claude Van Damme
10/18 Martina Navratilova
10/21 Patti Davis

IN ANIMAL STORIES

9/17 Roddy McDowall
9/23 Mickey Rooney
9/24 Lee Aaker
9/25 Tommy Norden
9/26 Edmund Gwenn
9/27 Claude Jarman, Jr.
10/08 Sigourney Weaver
10/14 Greg Evigan
10/16 Johnny Washbrook

RURAL LIFE, THE SOUTH

9/14 Hamlin Garland
9/16 Paul Henning
9/21 Larry Hagman
9/23 John Boyd Orr
9/24 Larry Gates
9/25 William Faulkner
9/26 Johnny Appleseed
9/26 Melissa Sue Anderson

9/26 Donna Douglas
9/27 Grazia Deledda
9/27 Sam Ervin
9/27 Kathleen Nolan
9/27 Lance Smith
9/28 Matthew Cowles
9/28 Al Capp
9/28 Kate Douglas Wiggin
9/29 Elizabeth Gaskell
10/01 Jimmy Carter
10/04 Jean-Francois Millet
10/07 Henry Wallace
10/13 Virgil
10/15 Jane Darwell
10/17 Irene Ryan
10/18 Inger Stevens
10/22 Stephen M. Babcock

LIBRARIANS

9/20 Herbert Putnam
10/01 Daniel Boorstin
10/12 Wilberforce Eames
10/13 Luther H. Evans
10/23 George Watterston

WRITERS

9/24 F. Scott Fitzgerald
9/25 William Faulkner
9/26 T. S. Eliot
9/30 Truman Capote

10/02 Graham Greene
10/02 Wallace Stevens
10/03 Gore Vidal
10/03 Thomas Wolfe
10/04 Damon Runyon
10/07 James Whitcomb Riley
10/14 E. E. Cummings
10/15 P. G. Wodehouse
10/16 Oscar Wilde
10/16 Eugene O'Neill
10/17 Arthur Miller
10/21 Samuel Taylor Coleridge

RESERVED, PRIVATE, SHY

9/17 David Souter
9/18 Greta Garbo
9/18 Ryne Sandberg
9/23 Gail Russell
9/25 Cheryl Tiegs
9/25 Heather Locklear
9/25 Barbara Walters
9/27 Patrick Muldoon
10/01 Jimmy Carter
10/03 Erik von Detten
10/05 Josie Bisset
10/06 Helen Wills
10/07 Ludmila Turischeva
10/08 Rona Barrett
10/10 Adlai Stevenson III
10/10 Henry Cavendish
10/13 Nancy Kerrigan

10/16 Suzanne Somers
10/17 Rita Hayworth
10/18 Lee Harvey Oswald
10/18 Laurie Dann
10/21 Zack Grienke
10/22 Joan Fontaine
10/22 Shelby Lynne
10/23 Johnny Carson

THE FENCES (SEPT.–OCT.)

The Earth was passing through Aries when the Fences were born. Their Sun sign is Libra. A lot of what we have come to associate with Aries – onrushing energy, impulsiveness, etc. – comes from its commonly asserted link to the vernal equinox. But Earth-in-Aries is an autumnal sign. It produces a more laid-back type of Aries that the one we are used to reading about. Many Fences are shy. The biggest myth about these people is that they are supposed to be so socially adept. In truth (see data), the sign is full of introverted loners!

Yet despite their occasional difficulties in relating to people, some Fences take the lead in fighting for worthy causes: nationalist leaders, civil rights leaders, animal rights leaders, leaders of the peace movement. The Fences also produce better military leaders than the Bridges: Dwight Eisenhower, Paul von Hindenburg, Horatio Nelson. Mars is the god of war, of fighting. When you crusade or protest, you separate yourself from those who disagree with your cause. Mars is separative, like a fence.

Another way you can separate yourself is to move away from the noisy crowds of the city and settle in the country. Nowadays, astrologers associate agriculture with Saturn, but it used to be under the rulership of Aries. The data confirm that Mars has never relinquished his dominion over ruralism. Country life is rugged, hardy, primal, unfrilled, and separate from the city, the cultural hub. Our keywords for the Fences are Protesting, Ruralism and Origins. The motto of Aries, "I am," is separative. It says, "I would rather be me than we." Our origins distinguish us from other people with different origins.

Our origins are of two types: ethnicity and childhood. In the data, the focus appears to be on others' ethnicity or race, but their origins separate them from yours. Moreover, if you happen to be in one of those groups yourself, that distinguishes you. The Fences are enormously nostalgic.

Notice how, even as adults, they retain things of childhood: cartoons, puppets, animals. Cartoons are Mars art because they distort, whereas Venus art is proportional. Mars is said to rule the animal kingdom as well.

Mars is like a red traffic light, alerting us to possible danger. Fittingly, the leaves turn red in autumn, especially in October, warning nature of hard times ahead. Mars is not for the faint-hearted. The Seventh House is not a peaceful one. It governs open enemies, litigation and war. It is also the house of marriage, but couples don't always get along. Since they are opposite sexes, by definition they are opposed. The war god requires that there be two sides. The challenge of the Seventh House is to achieve detente – not necessarily harmony (Venus).

Perhaps some Fences just want to get away from all the strife. We know they like peace and quiet, which is one reason they feel at home in libraries. The impressive list of writers may have to do partly with the fact that writing is something a person does alone, and in a quiet place.

Aries and Libra are opposite signs; therefore, they have opposite essences. Let us list again the keywords for each sign so that we can see the contrast between them:

Fences (Earth in Aries)	**Bridges** (Earth in Libra)
Protest	Accord
Ruralism	Culture
Origins (seeds, roots)	Flowers

KNEW PSYCHOLOGY

4/20 Philippe Pinel
4/21 Rollo May
4/30 Harvey Carr
5/02 Benjamin Spock
5/06 Sigmund Freud
5/10 Jean Houston
5/13 Henry A. Murray
5/15 Alvin Poussant

5/18 Anthony Storr
5/23 Franz Mesmer

SPIRITUAL LEADERS

4/25 Meadowlark Lemon
4/25 Randall Terry
5/08 Fulton J. Sheen
5/09 Kathryn Kuhlman
5/10 Kaufmann Kohler
5/11 Louis Farrakhan
5/13 Jim Jones 1931
5/17 Marshall Applewhite 1931
5/17 Ayatolla Khomeini
5/18 Pope John Paul II
5/20 Antoinette Blackwell

CLEVER IN CHESS, WAR

4/13 Garry Kasparov
4/14 Bogoliubow
4/17 Mikhail Botvinnik
4/27 Ulysses S. Grant
5/01 Duke of Wellington
5/03 Nona Gaprindashvili
5/14 Wilhelm Steinitz
5/15 Sebastien de Vauban
5/20 Max Euwe
5/23 Anatoly Karpov

KNEW ECONOMICS

4/19 David Ricardo
4/21 Max Weber
4/25 Edwin Seligman
4/27 Arthur Burns
4/28 Sidney Weintraub
5/05 Karl Marx
5/07 Lester C. Thurow
5/08 Friedrich von Hayek
5/15 Paul Samuelson
5/20 John Stuart Mill
5/20 Frederic Passy

PHILOSOPHERS, DEEP THINKERS

4/15 Thomas Hobbs
4/21 Hippolyte Taine
4/22 Immanuel Kant
4/25 Marcus Aurelius
4/26 Ludwig Wittgenstein
4/27 Herbert Spencer
5/01 P. Teilhard de Chardin
5/04 Johann Herbart
5/05 Soren Kierkegaard
5/07 David Hume
5/07 Rabindranath Tagore
5/09 Jose Ortega y Gasset
5/12 Niccolo Machiavelli
5/14 Socrates
5/18 Bertrand Russell
5/18 Rudolph Carnap

5/19 Johann Fichte
5/20 John Stuart Mill

LIBERALS IN GOVT.

4/20 John Paul Stevens
4/21 Edmund "Pat" Brown
4/25 William J. Brennan
4/27 Cory Booker
4/28 Elena Kagan
5/06 Tony Blair
5/08 Emanuel Celler
5/08 Harry Truman
5/10 Carl Albert
5/12 Mervyn Dymally
5/16 John Conyers
5/21 Al Franken

MISC. LIBERALS

4/15 Linda Bloodworth-Thomason
4/16 Charlie Chaplin
4/20 Jessica Lange
4/23 Michael Moore
4/24 Barbra Streisand
5/01 Judy Collins
5/03 Pete Seeger
5/06 George Clooney
5/11 Mort Sahl
5/13 Bea Arthur
5/13 Stephen Colbert
5/24 Bob Dylan

REVOLUTIONARIES

4/15 Kim Il-Sung
4/22 Vladimir Lenin
4/23 Bernadette Devlin
5/03 Emmanuel Sieyes
5/05 Karl Marx
5/05 Oliver Cromwell
5/06 Maximilian Robespierre
5/08 William Walker
5/14 Che Guevara
5/17 Ayatollah Khomeini
5/19 Ho Chi Minh
5/19 Pol Pot
5/20 F. Toussaint-L'Ouverture
5/20 Ramzi Yousef
5/24 Jean Paul Marat

DEFIANT MAVERICKS

5/11 Salvador Dali
5/12 Katharine Hepburn
5/13 Dennis Rodman
5/18 Reggie Jackson
5/18 Pernell Roberts
5/19 Malcolm X

MISC. RADICALS

4/13 Bruno Seghetti
4/22 Nicola Sacco
4/23 Timothy McVeigh

4/25 Randall Terry
4/25 Francesca Mambro
5/06 Berndt Baader
5/09 John Brown
5/09 Daniel Berrigan
5/09 A. Sommacampagna
5/15 Marco Costa
5/17 Patricia Soltysik
5/22 Ted Kaczynski
5/23 Rennie Davis

COMPOSED FILM MUSIC

4/16 Henry Mancini
4/18 Miklos Rozsa
4/26 Giorgio Moroder
5/10 Dimitri Tiomkin
5/10 Max Steiner 1888
5/11 Irving Berlin 1888
5/12 Burt Bacharach
5/18 Meredith Willson

POWERFUL WOMEN

4/23 Catherine de Medici
5/01 Isabella I
5/02 Catherine the Great
5/03 Golda Meir
5/07 Evita Peron
5/10 Ella Grasso
5/13 Maria Theresa
5/15 Madeleine Albright

FILM DIRECTORS

4/23 Frank Borzage
4/29 Fred Zinnemann
4/30 Jane Campion
5/02 Satyajit Ray
5/06 Orson Welles
5/08 Roberto Rossellini
5/09 James L. Brooks
5/10 Clarence Brown
5/10 Anatole Litvak
5/14 Robert Zemeckis
5/14 George Lucas
5/18 Frank Capra
5/18 Richard Brooks

FOOTBALL COACHES

4/16 Bill Belichick
4/19 Jack Pardee
4/21 Steve Owen
4/23 Bud Wilkinson
4/27 Chuck Knox
4/29 George Allen
4/30 Fielding Yost
5/06 Weeb Ewbank
5/06 John Vaught
5/20 Bud Grant
5/21 Ara Parseghian

CHORAL DIRECTORS

4/30 Robert Shaw
5/09 Harry Simeone
5/14 Norman Luboff

MURDEROUS TYRANTS

4/20 Adolf Hitler
4/28 Saddam Hussein
5/19 Pol Pot

THE DRILLS (APRIL–MAY)

The Earth was passing through Scorpio when the Drills were born. Their Sun sign is Taurus. The biggest myth about these people is that they are on the conservative side, or at least not very progressive. What do the data reveal? Rebels, radicals, revolutionaries, ardent liberals! How can these people possibly be Taurus? The answer is, they are not. Scorpio is the sign of transformation. Occasionally you run across a radically right-wing leader such as Hitler, Scorpio being the sign of extremes. Normally, though, the Drills are on the Left. Mars is the planet of liberalism, asserting his individuality by being a rebel, a divider.

Although Scorpio is a fixed sign, it seeks change, which seems like a paradox. Think of Scorpio as a spinning top. Spinning – or revolving – is symbolic of change. When the top is spinning, it has a certain stability in that it remains upright. When it stops spinning, it falls on its side. Thus, Scorpio needs change in order to function. Our three keywords for the Drills are: Change, Theorizing and Initiating.

There are two ways you can drill, vertically or horizontally. When you drill vertically, that symbolizes Scorpio's profound, penetrative intellect, delving deeply into subject matter to unearth the truth. Whether as philosopher, psychiatrist or spiritual leader, the Drills theorize their way to the answers others would never find.

You will notice quite a bit of initiating in the data. When you drill horizontally, that represents Scorpio's Mars style of leadership, an assertive style. The Second House is supposed to show your money and possessions – but Venus is not possessive. Mars is the possessive one. What sort of money is shown by the Second House? It's money you earned. It's certainly not a gift (Venus). It was earned through effort and competition (Mars concepts). We are always told that the Drills are stubborn – and why not? What could be more stubborn than fixed Mars?

STAGE ACTORS

10/18 George C. Scott
10/19 John Lithgow
10/22 Derek Jacobi
10/23 Sarah Bernhardt
10/24 Sybil Thorndike
10/24 F. Murray Abraham
10/25 Anthony Franciosa
10/27 Ruby Dee
10/28 Jane Alexander
10/28 Joan Plowright
10/30 Ruth Gordon
10/31 Barbara Bel Geddes
10/31 Sally Kirkland
10/31 Ethel Waters
11/10 Richard Burton
11/10 Claude Rains
11/11 Maude Adams
11/12 Kim Hunter
11/13 Edwin Booth
11/13 John Drew
11/15 James O'Neill
11/15 Sam Waterston
11/16 Burgess Meredith
11/22 Geraldine Page
11/22 Tom Conti

REGIONAL OR ETHNIC MUSIC

10/22 Franz Liszt
10/25 Johann Strauss
10/28 Howard Hanson

10/29 Daniel D. Emmett
10/30 Herschel Bernardi
11/06 John Philip Sousa
11/11 Elena Gerhardt
11/12 Aleksandr Borodin
11/16 W. C. Handy
11/23 Manuel de Falla
11/23 Jerry Bock
11/24 Lilli Lehmann

ASIANS IN THE ARTS

10/18 Victor Sen Yung
10/21 Hokusai
10/23 Ang Lee
10/24 B. D. Wong
10/25 Midori
10/27 Maxine Hong Kingston
10/28 Jack Soo
11/08 Kazuo Ishiguro
11/17 Isamu Noguchi

SCULPTORS

10/19 Umberto Boccione
10/22 Robert Rauschenberg
10/25 Pablo Picasso
10/29 Andrea Della Robbia
10/30 Emile Boardelle
10/30 John Rogers
11/01 Antonio Canova
11/02 Richard Serra

11/04 James E. Fraser
11/06 Seymour Lipton
11/10 Jacob Epstein
11/12 Auguste Rodin
11/12 Benvenuto Cellini
11/17 Isamu Noguchi
11/20 Maryon Kantaroff

SCULPTED THEMSELVES

10/18 Martina Navratilova
10/18 Jean Claude Van Damme
10/28 Bruce Jenner
10/30 Charles Atlas
11/03 Dolph Lundgren
11/09 Lou Ferrigno

COMPILED DATA, STATS

11/03 Samuel Lubell
11/09 Benjamin Banneker
11/13 Michel Gauquelin
11/18 George Gallup
11/19 William H. Sheldon

FOR THE WORKERS

10/17 Claude Henri
10/18 Melina Mercouri
10/26 Francois Mitterrand
10/26 Hillary Clinton
10/29 Louis Blanc

10/31 Tom Paxton
11/02 Patrick Buchanan
11/05 Eugene Debs
11/08 Bonnie Raitt
11/09 Leon Trotsky
11/11 Jules Guesde
11/12 Neil Young
11/13 Louis Brandeis
11/19 Tom Harkin
11/20 Norman Thomas
11/22 Straughton Lynd

EXPLORERS, FRONTIERSMEN

10/23 Bernt Balchen
10/25 Richard E. Byrd
10/31 G. Hubert Wilkins
11/02 Daniel Boone
11/03 Stephen Austin
11/03 Vilhjalmur Stefansson
11/07 James Cook
11/10 Donald MacMillan
11/11 Louis Bougainville
11/17 Pierre de La Verendrye
11/19 George Rogers Clark
11/21 Robert de La Salle
11/24 Father Bernard Hubbard

ASTRONOMERS

10/25 Henry Russell
10/25 Heinrich Schwabe

11/02 Harlow Shapley
11/08 Edmund Halley
11/09 Carl Sagan
11/09 Benjamin Banneker
11/15 William Herschel
11/20 Edwin Hubble

COLUMNISTS, EDITORS

10/16 Nicholas Von Hoffman
10/17 Jimmy Breslin
10/19 Jack Anderson
10/20 Morrie Ryskind
10/22 John Reed
10/24 Sarah Josepha Hale
10/27 Neil Sheehan
10/28 John Chamberlain
11/01 Larry Flynt
11/01 J. Jackson Kilpatrick
11/02 Patrick Buchanan
11/03 William Cullen Bryant
11/03 James Reston
11/04 Robert B. Considine
11/09 Elijah P. Lovejoy
11/14 Harrison Salisbury
11/15 Franklin P. Adams
11/16 Elizabeth Drew
11/16 Arthur Krock
11/19 Jeane Kirkpatrick
11/20 Alistair Cooke
11/21 Tina Brown
11/22 James Burnham

11/24 William F. Buckley
11/25 John F. Kennedy, Jr.

JUDGES

10/16 William O. Douglas
10/21 Judith Sheindlin
11/02 Rose Bird
11/03 Edward D. White
11/04 Benjamin Curtis
11/12 Harry Blackmun
11/13 Louis Brandeis
11/15 Felix Frankfurter
11/15 Joseph Wapner
11/20 Kenesaw Landis

JOCKEYS

10/17 Pat Valenzuela
10/21 Corey Nakatani
10/23 Javier Castellano
10/31 Dick Francis
11/05 Lester Piggott
11/08 Angel Cordero, Jr.
11/08 Eddie Maple
11/13 Earl Sande
11/21 Barbara Jo Rubin
11/24 Ramon Dominguez
11/24 John Velasquez

SOUTHERN SENATORS

10/18 Jesse Helms
11/02 Richard Russell
11/03 Russell Long
11/09 Bob Graham
11/13 Fred Harris
11/14 George Smathers
11/15 Howard Baker
11/18 Olin Johnston
11/24 Alben Barkley

SPORTS EXECS, ORGANIZERS

10/22 Joe Carr
10/25 Leland MacPhail
10/26 Ted Bassett
10/28 Bowie Kuhn
11/04 John J. O'Brien
11/06 James Naismith
11/06 James D. Norris
11/17 Frank Calder
11/18 James E. Sullivan
11/19 Ted Turner
11/22 Billie Jean King
11/24 Paul Tagliabue

THE ROCKS (OCT.–NOV.)

The Earth was passing through Taurus when the Rocks were born. Their Sun sign is Scorpio. The Rocks have their fingers in so many pies that at first glance it is difficult to pinpoint who these versatile people really are. Once you break them down into keywords, however, you find that they have the qualities they ought to have: Taurus qualities. One of the first things you'll notice in the data is that the Rocks are active in the arts, which you would expect of a Venus sign. Taurus is an earthy sign; thus, solid, tangible beauty appeals to them, such as in sculpture or a physically fit body. Our keywords for the Rocks are: Observing, Perseverance and Tradition.

Astronomers, explorers and columnists all have to be keen *observers*. Venus has a sedate side that is accentuated by the fixed nature of Taurus. The Rocks stay in one place long enough to observe what others may miss. Beauty is one of the things this Venus sign loves to observe. The beauty of the night sky undoubtedly appeals to astronomers. An explorer may well appreciate the beauty of the wilderness.

What do sculptors, bodybuilders and data compilers have in common? They all have to persevere. Sculpting is harder than painting because it has three dimensions. The Rocks are the hardest workers in the zodiac. That is one reason that they identify with the struggles of other hard workers. Another factor is that unions, co-ops, etc. are collaborations (Venus unifying). Jockeys collaborate with a horse, steadying and relaxing the animal with the Venus knack for pacification.

The Rocks are lovers of tradition. They like the traditional music of the place where they grew up. The theatre has a rich tradition that dates much farther back than film. Judges base their decisions on precedents. Southern senators are more traditional. Labor unions have a long, eventful history.

The Eight House is about unearned money, sex and death. Legacies and gifts come from love (Venus), not strife. Sex unites people (Venus); it doesn't drive them apart (Mars). The goddess Venus was herself a very sexual being. Mars does not rule death. Mars is the will to live, the fightingness in one's body and spirit that often enables us to cheat death. Mars never gives up. At his very core, he says, "I will survive." But as we grow old, we have to give up things we can no longer do: we have to compromise (Venus). The last thing we give up is our life. Death is the ultimate compromise. We associate flowers (Venus) with funerals and graves and "resting in peace."

Whether we are compiling data, cataloging the stars, or mapping the wilderness, we are putting something together, collecting, assembling – which is a basic function of Taurus. Amassing money is supposed to come under this heading too, but this may have been overstated because the data do not really show much preoccupation with money. There are some cases of stingy Taureans, like Hettie Green, the Witch of Wall Street. Taurus is such an enduring sign that we call these people the Rocks. What could be more enduring than a rock? Some rocks are billions of years old. Taurus is the Immovable Object, and Scorpio is the Irresistable Force. Let us contrast these opposites:

Rocks (Earth in Taurus)	Drills (Earth in Scorpio)
Observing	Theorizing
Perseverance	Initiating
Tradition	Change

Observing is different from theorizing because it implies the empirical method of gleaning truth. Perseverance is different from initiating because he who perseveres plows forward in the same direction, whereas he who initiates leads us off in a new direction. The apostle Peter must have been a Taurus. Jesus said, "Thou art a rock, and upon this rock I will build My church." Christ did not want His church to be transitory. He wanted it to endure, just as traditions endure, and perseverers endure. Taureans are very admirable people. No one is more dependable, and many of them are of sterling character – quite the opposite of the bad reputation accorded Sun-in-Scorpio people!

CONQUERORS, DICTATORS

6/19 Peter the Great
6/22 Cosimo de Medici
6/26 Louis XII
6/28 James I
6/30 Walter Ulbricht
7/05 Cecil Rhodes
7/06 Maximilian
7/07 Henry VIII
7/09 Julius Caesar
7/09 Hassan II
7/17 Alexander the Great
7/17 Nicholas I
7/18 Robert the Bruce
7/19 Ferdinand II
7/22 Arthur v. Seyes-Inquart
7/23 Haile Selasse

TOUGH SEA CAPTAINS

6/25 Louis Mountbatten
7/01 Charles Laughton (role)
7/05 David Farragut
7/06 John Paul Jones
7/17 James Cagney (role)

ALLEGATION OF ABUSE

6/12 Marv Albert
6/14 Donald Trump
6/18 Sean Eckhardt
6/20 Audie Murphy
6/23 Clarence Thomas
6/26 Michael Vick
6/30 Mike Tyson
7/02 Jose Canseco
7/06 Nicky Hilton
7/06 Alvin Harper
7/07 Henry VIII
7/09 O. J. Simpson
7/09 Fred Savage
7/11 Richie Sambora
7/12 Bill Cosby
7/21 Ernest Hemingway

BRUTAL, SADISTIC ROLE

6/22 Kris Kristofferson
6/28 Kathy Bates
6/30 Tony Musante
7/08 Kevin Bacon
7/22 Louise Fletcher
7/22 Danny Glover

ENTREPRENEURS

6/14 Donald Trump
6/24 Eleuthere du Pont

6/27 Ross Perot
7/01 Famous Amos
7/03 Stavros Niarchos
7/04 Meyer Lansky
7/04 Louis B. Mayer
7/05 Cecil Rhodes
7/05 P. T. Barnum
7/06 Harry F. Sinclair
7/08 John D. Rockefeller
7/10 Adolphus Busch
7/10 Richard King
7/11 John Wanamaker
7/12 George Eastman
7/12 Richard Simmons
7/13 Erno Rubik
7/14 Polly Bergen
7/14 Frederick Maytag
7/15 Amedeo Obici
7/16 Orville Redenbacher
7/17 John Jacob Astor
7/18 Richard Branson
7/23 Harry Cohn
7/23 Samuel Kress

CONSERVATIVES, THE G.O.P.

6/12 George H. W. Bush
6/17 Newt Gingrich
6/23 Clarence Thomas
6/24 George Petaki
7/02 Jon Sununu
7/03 Lamar Alexander

7/04 Calvin Coolidge
7/04 George Murphy
7/05 Henry Cabot Lodge
7/06 George W. Bush
7/07 Dick Armey
7/08 Phil Gramm
7/08 Nelson Rockefeller
7/08 George Romney
7/09 Donald Rumsfeld
7/09 Lindsey Graham
7/12 Mark Hatfield
7/13 Jack Kemp
7/14 Gerald Ford
7/15 Jeremiah Denton
7/18 S.I. Hayakawa
7/19 William Scranton
7/22 Robert Dole
7/22 Kay Bailey Hutchison
7/23 Anthony Kennedy

RELIGION'S FOUNDERS

6/28 John Wesley
7/04 St. John of the Cross
7/07 Henry VIII
7/13 Father Flanagan
7/15 Mother Cabrini
7/15 Truman B. Douglas
7/16 Mary Baker Eddy
7/20 John Calvin

LAWYERS

6/21 Percy Foreman
6/23 William P. Rogers
6/24 William B. Saxbe
6/26 Edward H. Levi
7/02 Thurgood Marshall
7/03 Gloria Allred
7/07 William Kunstler
7/07 Lawrence O'Brien
7/16 Richard Thornburgh
7/17 Benjamin Civiletti
7/20 Elliot Richardson
7/21 Janet Reno
7/21 Kenneth Starr

ENGINEERS, BUILDERS

6/26 Wilhelm Messerschmitt
6/29 George Goethals
7/05 William J. Rankine
7/08 Ferdinand von Zeppelin
7/09 Nikola Tesla
7/09 Elias Howe
7/12 R. Buckminster Fuller

PAINTERS

6/21 Rockwell Kent
7/03 John S. Copley
7/09 Peter Paul Rubens
7/10 Camille Pissaro

7/10 James A. M. Whistler
7/12 Amadeo Modigliani
7/12 Andrew Wyeth
7/15 Rembrandt
7/16 Jean B. C. Corot
7/16 George Catlin
7/17 Paul Delaroche
7/19 Edgar Degas
7/19 Marc Chagall
7/25 Thomas Eakins

THE HAMMERS (JUNE–JULY)

The Earth was passing through Capricorn when the Hammers were born. Their Sun sign is Cancer. The biggest myth about these people is that they are squishy, gentle creatures. According to the data, they are as tough as nails! You don't want a Hammer for an enemy – but he can be a staunch friend. Saturn is the planet of fear, and because they are insecure, the Hammers prefer to be in control. There is an authoritarian side to Capricorn. Whether as rulers or conquerors, as tough sea captains, or even as abusers, the Hammers tend to control. Churches are Saturnine in the sense that they have commandments you must obey, dogmas you must accept, and rituals you must perform. A hammer is a symbol of authority.

Hammers are also insecure about money, which motivates them to acquire it. They excel as businessmen and love to pile up huge profits! Think of Saturn as centripetal (acquisition, consolidation). Because of its slow movement, Saturn rules stability. Capricorns know that a rolling stone gathers no moss, so they stay put. The Hammers play for keeps. They want to nail down everything good in their lives and make it permanent. Typically, they are steadfast conservatives: cautious, thrifty, religious, worried about national security, and lovers of competition. They hate change, since they are apt to be winning the competition! They will do anything for their family, but they worry about high taxes and tend to feel that other people in society ought to learn to fend for themselves – the way they did.

Our keywords for Capricorn are: Controlling, Permanence and Constructing. Saturn rules structure. Painters and engineers construct. So do those who construct a new business or a new church. A hammer symbolizes construction. Capricorns are private people, not given to loquacity. The Fourth House is about your private life (Saturn), whereas the Tenth House governs your public life (Moon). Your home and your family are basic sources of stability in your life. They are your emotional foundation (Saturn). How could they be ruled by the inconstant, ever-changing Moon? They're not. The Fourth House governs real estate, other private property, and the grave – all Saturn concepts. Capricorn is said to be a climber – but when was the most famous mountain climber, Edmund Hillary, born? In July – not January.

WORLD LEADERS

12/17 W. L. MacKenzie King
12/18 Willy Brandt
12/19 Leonid Brezhnev
12/21 Kurt Waldheim
12/21 Benjamin Disraeli
12/23 Helmut Schmidt
12/24 Hamid Karzai
12/25 Anwar Sadat
12/25 Hu Jintao
12/26 Mao Tse-Tung
12/28 Woodrow Wilson
12/29 William Gladstone
12/30 Hideki Tojo
1/01 Cicero
1/02 Joseph Stalin
1/03 Ngo Dinh Diem
1/03 Clement Attlee
1/05 Konrad Adenauer
1/09 Richard Nixon
1/10 Lorenzo di Medici
1/11 John A. MacDonald
1/12 Pieter W. Botha
1/15 Gamal Abdul Nasser
1/16 Fulgencio Batista
1/17 David Lloyd George

U. S. POLITICAL LEADERS

12/20 John J. Sparkman
12/21 John W. McCormack
12/22 Jim Wright
12/26 Albert Gore, Sr.
12/29 Andrew Johnson
12/30 Alfred E. Smith
1/01 Barry Goldwater
1/01 James Oglethorpe
1/02 Dennis Hastert
1/03 Lucretia Mott
1/04 Everett Dirksen
1/05 Walter Mondale
1/06 Sam Rayburn
1/06 Charles Sumner
1/07 Millard Fillmore
1/09 Carrie Chapman Catt
1/11 Alexander Hamilton
1/12 James Farmer
1/13 Salmon P. Chase
1/14 Julian Bond
1/15 Martin Luther King, Jr.
1/17 L. Douglas Wilder
1/17 Benjamin Franklin
1/18 Daniel Webster
1/20 Richard Henry Lee

KIND HELPERS, HEALERS

12/25 Clara Barton
1/03 Millard Fuller
1/03 Father Damien

1/06 Danny Thomas
1/14 Albert Schweitzer
1/17 Tom Dooley
1/18 Danny Kaye

GOVERNMENT ADMINISTRATORS

12/13 George Shultz
12/18 Ramsay Clark
12/19 Donald Regan
12/25 Clark Clifford
12/31 George C. Marshall
1/02 Richard W. Riley
1/03 Carla Hills
1/03 Betty Furness
1/04 Lauro Cavazos
1/05 George Tenet
1/08 Sherman Adams
1/11 Juanita Kreps
1/13 Brock Adams
1/17 Newton Minow

EDUCATORS

12/27 William H. Masters
12/28 Woodrow Wilson
1/02 Wm. Lyon Phelps
1/02 John Hope Franklin
1/04 Louis Braille
1/04 Isaac Newton
1/05 Raisa Gorbachev
1/06 Alan Watts

1/08 Lowell Mason
1/08 Evelyn Wood
1/11 Eva Le Gallienne
1/12 Johann Pestalozzi
1/15 Ella Flagg Young
1/17 Robert M. Hutchins

LAW ENFORCERS

12/23 Ted Briseno
12/29 Tom Bradley
1/01 J. Edgar Hoover
1/03 Eddie Egan
1/06 Louis Freeh
1/17 Kip Keino
1/22 Joseph Wambaugh

VISIONS, VOICES BEYOND

12/23 Nostradamus
12/23 Joseph Smith
1/02 St. Therese de Lisieux
1/02 St. Ignatius of Loyola
1/05 Jeane Dixon
1/07 St. Bernadette
1/08 Arthur Ford
1/09 Ernest Bozzano
1/09 Phyllis Givens
1/15 Joan of Arc

BOUNDARY STRETCHERS

12/20 Uri Geller
12/21 Frank Zappa
12/25 Robert Ripley
12/25 Rod Serling
1/05 Marilyn Manson
1/07 Komar
1/08 David Bowie
1/10 Jim Bailey
1/12 Kreskin
1/17 Jane Horrocks
1/19 Frank Caliendo

DEFEATS, DOWNFALLS

12/14 Bill Buckner
12/18 Brian Orser
12/22 Steve Garvey
12/23 Paul Hornung
12/23 Susan Lucci
12/26 Gray Davis
12/30 Tiger Woods
12/30 Ben Johnson
12/31 Charles Cornwallis
1/01 Barry Goldwater
1/02 Julius La Rosa
1/02 Jim Bakker
1/05 Walter Mondale
1/09 Richard Nixon
1/11 Alexander Hamilton
1/18 Curt Flood
1/19 Robert E. Lee

UNUSUALLY VERSATILE

12/26 Steve Allen
1/01 Barry Goldwater
1/14 Albert Schweitzer
1/17 Ben Franklin

THE ANTENNAS (DEC–JAN.)

The Earth was passing through Cancer when the Antennas were born. Their Sun sign is Capricorn. These people never get the credit they deserve. They do more good in the world than any other sign, but regularly they are dismissed as merely "ambitious." In truth, they really care about people and really want to help them – and they're good at it too! The biggest myth about these people is that they are rather inarticulate loners. Actually, most of them are very sociable and talkative. The Moon rules the public, and Cancer's ability to relate to other people is unsurpassed.

Because of their knack for "tuning into people," the Antennas often turn to politics and government. The quick-moving Moon describes a quick, decisive mind – the kind of mind leaders have. A leader doesn't always have the best idea, but he has it first. The Moon is the Mother Principle, and Cancers are protective and nurturing, which makes them ideally suited for public service. Taking care of the sick also appeals to their humanitarian instincts and motivates some to become medical missionaries. The police might make you think of Mars or Saturn, but actually the profession attracts Lunar people because their job is to protect the public. The empathy that the Antennas feel toward others also makes them good teachers, ministering to the needs of their students.

Our keywords for Antennas are: Ministering, Impressionability and Phases. The Moon is responsive, receptive, sensitive to incoming stimuli. This enables some Antennas, like visionary saints and mediums, to pick up sights and sounds that others cannot tune into because they are not impressionable enough. Such visions and voices might seem "far out" to some people, but Cancer specializes in this sort of thing. Think of the Moon, zipping around the zodiac, as centrifugal, straining to reach the outer limits of experience, extending or surpassing existing boundaries.

Clearly, this sign couldn't possibly be ruled by restrictive Saturn, which sets boundaries and enforces them.

The Moon is ever-changing, and its phases symbolize change. There are two types of change: vertical and horizontal. Vertical change describes ups and downs of life, but Cancers experience more of a roller-coaster life than most people. They can drop from the highest heights to the lowest depths–and then perhaps get to the top again. Richard Nixon was "up" while ascending the political ladder, and "down" when he lost the election in 1960, up when he won the presidency in 1968, and down during the Watergate debacle. Horizontal change refers to versatility – switching from one activity or career to another.

The Tenth House is your public life (Moon) – what you do out among people. Your reputation is the "public opinion" of you. Contrary to what some have written, this house does not indicate someone who has power over you, such as a boss (Saturn). An oppressive person might well hold you back, but the Tenth House shows where and how you get ahead in your life. Let's compare Cancer with Capricorn:

Antennas (Earth in Cancer)	Hammers (Earth in Capricorn)
Ministering	Controlling
Impressionability	Constructing
Phases	Permanence

When you're constructing something, you are acting upon the environment, whereas impressionability means that the environment is acting upon you.

HOW THE ANCIENTS PROCEEDED

Students unfamiliar with the Earth sign zodiac might assume that it is something new, but actually it's as old as astrology. The oldest signs of the zodiac were Earth signs, not Sun signs. In ancient times, before there were any ephemerides (astronomical tables), people had to check out the sky to see where the planets were. Their first opportunity to see the night sky came right after sunset, as soon as the sky was dark enough. They would look to the east to see what stars and planets were rising, and base their forecast on that. Some ancient peoples cared a lot about the Full Moon, which could be seen rising in the east after sunset once a month.

In Egypt, the people associated what they experienced annually with the stars and the planets. For example, the military campaigns started when the Sun was in Gemini. But did they connect that event with Gemini? No – they associated it with Sagittarius the Archer, for that sign was rising in the east when the Gemini Sun was setting in the west. In other words, the original meaning of each sign, as interpreted by the ancients, was based on what was observed of people and events when the Sun was not in that sign, but opposite to it. At some point, someone evidently decided that the characteristics of each sign should be on full display when the Sun passes through that sign. Sun signs became popular, and Earth signs were sadly forgotten.

If Earth signs are more important than Sun signs, does that mean that we scrap everything that we have read about Sun traits? We think not. Astrologers have been observing human behavior for a long time now. It could be that they have associated certain traits with the right people, but the wrong sign. For example, we often have been told that Sun in Taurus people are stubborn. What does that have to do with Venus, the ruler of Taurus? Venus is all about harmony and collaboration. Mars is the stubborn one. The Mars person is contentious and resists compromise. We believe that the April-May people <u>are</u> stubborn, but it's not a Taurus trait. It's a Mars-Scorpio trait.

We are told that Sun in Gemini people get involved in too many projects at once, so that they seldom finish what they started. Couldn't this be a Jupiter-Sagittarius trait? Jupiter is the planet of expansion. Under his influence, a person reaches out in all directions seeking new experiences. He spreads himself too thin. He becomes overextended and overexpanded. We are told that Sun in Virgo is a perfectionist, but couldn't that be a form of Pisces idealism? We hear that Sun in Cancer is thrifty, but wouldn't that trait fit Saturn-Capricorn better? It is said that Sun in Aquarius is friendly, but wouldn't warm, outgoing Leo more logically be the friendly one? Traits like these don't lend themselves to research. And because of that, we should keep an open mind. Do you know 7,000 people?

We all owe a debt of gratitude to the ancients for laying out basic principles of astrology thousands of years ago. They were shrewd observers, but they were not infallible. They were human like the rest of us, and sometimes they made mistakes. Only through research can we ascertain which of their pronouncements are true, and which are misguided.

HOW AND WHY RULERSHIPS WORK

Where do sign rulerships come from? You could study Sun signs all your life and never find the answer, but Earth sign astrology makes it quite clear. The following table shows the Earth entering each sign, the date of entry, the speed of the earth on that date, and the planet ruling the sign. The numbers are minutes of arc. (There are sixty minutes in one degree.) The higher the number, the faster the Earth is traveling.

Entering	Date	Speed	Ruler
Aquarius	July 20	57.3	Saturn
Pisces	August 20	57.8	Jupiter
Aries	September 20	58.7	Mars
Taurus	October 20	59.8	Venus
Gemini	November 19	60.7	Mercury
Cancer	December 19	61.1	Moon
Leo	January 17	61.1	Moon
Virgo	February 16	60.5	Mercury
Libra	March 18	59.6	Venus
Scorpio	April 17	58.6	Mars
Sagittarius	May 18	57.7	Jupiter
Capricorn	June 18	57.2	Saturn

Notice that the Earth's speed when it enters Aquarius is almost the same as its speed when entering Capricorn. Note also that this speed is the slowest in the table. Therefore, Aquarius and Capricorn are ruled by Saturn, the slowest of the originally known planets. In other words, there is an analogy between the relative speed of the Earth and the relative speed of the other planets. Let's take another example. The Earth's speed when it enters Taurus is about the same as its speed when entering Libra – and this speed is the third fastest in the table. Therefore, Venus rules Taurus and Libra because Venus is the third fastest planet in the table.

Now you can see why the Sun cannot be the true ruler of Leo. The Sun, in its apparent movement through the sky, is not fast enough to rule Leo. Only the Moon is fast enough. Leo is ruled by a big, round, bright, showy Full Moon. Since the Sun is also big, round, bright and showy, it may have a special connection with Leo – but it is not the ruler.

The Earth sign zodiac is defined by the speed of the Earth. It is not defined by the four seasons (like the tropical zodiac) nor is it defined by the twelve constellations (like the sidereal zodiac). It evidently takes about a month for the speed of the Earth to change enough so that a different kind of person, represented by a different planet, will be born.

MILITARY HEROES

1/15 Joan of Arc
1/18 Israel Putnam
1/19 Robert E. Lee
1/20 Bertram Ramsey
1/21 Ethan Allen
1/21 Stonewall Jackson
1/21 John C. Breckinridge
1/21 John C. Fremont
1/24 Frederick the Great
1/25 George Pickett
1/26 Douglas MacArthur
1/26 Marc Mitscher
1/26 Charles XIV John
1/27 Hyman Rickover
1/28 Chinese Gordon
1/29 Light-Horse H. Lee

1/30 Nathaniel Banks
2/02 Albert S. Johnston
2/04 Tadeusz Kosciuszko
2/06 Jeb Stuart
2/08 William T. Sherman
2/09 Wm. Henry Harrison
2/09 Jeffrey Amherst
2/12 Omar Bradley
2/14 Winfield Hancock

ADMIRED PRESIDENTS

1/30 Franklin D. Roosevelt
2/06 Ronald Reagan
2/12 Abraham Lincoln
2/22 George Washington

SPORTS HEROES

1/17 Muhammad Ali
1/20 John Naber
1/21 Jack Nicklaus
1/24 Mary Lou Retton
1/25 Steve Prefontaine
1/26 Wayne Gretzky
1/31 Jackie Robinson
1/31 Nolan Ryan
2/04 Oscar De La Hoya
2/05 Henry Aaron
2/06 Babe Ruth
2/10 Mark Spitz
2/16 John McEnroe

2/17 Tommy Moe
2/17 Michael Jordan
2/17 Jim Brown
2/20 Charles Barkley

QUARTERBACKS

1/15 Drew Brees
1/18 Pat Sullivan
1/19 Terry Hanratty
1/23 Pat Haden
1/28 Daunte Culpepper
1/29 Bill Nelsen
2/01 Wade Wilson
2/03 Bob Griese
2/03 Fran Tarkenton
2/05 Craig Morton
2/05 Roger Staubach
2/09 Danny White
2/14 Drew Bledsoe
2/14 Jim Kelly
2/14 Steve McNair
2/15 Ken Anderson
2/15 John Hadl
2/17 Billy Guy Anderson
2/17 David Klinger
2/17 Neil Lomax

RAN FOR PRESIDENT

1/21 John C. Breckinridge
1/21 John C. Fremont

1/31 James G. Blaine
2/03 Horace Greeley
2/05 Adlai Stevenson
2/06 Aaron Burr
2/09 Samuel J. Tilden
2/12 Peter Cooper
2/15 John B. Anderson
2/15 John Bell
2/18 Wendell Wilkie

FRIENDLY, WELL-LIKED

1/14 Andy Rooney
1/16 Dizzy Dean
1/17 Betty White
1/19 Dolly Parton
1/26 Bob Uecker
1/29 Oprah Winfrey
2/02 Carroll Righter
2/06 Tom Brokaw
2/06 Ronald Reagan
2/11 Sarah Palin
2/17 Frances A. Genter

BENIGN TV PARENTS

1/14 Guy Williams
1/19 Jean Stapleton
1/22 John Wesley Shipp
1/22 Bill Bixby
1/26 Bob Uecker
1/27 Donna Reed

1/29 John Forsythe
2/04 Conrad Bain
2/09 Judith Light
2/09 Charles Shaughnessy
2/09 Peggy Wood
2/12 Lorne Green
2/12 Joanna Kerns
2/14 James Eckhouse
2/14 Florence Henderson
2/14 Brian Kelly
2/16 Hugh Beaumont
2/22 Robert Young

POPULAR COMICS

1/17 Andy Kaufman
1/20 George Burns
1/23 Ernie Kovaks
1/24 John Belushi
1/24 Yakov Smirnoff
1/26 Ellen DeGeneres
1/28 Mo Rocca
1/29 Irwin Corey
2/02 Tom Smothers
2/03 Shelley Berman
2/03 Joey Bishop
2/04 David Brenner
2/05 Red Buttons
2/07 Chris Rock
2/08 Robert Klein
2/10 Jimmy Durante

2/12 Arsenio Hall
2/14 Jack Benny

IRREPRESSIBLE TALKERS

1/15 Charo
1/17 Muhammad Ali
1/20 Ozzie Guillen
1/31 Carol Channing
2/06 Zsa Zsa Gabor
2/08 Jack Lemmon

GAME SHOW HOSTS

1/17 Warren Hull
1/19 Paul Rodriguez
1/31 Garry Moore
2/12 Joe Garagiola
2/14 Hugh Downs
2/15 Geoff Edwards
2/18 Bill Cullen
2/20 John Daly

SAD VIOLINS, CELLOS

1/20 Ernest Chausson
1/20 Mischa Elman
1/25 Jacqueline Du Pres
1/27 Edouard Lalo
1/30 Lynn Harrell
2/01 Victor Herbert
2/02 Jascha Heifetz

2/02 Fritz Kreisler
2/02 Pablo de Sarate
2/03 Felix Mendelssohn
2/05 Ole Bull
2/17 Henri Vieuxtemps
2/19 Luigi Boccherini

OPERA SINGERS

1/16 Marilyn Horne
1/20 Norman Cordon
1/21 Placido Domingo
1/22 Rosa Ponselle
1/22 William Warfield
1/29 Justino Diaz
1/31 Mario Lanza
2/01 Flaviano Labo
2/02 Jussi Bjoerling
2/02 Martina Arroyo
2/02 Lisa Della Casa
2/04 Martti Talvela
2/06 Richard Bonelli
2/08 Ferdinand Franz
2/09 Hildegard Behrens
2/10 Adelina Patti
2/10 Alessandro Bonci
2/10 Leontyne Price
2/10 Cesare Siepe
2/13 Eileen Farrell
2/13 Feodor Chaliapin
2/13 Sophie Arnould
2/14 Renee Fleming

2/14 Maria Labia
2/20 Mary Garden

IN SCI-FI ROLE

1/19 Tippi Hedron
1/20 DeForest Kelley
1/22 Bill Bixby
1/22 John Wesley Shipp
1/23 Richard Dean Anderson
1/23 Gil Gerard
1/29 Marc Singer
1/30 Hugh Marlowe
1/30 David Wayne
1/31 John Agar
1/31 Suzanne Pleshette
2/01 Billy Mumy
2/03 Blythe Danner
2/04 Gary Conway
2/06 Francois Truffaut
2/07 Buster Crabbe
2/08 Brooke Adams
2/10 Neva Patterson
2/11 Leslie Nielsen
2/12 Lorne Greene
2/14 Andrew Prine
2/15 Claire Bloom
2/15 Kevin McCarthy
2/16 LeVar Burton
2/19 Cedric Hardwicke

VIVID IN VILLAIN ROLE

1/14 Faye Dunaway
1/21 Telly Savalas
1/22 Linda Blair
1/22 Piper Laurie
1/23 Humphrey Bogart
1/23 Dan Duryea
1/23 Rutger Hauer
1/24 Ernest Borgnine
1/26 Paul Newman
1/30 Dorothy Malone
1/31 Jessica Walter
2/03 Morgan Fairchild
2/03 Thomas Calabro
2/04 Ida Lupino
2/05 John Carradine
2/05 Charlotte Rampling
2/06 Rip Torn
2/10 Judith Anderson
2/11 Kim Stanley
2/14 Vic Morrow
2/15 Gale Sondergaard
2/18 Jack Palance
2/18 Edward Arnold
2/19 Lee Marvin
2/21 Gary Lockwood

NOVELISTS

1/12 Jack London
1/14 John Dos Passos
1/22 Joseph Wambaugh

1/23 Stendhal
1/24 Edith Wharton
1/25 Somerset Maugham
1/25 Virginia Woolf
1/27 Lewis Carroll
1/28 Colette
1/29 Romain Rolland
1/31 Zane Grey
1/31 Norman Mailer
1/31 John O'Hara
2/02 James Joyce
2/02 Ayn Rand
2/03 James A. Michener
2/07 Charles Dickens
2/07 Sinclair Lewis
2/08 John Grisham
2/08 Jules Verne
2/09 Alice Walker
2/10 Boris Pasternak
2/11 Sidney Sheldon
2/18 Toni Morrison
2/19 Carson McCullers

INVENTORS

1/17 Benjamin Franklin
1/18 Ray Dolby
1/19 Henry Bessemer
1/19 James Watt
1/21 John Fitch
1/31 Irving Langmuir
2/05 Hiram Maxim

2/06 Charles Wheatstone
2/11 Thomas Edison
2/14 G. W. Gale Ferris
2/15 Cyrus McCormick
2/17 Fred E. Ives
2/17 Rene Laennec
2/18 Alessandro Volta

ABSTRACT ARTISTS

1/24 Robert Motherwell
1/28 Jackson Pollack
1/29 Barnett Newman
2/04 Fernand Leger
2/08 Franz Marc
2/11 Carlo Carra
2/12 Max Beckmann

THE LIGHTS (JANUARY–FEBRUARY)

The Earth was passing through Leo when the Lights were born. Their Sun sign is Aquarius. When astrologers first started using Sun signs, they knew that Aquarius was supposed to be a Saturn sign. Eventually, however, they realized that the Lights were nothing like Saturn. But instead of giving them their rightful ruler – the Full Moon – astrologers assigned the Lights to Uranus, which they considered a planet of change and eccentricity. They forgot that the Moon is also a "planet" of change. Moreover, the root of the word "lunacy" is Luna, the Moon. Actually, we believe the eccentricity of this sign is overstated. Overly eccentric people are apt to be unpopular, and the Lights are the most popular sign in the zodiac. Our keywords for them are Spotlight, Personality and Inspiration.

Leos frequently occupy the spotlight. In this sign we find military heroes, sports heroes, three categories of actors, opera singers and violin soloists. There is also a lot of leadership: generals, presidents, those who ran for president and quarterbacks. In the category of Personality, we have popular comics, game show hosts, miscellaneous "personalities," gabby people and many of the actors. The warm, radiant personality of the Lights comes from the Moon (people persons) and perhaps also the Sun.

The Moon is responsive and receptive, and thus confers an abundance of imagination. Inventors, novelists and abstract painters all attest to the fact that Leos are truly inspired. A brilliant idea is often symbolized by a light bulb. Because of this fact, because of the spotlight, and because of their sparkling personalities, we chose to call these people the Lights. This sign has a reputation for being radical, but the data do not really confirm that. Scorpio is the true rebel. If the Lights were as radical as the Drills, they probably would be less popular.

The Eleventh House is a sociable house (Moon). It governs friends and gatherings. We imagine (Moon) achieving our hopes and wishes, which are also ruled by this house. Because of its phases, the Moon is regarded as a lover of novelty, a trait believed to be possessed by February people.

FASHION DESIGNERS

7/22 Oscar de la Renta
7/30 Giorgio Armani
7/31 Renie
8/01 Yves St. Laurent
8/04 Laura Biogiotti
8/o6 Jean Desses
8/08 Rudi Gernreich
8/09 Michael Kors
8/10 Marcel Vertes
8/10 Betsey Johnson
8/15 Gianfranco Ferre'
8/19 Coco Chanel
8/22 Theoni Aldredge
8/22 Marc Bohan

ARCHITECTS

7/14 Robert Adam
7/23 Arata Isozaki
7/29 Inigo Jones
8/03 Charles Bulfinch
8/09 Giorgio Visari
8/12 Robert Mills
8/20 Eero Saarinen

SCENIC DESIGNERS

7/29 William Menzies
8/03 Alexander Trauner
8/18 Georges Wakhevitch
8/19 Charles D. Hall
8/21 Hans Dreier

BEAUTICIANS, COSMETOLOGISTS

8/01 Linda Marshall
8/05 Anita Colby
8/08 Connie Stevens
8/11 Arlene Dahl
8/15 Lori Nelson
8/17 Hazel Bishop
8/18 Max Factor, Jr.

WERE CHEERLEADERS

7/26 Sandra Bullock
7/28 Sally Struthers
7/30 Vivica A. Fox
8/16 Angela Bassett
8/16 Kathie Lee Gifford

MODELS

7/23 Stephanie Seymour
7/23 Angie Kelley
7/25 Iman
7/29 Alexandra Paul

7/31 France Nuyen
8/01 Mariann Molski
8/05 Anita Colby
8/10 Angie Harmon
8/15 Abby Dalton
8/19 Randi Oakes
8/24 Claudia Schiffer

BEAUTY PAGENT QUEENS

7/16 Bess Myerson
7/21 Aly Landry
7/30 Delta Burke
8/06 Jon Benet Ramsey
8/08 Deborah Norville
8/16 Kathie Lee Gifford
8/17 BeBe Shopp
8/18 Katie Harman
8/20 Jacquelyn Mayer
8/20 Courtney Gibbs

SCREEN BEAUTIES

7/18 Audrey Landers
7/20 Theda Bara
7/20 Natalie Wood
7/24 Jennifer Lopez
7/24 Lynda Carter
7/29 Clara Bow
8/02 Myrna Loy
8/03 Dolores Del Rio
8/05 Loni Anderson

8/07 Charlize Theron
8/08 Connie Stevens
8/10 Norma Shearer
8/10 Rhonda Fleming
8/11 Arlene Dahl
8/14 Halle Berry
8/16 Madonna
8/16 Julie Newmar
8/16 Lesley Ann Warren
8/17 Maureen O'Hara
8/18 Madeleine Stowe
8/19 Jill St. John
8/19 Debra Paget
8/21 Kim Cattrall
8/22 Valerie Harper
8/23 Barbara Eden

SITCOM ACTRESSES

7/18 Harriet Nelson
7/23 Edie McClurg
7/25 Estelle Getty
7/26 Vivian Vance
7/26 Gracie Allen
7/28 Sally Struthers
7/28 Lori Loughlin
7/28 Georgia Engel
7/30 Lisa Kudrow
7/30 Delta Burke
8/01 Tempestt Bledsoe
8/06 Lucille Ball
8/12 Jane Wyatt

8/12 Marjorie Reynolds
8/14 Jackee
8/14 Susan St. James
8/14 Alice Ghostley
8/15 Debra Messing
8/15 Rose Marie
8/16 Julie Newmar
8/19 Marie Wilson
8/22 Valerie Harper
8/22 Cindy Williams
8/23 Shelley Long
8/23 Barbara Eden

SOAP ACTRESSES

7/18 Darlene Conley
7/19 Helen Gallagher
7/21 Chrishell Stause
7/23 Beth Ehlers
7/24 Maeve McGuire
7/25 Katherine Kelly Lang
7/26 Kathryn Hays
7/30 llene Kristen
7/31 Susan Flannery
8/02 Lisa Brown
8/04 Crystal Chappell
8/05 Erika Slezak
8/09 Beverlee McKinsey
8/18 Taylor Miller

GOOD COOKS

8/01 Dom DeLuise
8/03 Martha Stewart
8/15 Julia Child
8/16 Kathie Lee Gifford
8/19 Jill St. John
8/20 Al Roker
8/25 Rachael Ray

BASEBALL MANAGERS

7/17 Lou Boudreau
7/18 Joe Torre
7/27 Leo Durocher
7/30 Casey Stengel
7/31 Hank Bauer
8/04 Dallas Green
8/07 Bill McKechnie
8/09 Ralph Houk
8/12 Fred Hutchinson
8/13 Fielder A. Jones
8/14 Earl Weaver
8/15 Tom Kelly
8/16 Buck Rodgers
8/20 Al Lopez
8/22 Ned Hanlon

PORTRAYED CLERGY

7/31 Don Murray
8/05 John Huston

8/13 John Beal
8/15 Zeljko Ivanek
8/18 Edward Norton
8/20 Peter Davies

HISTORICAL NOVELISTS

7/24 Alexandre Dumas
8/08 Sarah Dunant
8/11 Alex Haley
8/15 Sir Walter Scott
8/16 Georgette Heyer
8/16 Anthony Price
8/20 Vilhelm Moberg
8/21 Mary Margaret Kaye

CONSERVATIVE OPINION

7/18 Steve Forbes
7/19 William Rusher
7/20 M. Stanton Evans
7/31 William J. Bennett
7/31 Milton Friedman
8/07 Alan Keyes
8/11 Jerry Falwell
8/14 Lynne Cheney
8/15 John Silber
8/15 Lewis Lehrman
8/15 Phyllis Schlafly
8/19 Mary Matalin
8/24 Mike Huckabee

THE PATTERNS (JULY–AUG.)

The Earth was passing through Aquarius when the Patterns were born. Their Sun sign is Leo. The Patterns are absolutely nothing like the Aquarius we read about–and there's no reason why they should be. The original Aquarius, as defined by the ancients, was a Saturn sign. It had nothing to do with Uranus, which was not discovered until many centuries later. The presence of conservative thinkers in the data confirms that this is a Saturn sign. Historical novelists, since they write about the past, are also under Saturn. Our keywords for this sign are: Plans, Appearance and Parenting.

Whether as fashion designers, building designers or Hollywood production designers, the Patterns always have to have a plan. Fashion designers sketch the clothing before it is made. Architects draw a blueprint before a house is built. We don't know if scenic designers sketch their plan, but they certainly have to have one. Saturn is the Great Planner. He is too insecure to go forward without a carefully laid plan. Like the Hammers, most Patterns are religious. They like to have a blueprint for living. Cooks follow recipes as their plan of action.

Models, beauty pageant winners and screen beauties attest to the fact that Aquarius rules appearance. Beauty is mostly about bone structure, which is ruled by Saturn. Also, there are certain standards of beauty to which a model or pageant queen must conform, and Saturn is the planet of conformity. Cosmetics help a woman conform to these standards.

Many sitcoms–and virtually all soap operas–are about families. There is a domestic side to Aquarius. Baseball managers, clergy and cooks all occupy parental roles. But the Patterns are less strict parents than the Hammers. Saturn is a negative planet, but Aquarius is a positive sign. The result is a more mellow version of Saturn than Capricorn (a negative sign) produces. Although they may lack the showy personality of a Leo, the Patterns are very nice people–very sweet and genial.

A design forms a type of pattern. Even your face forms a kind of pattern. On the domestic front, such things as sofas, curtains and rugs can have a pattern. Although not quite in the same league as Capricorn, Aquarians have considerable business acumen. Henry Ford, Marshall Field and Bernard Baruch were Patterns. Fashion houses have become big business.

The Fifth House governs children, love affairs, gambling and hobbies. Your children enable you to live on through them because they have a genetic blueprint patterned after your own. Your role as their parent is to set boundaries (Saturn). In a love affair, you stake a claim to someone's heart, at least temporarily. Gambling is a form of business investment, like the stock market. Many poker players, racehorse bettors and other gamblers play the odds and try to proceed logically (Saturn). They don't rely on pure luck, which would come under Jupiter and Uranus. A hobby is apt to involve either study or craftsmanship or collecting, all of which can be associated with Saturn. Let us now contrast the Patterns with their opposites, the Lights:

Patterns (Earth in Aquarius)	**Lights** (Earth in Leo)
Plans	Inspirations
Appearance	Personality
Parenting	Spotlight

Parenting is different from Spotlight because, in a typical family, it is the children who occupy the spotlight. The children are the "stars," and the parents are the "directors." Aquarius, as we have known it in the past, is the only sign that does not exist. Libra traits can be found in April, Capricorn traits in July, Gemini traits in December – but the Sun-in-Aquarius traits are not found in August. The scientists are in March. The radicals are in May. The February people are like Leo. It is time to wipe away a tear, raise a glass in remembrance and say, "Farewell, Aquarius." It was nice knowing you – except that we never did.

TRANSPORT, TRAVEL

2/12 Peter Cooper
2/17 Montgomery Ward
2/20 Enzo Ferrari
2/25 Charles Freer
2/25 Edward Harriman
3/03 George Pullman
3/06 Homer Ferguson
3/09 Leland Stanford
3/12 Clement Studemaker
3/15 Gerardus Mercator
3/17 Gotlieb Daimler
3/18 Rudolf Diesel

TV EXECUTIVES

2/22 Sheldon Leonard
2/27 David Sarnoff
3/02 Desi Arnaz
3/05 Lawrence Tisch
3/06 William J. Bell
3/14 Dwight Hemion
3/19 Burt Metcalfe
3/20 Jack Barry
3/20 Ozzie Nelson

SCIENCE, MATH

2/11 Josiah Gibbs
2/11 Leo Szilard
2/12 Julian Schwinger

2/13 William Shockley
2/15 Alfred North Whitehead
2/17 Otto Stern
2/20 George Smoot
2/22 Heinrich Hertz
2/25 Galileo Galilei
2/26 Camille Flammarian
2/28 Nicolaus Copernicus
2/28 Rene Reaumur
3/04 George Gamow
3/07 John Herschel
3/09 Howard Aiken
3/11 Vannemar Bush
3/12 Gustav Kirchhoff
3/12 Simon Newcomb
3/13 Percival Lowell
3/14 Albert Einstein
3/14 Giovanni Schiaparelli
3/16 Georg Simon Ohm
3/21 Jean Fourier
3/22 Robert Millikan
3/23 Wernher von Braun

ASTRONAUTS

2/19 Joseph Kerwin
3/01 Deke Slayton
3/06 L. Gordon Cooper
3/06 Valentina Tereshkova
3/09 Yuriy Gagarin
3/12 Walter Schirra
3/14 Frank Borman

3/14 Eugene Cernan
3/15 Alan Bean
3/16 R. Walter Cunningham
3/16 Vladimir Komarov
3/17 James Irwin
3/17 Thomas Mattingly

BULLFIGHTERS

2/16 Antonio Ordonez
2/17 Carlos Arruza
2/20 Cristina Sanchez
2/25 Domingo Ortega
2/27 Desperdicios
3/08 Juan Silveti
3/14 Pepe-Hillo
3/18 Chiclanero

RACE CAR DRIVERS

2/12 Brad Keselowski
2/14 Ronnie Peterson
2/15 Graham Hill
2/20 Bobby Unser
2/20 Roger Penske
2/22 Niki Lauda
2/24 Alain Prost
2/25 Davey Allison
2/27 Ted Horn
2/28 Mario Andretti
3/04 Buck Baker
3/07 Janet Guthrie

3/09 Danny Sullivan
3/10 Matt Kenseth
3/11 Troy Ruttman
3/12 Johnny Rutherford
3/13 Marco Andretti
3/13 Lyn St. James
3/14 Jim Clark
3/14 Lee Petty
3/14 Bill Rexford
3/16 Gijs van Lennep
3/18 Mark Donohue
3/21 Ayrton Senna
3/23 Craig Breedlove

DRUG OR ALCOHOL USE AMONG ACTORS

2/14 Ken Wahl
2/15 Chris Farley
2/15 John Barrymore
2/17 Barry Humphries
2/17 Wayne Morris
2/19 Margaux Hemingway
2/20 Drew Barrymore
2/20 Kelsey Grammer
2/22 Robert Young
2/23 Peter Fonda
2/24 James Farentino
2/26 William Frawley
2/27 Elizabeth Taylor
3/02 Desi Arnaz
3/03 Gia Scala
3/06 Tom Arnold

3/07 Daniel J. Travanti
3/08 Camryn Manheim
3/12 Liza Minnelli
3/15 Macdonald Carey
3/17 Mercedes McCambridge
3/17 Rob Lowe

GAY ROLES (THEN DARING)

2/26 Tony Randall
3/05 Rex Harrison
3/08 Aidan Quinn
3/09 Kerr Smith
3/14 Billy Crystal
3/15 Chris Bruno
3/18 Brad Dourif
3/19 Glenn Close
3/20 William Hurt
3/21 Matthew Broderick

PSYCHIC ABILITY

2/13 Robert Ferguson
2/17 C. W. Leadbeater
2/22 Sybil Leek
3/01 Brenda Crenshaw
3/10 Kelly Quinn
3/15 Fran Sharon
3/16 Jz Knight
3/16 Lucille Van Tassel
3/17 Eileen Garrett
3/18 Edgar Cayce

SPARKED CONTROVERSY

2/12 Charles Darwin
2/14 Woody Hayes
2/16 John McEnroe
2/20 Patricia Hearst
2/20 Charles Barkley
2/22 Charles O. Finley
2/22 Christine Keeler
2/25 Galileo
2/25 Bobby Riggs
2/27 Gerald L. K. Smith
2/27 Lee Atwater
3/01 Robert Bork
3/08 Dick Allen
3/08 Jim Bouton
3/09 Gge. Lincoln Rockwell
3/12 Andrew Young
3/12 Jack Kerouac
3/12 Darryl Strawberry
3/13 L. Ron Hubbard
3/13 William Casey
3/16 Jerry Lewis
3/18 Vanessa Williams
3/19 Earl Warren
3/20 B. F. Skinner
3/22 Pat Robertson

REFORMERS

2/12 John L. Lewis
2/15 Susan B. Anthony
2/16 Gretchen Wyler

2/19 Karen Silkwood
2/22 Edward Kennedy
2/22 David Dubinsky
2/23 W. E. B. Du Bois
2/24 Michael Harrington
2/24 Edward James Olmos
2/27 Ralph Nader
2/27 John Steinbeck
2/27 Charlayne Hunter-Gault
3/01 Yitzhak Rabin
3/02 Mikhail Gorbachev
3/02 Carl Schurz
3/07 Thomas Masaryk
3/09 Ernest Bevin
3/10 Vernon Dahmer
3/11 Ralph Abernathy
3/13 Charles Grey
3/16 Daniel P. Moynihan
3/17 Bayard Rustin
3/17 Myrlie Evers-Williams
3/19 Wm. Jennings Bryan
3/21 Dr. George Lundberg

TV COPS, DETECTIVES

2/18 George Kennedy
2/18 Cybill Shepherd
2/19 Lee Marvin
2/21 William Petersen
2/21 Tyne Daly
2/22 Kyle MacLachlan
2/24 Edward James Olmos

2/24 Steven Hill
2/27 Van Williams
3/01 Mark-Paul Gosselaar
3/01 Dirk Benedict
3/01 Robert Conrad
3/02 Al Waxman
3/05 James B. Sikking
3/05 Michael Warren
3/06 Martin Kove
3/07 Daniel J. Travanti
3/12 Mandel Kramer
3/14 Adrian Zmed
3/16 Erik Estrada
3/17 Don Mitchell
3/18 Peter Graves
3/18 Kevin Dobson
3/19 Bruce Willis
3/20 Hal Linden

POP-JAZZ MUSICIANS

2/10 Chick Webb
2/16 Wayne King
2/19 Stan Kenton
2/27 Dexter Gordon
2/29 Jimmy Dorsey
3/01 Glenn Miller
3/06 Wes Montgomery
3/10 Donn Trenner
3/10 Bix Beiderbecke
3/11 Lawrence Welk
3/12 Paul Weston

3/13 Sammy Kaye
3/13 Ina Ray Hutton
3/14 Quincy Jones
3/14 Les Brown
3/14 Les Baxter
3/14 Luther Henderson, Jr.
3/15 Harry James
3/15 Jimmy McPartland
3/16 Tammy Flanagan
3/18 Kai Winding
3/19 Ornette Coleman
3/20 Larry Elgart
3/20 Marian McPartland
3/21 Mort Lindsey

THE SLINGSHOTS (FEB.–MAR.)

The Earth was passing through Virgo when the Slingshots were born. Their Sun sign is Pisces. Based on what we read about Pisces – sensitive, emotional, romantic and so forth – we might assume that the Slingshots are a more or less feminine type of sign – but it's not true. The data show masculine interests like science, machines and daredevil activities. Even their choice of entertainment seems masculine: they like cops and robbers and jazz. Wouldn't Pisces prefer a love story or a love song? The answer to the riddle, of course, is that these people are not Pisceans. They're Virgos.

The biggest myth about the Slingshots is that they are rather timid souls. Nothing could be farther from the truth! Whether as bullfighters, race car drivers or astronauts, the Slingshots intrepidly court danger no matter what the risks. These people love speed, be it autos or spaceships. Let us remember that their ruler, Mercury, is very fast. It is close to the Sun, which calls to mind a moth circling a flame. The way Mercury hurtles through space symbolizes recklessness and instability, which can lead these daredevils into drugs. They are afraid of nothing – even things that can destroy them. They also like to challenge the powerful elite by demanding reforms or spreading controversial ideas. The more people line up to debate them, the better they like it. They enjoy being the underdog!

Our first two keywords for Virgo are Intrepidity and Debate. The third one is Efficiency. Machines, which promote efficiency, are bound to appeal to an earthy sign ruled by Mercury. Virgos love to analyze, so naturally they are drawn to science and math. Their technological cleverness gives them an interest in modes of efficient transportation. Many auto racers know a lot about the cars they drive, and astronauts have to know all about the rockets they pilot. Virgo also rules differentiation, and science is always coming up with a new product or a new idea that's different from what we had before.

Mercury is the smallest planet, and science deals with some very small things, like atoms and molecules. The Virgoan himself is small when stacked up against the challenges he faces and the opposition he encounters. He is like David facing Goliath. The Slingshot is a good name for Virgo, especially since a slingshot is a kind of simple machine.

Virgo is a whiz at details. ESP is under this sign because a prediction is only as good as its detail. Anyone can forecast, "It will snow next winter." But if you say, "It will snow thirteen inches next February 17 in Cleveland" – and that turns out to be true – that's a good prediction! ESP is associated with the solar plexus, which is ruled by Virgo. It's a trip into the future, wing-footed Mercury being associated with travel. We have never seen any proof that Neptune rules ESP, and we doubt that such a slow planet could. ESP should be under quick-moving planets. Psychic flashes come fast. The Twelfth House is about seclusion, and we do our best thinking (Mercury) when we're off by ourselves. It is also the house of "self-undoing," and what gets us into more trouble than our brains, or the lack of them? In mythology, Mercury was full of mischief. In astrology, he is tricky, duplicitous and light-fingered. We consider Mercury malefic because of the order of planetary speeds: Moon benefic, Mercury malefic, Venus benefic, Mars malefic, Jupiter benefic, and Saturn malefic.

MASKED IN TV ROLE

9/14 Clayton Moore
9/19 Adam West

POOR PRESS RELATIONS

8/17 Sean Penn
8/25 Albert Belle
8/27 Tommy Sands
8/29 Michael Jackson
8/30 Ted Williams

8/31 Arthur Godfrey
9/10 Roger Maris

UNMASKED BY SCANDAL

8/18 Roman Polanski
8/19 Bill Clinton
8/27 Pee Wee Herman
8/29 Ingrid Bergman
9/04 Anthony Weiner
9/08 Mark Foley
9/09 Hugh Grant
9/11 Robert Packwood

ISOLATIONIST STANCES

9/02 Hiram W. Johnson
9/08 Robert A. Taft
9/12 Henry Waxman
9/21 H. G. Wells

THE DISABLED

8/19 Bill Shoemaker
8/24 Max Cleland
8/24 Marlee Matlin
8/25 George Wallace
8/26 Rick Hansen
8/26 Chris Burke
8/27 Bob Kerrey
8/29 James S. Brady
8/31 Itzhak Perlman

9/05 Graham Salmon
9/07 Daniel Inouye
9/10 Jose Feliciano
9/13 Rosemary Kennedy
9/19 Jim Abbott
9/22 Andrea Bocelli
9/23 Ray Charles
9/25 Christopher Reeve

PRODUCERS, SHOWMEN

8/18 Gus Edwards
8/22 Daniel Frohman
8/27 Sam Goldwyn
8/31 Dore Schary
9/05 Darryl F. Zanuck
9/06 Billy Rose
9/09 Arthur Freed
9/09 Joseph E. Levine
9/09 Max Reinhardt
9/13 Jesse Lasky
9/14 Hal Wallis
9/15 Leland Hayward
9/16 Jerry Wald
9/17 Joseph Pasternak

HIGH ACHIEVERS: SPORTS

8/29 Bob Beamon
8/30 Ted Williams
8/31 Edwin Moses
9/01 Rocky Marciano

9/03 Shaun White
9/12 Jesse Owens
9/19 Al Oerter

ATHLETIC COACHES

8/16 Amos Alonzo Stagg
8/21 Toe Blake
8/22 Bill Parcells
8/23 Howard Jones
8/27 Frank Leahy
8/30 Jerry Tarkanian
8/31 Pete Newell
9/02 Adolph Rupp
9/02 John Thompson
9/02 Glen Sather
9/03 Dick Motta
9/04 Vince Dooley
9/06 Phil Johnson
9/07 Al McGuire
9/07 Paul Brown
9/07 Jacques Lemaire
9/07 Bora Milutinovic
9/11 Bear Bryant
9/11 Tom Landry
9/11 Franz Beckenbauer
9/13 Bela Karoliy
9/14 Larry Brown
9/17 Phil Jackson
9/18 Scotty Bowman
9/20 Red Auerbach

CRITICS

8/19 John Dryden
8/28 Paul Henry Lang
9/02 Cleveland Amory
9/11 Paul Bekker
9/12 H. L. Mencken
9/14 Eric Bentley
9/14 Van Gordon Sauter
9/15 Robert Benchley
9/18 Howard Clurman
9/18 Samuel Johnson
9/23 Nicholas Johnson

DRUMMERS

8/19 Ginger Baker
8/23 Keith Moon
8/28 Clem Cattini
8/28 Danny Saraphine
9/01 Gregg Errico
9/03 Donald Brewer
9/11 Mickey Hart
9/11 Jon Moss
9/12 Neil Peart
9/16 Joe Butler

MEDICINE, PHYSIOLOGY

8/20 Roger Sperry
8/22 Denton Cooley
8/24 Albert Claude

8/25 E. Theodor Kocher
8/25 Hans Krebs
8/25 Frederick Robbins
8/26 Albert Sabin
8/31 Hermann von Helmholtz
9/04 Max Delbruck
9/05 Susumu Tonegawa
9/07 Michael De Bakey
9/09 Luigi Galvani
9/13 Walter Reed
9/18 Ben Carson
9/20 Sister Elizabeth Kenny
9/26 Ivan Pavlov

ZOOLOGY

8/23 Baron de Cuvier
9/07 Georges-Louis Buffon
9/10 Stephen Jay Gould
9/12 James Hall
9/20 George Grinnel

THE TOWERS (AUG.–SEPT.)

The Earth was passing through Pisces when the Towers were born. Their Sun sign is Virgo. These people take pride (Jupiter) in their work (Sixth House) and tend to be perfectionists about it. Yet the more perfect their work is, the more attention they attract – even acclaim – and they don't like the spotlight. The more praise they receive, the more pressure they feel to try to live up to the accolades. Shyness is a form of pride, and Towers are shy about talking to the press. Pisces actors are even comfortable wearing masks, which some other actors might be too vain to do. Producers and athletic coaches are on the sidelines – not in the spotlight. Yet they do crucial work. So do drummers, but they are always at the back of the band. Doctors work their magic behind closed doors; they don't want an audience. Isolationists don't want to be involved with other nations. We call this general Pisces tendency "Disengagement," our first keyword. Our others are Superiority and Impairment. Neptune, often linked to Pisces, can bring scandal.

Superiority refers to coaches, critics and doctors – all of whom have superior (Jupiter) knowledge that causes the rest of us to value their opinions and defer to their wisdom. These elite experts theoretically tower above us, so we call Pisceans the Towers. Moreover, an "ivory tower" existence describes many Pisceans who disengage. Impairment refers to the surprisingly large number of disabled Towers. Virgo is the sign of efficiency; therefore, its opposite, Pisces, is the sign of inefficiency.

We are told that Pisces is a sympathetic sign. Who can think of anyone more sympathetic that Mother Teresa? She was born August 27. Doctors and nurses feel sympathy for their sick, suffering patients. Whereas Virgo differentiates, Pisces is about sameness. Doctors want to "make 'em all alike"; that is, they want to make their patients healthy like the rest of us. Both Virgo and Pisces like science. Isn't it fitting that sympathetic Pisces would prefer life science, while analytical Virgo would prefer mathematical science? Jupiter is often called "the Great Healer."

Producers bask in Jupiter opulence. In many places, crops are gathered in August or September, for the harvest reflects Jupiter abundance. Pisces is the sign of hospitalization. However, your Sixth House of illness is not a death house. It therefore represents your triumph (Jupiter) over illness. You are the master (Jupiter) over pets, servants and employees (all shown by the Sixth House). Compare the Towers with Slingshots:

Towers (Earth in Pisces)	Slingshots (Earth in Virgo)
Disengagement	Debate
Superiority	Intrepidity
Impairment	Efficiency

Intrepidity is different from Superiority because the elite Towers, operating as they do from a position of strength, have no need to be brave. In the David and Goliath saga, they are Goliath, Jupiter being the largest planet.

FINANCIERS, BANKERS

5/20 Stephen Girard
5/26 Samuel Allerton
5/27 Cornelius Vanderbilt
5/27 Jay Gould
5/27 Adolph Lewisohn
6/03 Bert Lance
6/06 Kirk Kerkorian
6/09 Robert McNamara
6/12 David Rockefeller
6/17 Harold Bache
6/21 Joseph Rainey

WEALTH, LAVISHNESS

5/16 Liberace
5/21 Mr. T
5/22 Barbara Villiers
5/27 Allan Carr
5/31 Prince Rainier
6/03 Josephine Baker
6/09 Cole Porter
6/10 F. Lee Bailey
6/13 Aly Khan
6/14 Donald Trump

TORY PRIME MINISTERS

5/28 Wm. Pitt the Younger
5/30 Henry Addington
6/05 3rd Earl of Bute
6/07 2nd Earl of Liverpool
6/12 Anthony Eden

STARS IN THE G.O.P.

5/20 James Stewart
5/26 John Wayne
5/28 Elisabeth Hasselbeck
5/29 Bob Hope
5/31 Clint Eastwood
6/01 Pat Boone

FASHION EXPERTS

5/12 Linda Dano
5/27 Lee Meriwether
6/06 Louis Godey
6/07 Beau Brummell
6/08 Joan Rivers
6/17 Venus Williams

SADISTIC BUTCHERS

5/21 Jeffrey Dahmer
5/25 Joel Steinberg
5/27 Wayne Williams
6/01 David Burkowitz
6/02 Peter Sutcliffe
6/06 Neville Heath
6/08 Lt. William Calley
6/15 Marvin Lemons
6/17 John Norman Collins

WERE TEEN IDOLS

5/30 Robert Logan
6/01 Pat Boone
6/03 Tony Curtis
6/04 Parker Stevenson
6/04 Scott Wolf
6/05 Chad Allen
6/05 Mark Wahlberg
6/08 James Darren
6/08 Don Grady

6/09 Johnny Depp
6/09 Michael J. Fox
6/11 Joshua Jackson

INVINCIBLE HEROES

5/16 Pierce Brosnan
5/19 Bruce Bennett
5/21 Mr. T
5/21 Raymond Burr
5/23 Douglas Fairbanks, Sr.
5/26 John Wayne
5/26 Jim Arness
5/30 Clint Walker
5/31 Clint Eastwood
5/31 Sharon Gless
6/01 Edward Woodward
6/02 Johnny Weissmuller
6/02 Stacy Keach
6/04 Angelina Jolie
6/05 William Boyd
6/13 Basil Rathbone
6/14 Gene Barry
6/14 Lash La Rue
6/17 Ralph Bellamy
6/18 Richard Boone
6/20 Errol Flynn
6/20 Audie Murphy
6/20 Danny Aiello
6/21 Ron Ely
6/22 Lindsay Wagner

"TAMED" WILD ANIMALS

6/10 Clyde Beatty
6/10 Carl Hagenbeck
6/13 Siegfried Fischbacher

SITCOM ACTORS

5/17 Bob Saget
5/18 Dwayne Hickman
5/20 Bronson Pinchot
5/23 Drew Carey
5/24 Gary Burghoff
6/01 Andy Griffith
6/02 Jerry Mathers
6/08 Jerry Stiller
6/09 Bob Cummings
6/09 Michael J. Fox
6/12 Jim Nabors
6/13 Tim Allen
6/15 Neil Patrick Harris
6/17 Thomas Hayden Church
6/17 Mark Linn-Baker
6/20 John Goodman
6/21 Michael Gross
6/22 Freddy Prinze

OMNIPOTENT TV DOCTORS

5/18 Pernell Roberts
5/31 Gregory Harrison
6/04 Noah Wyle

6/04 Scott Wolf
6/10 Shane West
6/11 Chad Everett
6/11 Hugh Laurie
6/15 Neil Patrick Harris
6/18 Richard Boone

OMNISCIENT LAWYERS

5/16 Debra Winger
5/20 James Stewart
5/21 Raymond Burr
5/23 John Payne
5/25 Dixie Carter
5/25 Hillary B. Smith
5/31 Sharon Gless
6/01 Andy Griffith
6/11 Stephen Schnetzer
6/14 Burl Ives
6/18 E. G. Marshall
6/21 Monte Markham

ROCK SINGERS

5/12 Steve Winwood
5/13 Stevie Wonder
5/13 Richie Valens
5/16 Janet Jackson
5/20 Cher
5/24 Lenny Kravitz
5/26 Stevie Nicks
5/28 Gladys Knight

5/28 John Fogerty
5/29 Melissa Etheridge
5/31 Corey Hart
6/01 Alanis Morissette
6/03 Deniece Williams
6/05 Marky Mark
6/06 Gary U.S. Bonds
6/07 Prince
6/07 Tom Jones
6/09 Jackie Wilson
6/11 Joey Dee
6/14 Boy George
6/17 Barry Manilow
6/18 Paul McCartney 1942
6/20 Brian Wilson 1942
6/20 Lionel Richie
6/22 Cyndi Lauper

POP SINGERS

5/14 Bobby Darin
5/18 Perry Como
5/20 Joe Cocker
5/23 Rosemary Clooney
5/23 Jewel
5/23 Helen O'Connell
5/25 Leslie Uggams
5/26 Peggy Lee
6/01 Pat Boone
6/08 Nancy Sinatra
6/09 Les Paul
6/10 Judy Garland

6/12 Vic Damone
6/14 Burl Ives
6/15 Harry Nilsson
6/17 Dean Martin
6/20 Anne Murray

FURNITURE MAKERS

5/21 Marcel Breuer
5/24 George Nakashima
6/05 Thomas Chippendale
6/17 Charles Eames

WROTE POP MUSIC

5/12 Burt Bacharach
5/13 Arthur Sullivan
5/18 Meredith Willson
5/24 Bob Dylan
5/27 Harold Rome
5/31 Peter Yarrow
6/07 Charles Strouse
6/09 Cole Porter
6/10 Frederick Loewe
6/12 Richard B. Sherman
6/14 Cy Coleman
6/17 Sammy Fain
6/18 Paul McCartney

WROTE LYRICS

5/17 Howard Ashman

5/22 Bernie Taupin
5/25 Hal David
5/27 Julia Ward Howe
5/29 G. K. Chesterton
6/10 Al Dubin
6/18 Sammy Kahn
6/21 Mack Gordon

BECAME RELIGIOUS

5/12 Stephen Baldwin
5/16 Jonathan Jackson
5/19 Malcolm X
5/21 Mr. T
5/23 Rennie Davis
5/23 Lauren Chapin
5/24 Bob Dylan
5/24 Kristin Scott Thomas
5/25 Connie Sellecca
5/26 Phillip Michael Thomas
5/29 Lisa Whelchel
5/30 Stepin Fetchit
6/01 Pat Boone
6/04 Dennis Weaver
6/05 Bill Moyers
6/05 Mark Wahlberg
6/07 Prince
6/09 Bob Cummings
6/10 June Haver
6/14 Lash La Rue
6/18 Kay Kyser
6/19 Ayman al-Zawahiri

6/21 Michael Gross
6/23 Wilma Rudolph
6/24 Ralph Reed

REPORTERS, NEWSMEN

5/12 Howard K. Smith
5/17 Kathleen Sullivan
5/19 Jim Lehrer
5/19 David Hartman
5/20 Adela Rogers St. John
5/20 Ron Reagan
5/22 Bernard Shaw
5/24 Elsa Maxwell
5/30 Frank Blair
6/02 Clarence Page
6/03 Anderson Cooper
6/04 Charles Collingwood
6/05 Bill Moyers
6/07 Ray Scherer
6/09 Marvin Kalb
6/09 Jerry Dumphy
6/10 Jeff Greenfield
6/11 Lawrence Spivak
6/11 Greta Van Susteren
6/17 John Hersey
6/18 Tom Wicker
6/21 Carl Stokes
6/22 Ed Bradley
6/22 Barry Serafin
6/22 Brit Hume

NEWSPAPER PUBLISHERS

5/17 Harry Chandler
5/24 Samuel Newhouse
5/25 Lord Beaverbrook
6/05 Lord Thomson of Fleet
6/10 Robert Maxwell
6/16 Katharine Graham

ADVERTISERS

5/24 Douglas Leigh
5/25 Mary Lawrence
6/16 Raymond Rubicam
6/23 David Ogilvy

PRESS SECRETARIES

5/12 Ron Ziegler
5/22 Jay Carney
5/25 Ron Nessen
6/01 Tony Snow
6/05 Bill Moyers
6/08 Lyn Nofsiger
6/14 Pierre Salinger

THE TRUMPETS (MAY–JUNE)

The Earth was passing through Sagittarius when the Trumpets were born. Their Sun sign is Gemini. Jupiter, their ruler, is the largest of all the planets by far. It is impressive-looking and attention-grabbing, and the Trumpets are much the same. They care a lot about the good opinion of society and crave respectability. Notice that, in various acting categories, they always prefer to play the hero: omnipotent doctors, omniscient lawyers, invincible action heroes.

As teen idols, rock stars and pop singers, the Trumpets are idolized by an adoring public, which boosts their egos (Jupiter pride). Performing is one of their favorite ways of attracting attention, and that includes amusing comedians and bold lion tamers. The music they sing is popular music, and much of their acting is on TV – assuring them a mass audience and mass appeal. A lot of comedy is based on exaggeration (Jupiter) of the normal, and humor itself is under Jupiter and Neptune rulership.

Another aspect of respectability is having money. Not every Sagittarian can be rich, but many noted wealthy people are under this sign. Jupiter rules abundance, privilege, aristocracy, pomposity, ostentation and bon vivants. It's small wonder that bankers, financiers and people who "live large" are often Trumpets. They need to feel good about themselves and their place in the world. Money helps them to do this. Politically, they are often on the Right (Tories), but not always (reporters). They learn about fashion because it's important to them to dress correctly. Sagittarians are the most religious sign in all the zodiac. Devotion to their God and their church is another aspect of their respectability.

Our first two keywords are Performing and Respectability. The third one is Spreading. Jupiter is the planet of expansion, and the Trumpets are eager to expand their horizons. Reporters spread the news, often to a very wide audience. Advertisers spread the word about their products.

Publishers spread their books and periodicals all over the country and often worldwide. Some newspapers are called The Clarion. Some religious people consider it their duty to spread the Word of God.

Of all the data on Sagittarius, the item that seems the most out of place is the category of sadistic butchers. They're certainly not respectable! We can only assume that they feel omnipotent by lording it over their victims before killing them. Presumably this sign produces songwriters for the same reason that it produces singers: because Jupiter has a musical side. It is the planet of relaxation. Some people relax through laughter and comedy, and some people relax through music. Jupiter is audio - sensitive; Saturn is visually sensitive.

The Third House governs your neighborhood, your early schooling, and your relatives. In your own neighborhood, you can be a big fish (Jupiter) in a little pond. A child doesn't think for himself very much; he accepts on faith (Jupiter) what he is told by teachers, parents and clergy. Relatives are often generous (Jupiter) in helping you out. The Trumpets are the most charming people in all the zodiac. That's because optimistic Jupiter gives them confidence, which is always an appealing trait.

PLAYWRIGHTS

11/14 George S. Kaufman
11/21 Oliver Goldsmith
11/24 Garson Kanin
11/26 Eugene Ionesco
11/26 Emlyn Williams
11/30 David Mamet
12/01 Voltaire
12/12 John Osborne
12/13 Marc Connelly
12/15 Maxwell Anderson
12/16 Noel Coward
12/18 Abe Burrows
12/18 Ossie Davis

12/18 Christopher Fry
12/19 Jean Genet
12/19 Howard Sackler
12/21 Jean Racine

HUMORISTS, SATIRISTS

11/18 Clarence Day
11/18 William S. Gilbert
11/22 Terry Gilliam
11/28 Randy Newman
11/29 Joel Coen
11/29 Gary Shandling
11/30 Mark Twain
11/30 Abbie Hoffman
11/30 Allan Sherman
12/01 Woody Allen
12/04 Samuel Butler
12/07 Joyce Cary
12/07 Johann Nestroy
12/08 Joel Chandler Harris
12/10 Jonathan Swift
12/11 Alfred de Musset
12/16 Jane Austen

KNEW ABOUT WORDS

11/24 William F. Buckley
11/26 Ferdinand de Saussure
12/06 Friedrich Muller
12/07 Noam Chomsky
12/09 Phil Appleby

12/09 Collice Portnoff
12/15 Ludwik Zamenhoff
12/17 William Safire

WITTY TALKERS

11/14 George S. Kaufman
11/15 Franklin P. Adams
11/20 Richard Dawson
11/23 Steve Harvey
11/24 William F. Buckley
11/25 John Larroquette
11/26 Robert Goulet
11/28 Jon Stewart
11/30 Winston Churchill
11/30 Donald Ogden Stewart
12/03 Michael Musto
12/07 Heywood C. Broun
12/09 Hermione Gingold
12/11 Teri Garr
12/11 Sally Eilers
12/13 Marc Connelly
12/18 Abe Burrows
12/21 Andy Van Slyke

CHILD PRODIGIES

11/26 Norbert Weiner
12/13 Queen Silver
12/19 John Candies

VENTRILOQUISTS

12/15 Jimmy Nelson
12/15 Tim Conway
12/21 Paul Winchell

MURDERERS, GANGSTERS

11/15 William Heirens
11/21 Vito Genovese
11/22 Joey Adonis
11/23 Billy the Kid
11/23 Dennis Nilsen
11/24 Ted Bundy
11/24 Lucky Luciano
11/24 Charles Starkweather
11/26 Bruno Hauptmann
12/02 Charles "Tex" Watson
12/02 Richard Tingler, Jr. 1940
12/03 Patricia Krenwinkel
12/04 Gary Gilmore 1940
12/06 Baby Face Nelson
12/06 Richard Speck
12/10 Thomas Hamilton
12/18 Edmund Kemper
12/24 Dean Corll

DRUGS: MUSIC WORLD

11/27 Jimi Hendrix
11/30 Billy Idol
12/02 Britney Spears

12/03 Ozzy Osbourne
12/04 Dennis Wilson
12/05 Little Richard
12/08 Gregg Allman
12/08 Sammy Davis Jr.
12/08 Jim Morrison
12/11 Nikki Sixx
12/13 Lillian Roth
12/18 Keith Richard
12/19 Edith Piaf

ACTORS IN MUSICALS

11/26 Robert Goulet
11/30 Mandy Patinkin
12/01 Cyral Ritchard
12/05 Larry Kert
12/08 John Rubinstein
12/09 Donny Osmond
12/13 Robert Lindsay
12/13 Christopher Plummer

OPERA COMPOSERS

11/16 Paul Hindemith
11/22 Benjamin Britten
11/23 Manuel de Falla
11/25 Virgil Thomson
11/29 Gaetano Donizetti
12/07 Pietro Mascagni
12/11 Hector Berlioz
12/16 Zoltan Kodaly

12/16 Ludwig van Beethoven
12/18 Carl Maria von Weber
12/22 Giacomo Puccini

CATCHERS (BASEBALL)

11/19 Bob Boone
11/19 Roy Campanella
11/24 Steve Yeager
11/27 Mike Scioscia
11/29 Bill Freehan
11/30 Ivan Rodriquez
12/07 Johnny Bench
12/07 Ozzie Virgil
12/20 Gabby Hartnett
12/23 Victor Martinez

THE RAPIERS (NOV.–DEC.)

The Earth was passing through Gemini when Rapiers were born. Their Sun sign is Sagittarius. Their ruler is Mercury, planet of reading, writing and thinking. Geminis know more about words than anybody, and their large vocabulary makes them highly articulate. Their cleverness can be seen in their witty jokes, witty writings, and skill at ventriloquism. Our first keyword for the Rapiers is Verbalizing. They do a lot of writing and speaking; they're very verbal. With rapier speed, they blurt out their quips. They don't need to be supplied with jokes like sitcom actors. Some of their commentary is Satire, our second keyword. Like fast-moving Mercury, their minds are very quick. Most are voracious readers, but they tend to skim over the surface of things. Most are not deep thinkers like the Drills, but they do form clever insights about life.

Our third keyword is Targeting. Murderers target their victims. The rapier can be a deadly weapon. Humor targets the butt of the joke. Some humor is a form of aggression, wherein jokes are used as a weapon. Murderers are impatient: they don't want to wait until their victim dies on his own. Swift-moving Mercury rules impatience, plus a lack of self-control that can lead to drug use. Mercury haste also results in tactlessness.

The Rapiers are musical, possibly because music has a mathematical foundation. There are so many beats to the measure, quarter notes and half notes, etc. Some of the most notably musical Geminis were Beethoven, Frank Sinatra and Maria Callas. There are of course numerous other examples. This sign and its opposite, Sagittarius, both have a special connection to rhythm.

The Ninth House rules long trips and higher education. Journeying a long distance calls for high-speed travel (Mercury). In a faraway land, or on a sprawling campus, you are a little fish (Mercury) in a big pond. College students do more reading and writing than they ever did before.

They have an inquiring mind (Mercury). They don't accept things on faith, the way they did as children. The presence of child prodigies in the data shows how bright Geminis can be. It could be argued that some are wasting their considerable brain power on activities of no great moment.

Now let's compare the Rapiers and the Trumpets:

Rapiers (Earth in Gemini)	Trumpets (Earth in Sagittarius)
Verbalizing	Performing
Satire	Respectability
Targeting	Spreading

Performers recite words written by others; they don't have to be verbal. Like a pin pricking a balloon, satire deflates the "respectable." Targeting zeroes in on a center; spreading stretches outward from the center.

PART TWO

ANALYSIS OF THE SIGNS AND THEIR PLANETARY RULERS

COMPUTING OUR FINDINGS

In the following tabulation, "A" equals Art, "E" equals Entertaining, "S" equals Science, and "H" equals Helping. Actors were considered entertainers unless they were acclaimed enough to be counted as artists. Science includes also business and law – anything practical and logical. Helpers are nearly all involved in either government or medicine. Unusually high numbers are underlined. Note that the signs, sign elements and sign rulers are all according to <u>Earth</u> signs. Libra is the best artist, Leo is the best entertainer, Virgo is the best scientist, and Cancer is the best helper. Isn't that exactly what you would expect?

	A	**E**	**S**	**H**
LIB	<u>18</u>	3	4	5
AQU	7	16	5	3
GEM	11	5	0	0
ARI	9	14	2	14
LEO	12	<u>22</u>	6	12
SAG	14	20	10	1
CAP	3	2	18	10
TAU	10	0	14	7
VIR	6	14	<u>31</u>	6
CAN	0	2	0	<u>20</u>
SCO	6	1	2	13
PIS	4	1	7	10
AIR	<u>36</u>	24	9	8
FIRE	35	<u>56</u>	18	27

EARTH	19	16	63	23
WATER	10	4	9	43

	A	E	S	H
VENUS	28	3	18	12
SATURN	10	18	23	13
MERCURY	17	19	31	6
MARS	15	15	4	27
MOON	12	24	6	32
JUPITER	18	21	17	11

The above numbers are percentages. They show what portion of the birthdays in this book fall under each of the four occupational categories. Note that Venus signs are best at the arts, Moon signs are best at relating to people, and signs of the element earth enjoy subjects that are practical and logical. All that sounds reasonable, based on what we have been taught about planets and elements. But note that all of the above numbers are based on Earth signs! Look what happens if you use tropical Sun signs instead: Mars becomes the artistic planet, taciturn Saturn becomes best at handling people, and the emotional water signs do the most practical things! Would any of that make sense? Of course not.

Here we will try to show how each unique element and each unique planet combine to form each unique sign.

ELEMENT		**PLANET**	
Earth:	Practical pursuits	Saturn:	Constructing
Air:	Abstract Feeling, as in Art	Venus:	Interacting
Water:	Aid and Comfort	Mercury:	Intellectualism
Fire:	Entertainment, as in Humor	Moon:	The Public
		Mars:	Aggressiveness
		Jupiter:	The Magnified

SIGN	ACTIVITY	DESCRIPTION
Earthy Saturn	Business, Engineering	Practical Constructing
Airy Saturn	Designing	Artistic Constructing
Earthy Venus	Law, Journalism	Practical Interacting
Airy Venus	Music, Acting	Artistic Interacting
Earthy Mercury	Science, Mechanics	Practical Intellectualism
Airy Mercury	Writing	Artistic Intellectualism
Watery Moon	Government	Public Aid
Fiery Moon	Stand-Up Comedy	Public Humor
Watery Mars	Revolution	Aggressive Aid
Fiery Mars	Cartoons, Puppets	Aggressive Humor
Watery Jupiter	Medicine	Magnified Aid
Fiery Jupiter	Clowning Comedy	Magnified Humor

Of course, the signs have broader meanings than what we have shown here, but these examples will help the reader to see how logical and orderly astrology is, as is the universe it reflects.

Let us now consider the three modes of action. Cardinal signs display the most leadership ability. These people are the most active in government and politics, wielding power and exerting influence on a national level. Fixed signs more often become power centers on a more localized level. They can lead an army, large or small, as a general or a quarterback. They also excel in guiding activities like coaching, directing and counseling. Mutable signs do not usually exhibit much leadership.

Mutable signs have the least self-control, and fixed signs have the most. Out of 918 murders, mutable people committed half of them! Cardinal folks perpetrated one-third, which is normal, and fixed persons committed just one-sixth of the killings. Indications are that mutable signs are more apt to become addicts as well. On a more positive note, mutable people are the most musical group in the zodiac.

Because of their musical bent and their out-of-control behavior, we may say that Neptune co-rules all four mutable signs. Pluto, which is much more literary than astrologers realize, co-rules the cardinal signs. We find creative writers in Libra and Aries, lone wolves in Aries, political power in Cancer and Capricorn, and economic power in Capricorn. Uranus, planet of visualization and spacial relations, co-rules the fixed signs: Aquarius (designers), Taurus (sculptors), Scorpio (directors) and Leo (astrologers).

THE SIDEREAL ZODIAC

During our descriptions of the twelve Earth signs, we avoided mentioning the sidereal zodiac because we preferred to discuss it afterward. First, let us list the signs of the sidereal zodiac alongside the corresponding Earth signs.

Earth Sign	Sidereal Sign
Aries (Fences)	Virgo
Taurus (Rocks)	Libra
Gemini (Rapiers)	Scorpio
Cancer (Antennas)	Sagittarius
Leo (Lights)	Capricorn
Virgo (Slingshots)	Aquarius
Libra (Bridges)	Pisces
Scorpio (Drills)	Aries
Sagittarius (Trumpets)	Taurus
Capricorn (Hammers)	Gemini
Aquarius (Patterns)	Cancer
Pisces (Towers)	Leo

Notice that you can usually see a few similarities between each Earth sign and its corresponding sidereal sign. Aries and Virgo are both hard-working signs. Taurus and Libra are both artistic. Gemini is sharp-witted and Scorpio is sharp-tongued. Cancer and Sagittarius are both generous and giving. Leo and Capricorn both can take charge, control and organize. Virgo and Aquarius are both intellectual. Libra and Pisces are both romantic. Scorpio and Aries both are assertive and able to command. Sagittarius and Taurus are both financially fortunate. Aquarius makes a good architect, and Cancer is said to rule homes and other buildings. In other words, we believe that Siderealists saw in the Earth-sign traits qualities which they thought fitted their sidereal signs.

Let us examine how Siderealists mistook various Earth signs for their sidereal signs. It was inevitable that they would do this because they did not know of the Earth sign zodiac and thought it appropriate to use the twelve constellations as their point of reference.

They saw that the Fences had a connection to rural life. Virgo the Virgin is supposed to be holding corn or wheat, which suggested the harvest, so agriculture came to be associated with Virgo. They also noticed that the Fences were not very sociable, so Virgo became known as an introvert.

It was easy to mistake Taurus for Libra because they are both Venus signs. Both are artistic and attractive. Siderealists saw that the Rocks made good judges, so they assigned that trait to Libra, which they thought resembled scales of justice.

Siderealists probably noticed that the Rapiers can be violent and even deadly, which made them think of the poisonous sting of a scorpion, which they thought they saw in the sky. Both Gemini and Scorpio have sharp intellects and engage in a search for knowledge.

When Siderealists looked over the Antennas, they saw that there was much altruism on display: statesmen, educators, missionaries – even saints – so these things became associated with Sagittarius. They have nothing to do with archery, but they do reflect the fact that Jupiter was considered virtuous, benevolent, and worthy of esteem.

There is a parental side to the Lights. Presidents are father figures, and the sign produces kindly TV parents as well. Since Capricorn is a parental sign too, it's easy to see how Leo was mistaken for Capricorn. The Lights enjoy the sad music of violins and tragic operas, and Saturn is considered melancholy.

The notion that Virgos are scientific goes back at least as far as Ptolemy, and our data show that they are mechanically clever as well. Political reformers also are often Slingshots. All of these traits therefore became associated with sidereal Aquarius.

Since Venus is said to be exalted in Pisces, that sign has something in common with Libra. Both are considered romantic, sentimental and easy-going. Our data show that musicians, actors and mystics often are found among the Bridges, which caused these things to be associated with Pisces.

Earth-in-Scorpio and sidereal Aries have Mars in common, so it was easy to confuse the two. Siderealists saw that the Drills are strong, forceful, passionate leaders, capable of ferocity and destruction. In their role as revolutionaries, they bring about new beginnings, like the phoenix rising from the ashes. Leadership and new beginnings were therefore assigned to Aries.

In the Trumpets' data, we find financiers, bankers and lavish living. This preoccupation with money and wealth thus came to be associated with Taurus. The Trumpets also make good singers, and Taurus is considered ruler of the throat.

Earth-in-Capricorn and sidereal Gemini have a little in common because their rulers – Saturn and Mercury, respectively – are both capable of logic and pragmatism. Siderealists must have noticed that the greatest businessmen were Hammers. Since in mythology, Mercury was called the god of commerce, they associated business with Gemini.

The Patterns, as we saw in our data for that sign, have a domestic side. They make good cooks and like to act in stories about families. They are parental when they portray clergy or manage a baseball team. It therefore is not surprising that Siderealists mistook these people to be Cancer.

In the data on the Towers, we found that they excel as showmen. They display pride and are often in a position of being superior in knowledge and expertise. For these reasons, Siderealists thought they were observing Leo traits.

There are several Earth signs that really don't fit the sidereal zodiac very well. The Towers are one of them. All the evidence shows that, whether deliberately or circumstantially, they tend to avoid the spotlight. How then could they be Leo? That sign is supposed to love attention! Leo is the spotlight!

Another bad fit would appear to be the Hammers. Why would Gemini, a supposedly experimental sign, be so conservative? And what about the authoritarian attitude? These things have nothing to do with Mercury, but they're right up Saturn's alley.

We don't think the Lights fit their sidereal sign too well either. If you use the sidereal system, instead of Leo being the foremost entertainer in the zodiac, that honor would go to reserved Capricorn, an unlikely candidate.

Another factor to consider are our keywords for each sign, which, the reader will recall, were derived directly from the research data. These keywords do not fit the sidereal signs nearly as well as the Earth signs.

We tested all three zodiacs to see how reliable each one is. We awarded points to each zodiac according to how well each one fitted each occupation in the data. The final score: Earth signs 399, sidereal signs 323, and tropical signs 274. We invite the reader to conduct his own test, and you will see that the Earth sign zodiac works the best.

PLANETARY SPEED

A lot of what the planets "mean" is based on their speed through the zodiac. Let's start with the two fastest, the Moon and Mercury. The Moon rules conversation and produces gabby people. Mercury rules thinking and produces clever people. By apparent motion, the Moon is faster than Mercury – and talking is faster than thinking. Otherwise, you would not see so many people putting their foot in their mouth. Our brains can never hope to keep pace with our flapping mouths!

Yet the mind is faster than the body. You can tell that just by writing a letter. Your mind will race ahead of your pen. Even if you type eighty words a minute, your brain is still faster. Venus and Mars denote physical action. The faster Venus depicts rapid action: violence, vehemence, energy, vitality. The slower Mars indicates more strategic action. The person ruled by Mars is competitive with the Venus person because his action is better thought out. Even so, Venus has the advantage of greater speed. Mars is like a person running down the stairs, racing someone who is sliding down the banister. Thus, the Venus person is all smiles, while the Mars person wears a scowl.

Jupiter describes a person who has already "made it" and now has time for relaxation. Perhaps he owns the company where he works. He takes the time to smell the roses along the way, to laugh and to enjoy music. He doesn't hurry too much because that would be incompatible with dignity. (Did you ever see Queen Elizabeth run?) Picture Jupiter as an older man than Mars – someone like Donald Trump – strutting about, enjoying his success.

The Saturn person has a long road to travel, and he is having trouble keeping up. For him, life is a struggle, but he keeps plugging away. Like the tortoise who beat the hare, he intends to win in the end through hard work and perseverance. If he has to do the work of ten men half his age (he is getting old), he'll do that. Although not very well-liked, he gets promotions from time to time because he earns them. A conservative, he doesn't want any changes because he believes the current system favors him in the long run. A long time ago, he formed a 29-year plan for success, and he's sticking to it.

The Uranus-ruled person would require eighty-four years to reach his goals. He'd be long since retired by then, so he knows he's got no shot. He is frustrated, fed up, ready to chuck everything and make a new start, perhaps in a new locality far away. He has a strong will power to make the necessary changes. Upheavals can keep him awake at night, however. He becomes accident-prone due to insufficient sleep. All the stress in his life takes a toll, but he is not discouraged. He firmly believes he can change his life via ingenuity.

The persons symbolized by Neptune and Pluto are like school dropouts who were too slow to keep up in class. They have given up trying to compete. The Neptune person creates an elaborate fantasy world and craves thrills and sensations to rescue him from his malaise. The Pluto person, so far away from the solar family, never wanted to belong anyway. He prefers a life of solitude. He lives by his own rules because he is too alienated from society to share its values.

The twelve signs are basic ontological principles, and the planets are a part of that universal reality. There were twelve apostles, twelve gates to the city and twelve signs. The signs are like twelve different facets of a supreme intelligence. In our view, astrology has always existed. Cavemen were influenced by the planets just as much as men of today. The Babylonians and Egyptians did not invent astrology – they merely developed it. We would not even say that they discovered it because who knows how long ago the very first person looked out at the night sky and thought it might be significant. 5,000 B.C.E.? 10,000 B.C.E? No one knows.

MORE RESEARCH RESULTS

The following tabulations show which elements, planets and signs were found to be important for engaging in which vocational activities. When a planet is listed, it refers to the two signs ruled by that planet. For example, if Saturn is listed first, this means that the combined total for Capricorn and Aquarius was highest. There are hardly any surprises in the research, which proves two things. First, it shows that astrologers have been right all along in what they have said about planets, signs and elements. Secondly, it proves that one must always use the Earth sign zodiac to obtain results that verify what astrologers believe.

146 Top Comedians:	88 Fiction Writers	101 Physical Scientists	43 Life Scientists
45 Fire	35 Air	32 Earth	16 Water
39 Air	24 Fire	27 Water	13 Earth
35 Water	16 Earth	24 Air	8 Air
27 Earth	13 Water	18 Fire	6 Fire

Fiery and airy people like to do things that are more or less fun, such as performing and the arts. Earthy and watery persons are more serious-minded in their outlook. Earthy signs prefer working with things and practical concepts, while water signs like to work with people. It could be that watery folks are not attracted to writing because that's something one does alone.

69 Top Artists	120 Great Actors	129 Top Politicians	77 Talk Show Hosts
17 Venus	33 Venus	33 Moon	23 Moon
14 Saturn	21 Mars	21 Mercury	16 Mercury
13 Jupiter	19 Moon	21 Venus	14 Venus
12 Mars	18 Mercury	20 Mars	9 Mars
8 Mercury	15 Saturn	19 Jupiter	8 Saturn
5 Moon	14 Jupiter	15 Saturn	7 Jupiter

Notice that the rankings for politicians are in the exact order of planetary speed – and the order is almost the same for talk show hosts! This happens because talking is one of the fastest things people do. The quick-moving Moon easily "won" both categories, while slow Saturn and Jupiter did the worst. The latter pair trailed also for actors, but here Venus, the artistic planet, was the runaway winner. Because of Venus emotions and creativity, she won among artists (mostly painters) as well. Notice, however, that all the other planets below Venus are in exactly the reverse order of their speeds. That's because the artist's careful work requires a lot of patience – and almost no talking.

111 Top Military	34 Noted Dictators	30 Famous Tycoons	101 Physical Scientists
27 Mars	11 Saturn	12 Saturn	23 Mercury
19 Moon	8 Mars	8 Jupiter	21 Saturn
18 Venus	4 Jupiter	4 Mercury	17 Mars
17 Saturn	4 Mercury	3 Moon	16 Jupiter
15 Mercury	4 Venus	2 Mars	12 Moon
15 Jupiter	3 Moon	1 Venus	12 Venus

The tabulation for military men shows that, although Leo produces the highest quality generals, the Mars signs are highest in <u>quantity</u>. Mars is, of course, the god of war in mythology. Mars made a good showing among dictators as well, but here the winner was Saturn, a restrictive, authoritarian symbol. The most unselfish and compassionate planet, the Moon, finished last. Practical, conservative Saturn led among business tycoons as well, but here Mars did not do well because both his signs tend to be liberal. Logical Mercury and Saturn head the science list, while the two most emotional planets trail.

58 Great Poets	69 Top Composers	66 Noted Singers	94 Great Athletes
15 Sag & Gem	20 Sag & Gen	17 Sag & Gem	25 Jupiter
10 Sco & Tau	12 Sco & Tau	12 Lib & Ari	17 Mars
9 Vir & Pis	11 Lib & Ari	12 Vir & Pis	17 Mercury
9 Leo & Aqu	10 Vir & Pis	11 Leo & Aqu	16 Saturn
8 Lib & Ari	9 Can & Cap	10 Sco & Tau	10 Moon
7 Can & Cap	7 Leo & Aqu	4 Can & Cap	9 Venus

As you can see, the Gemini-Sagittarius polarity did best in three different disciplines that involve rhythm. We are not quite sure exactly why this is so, but we don't think it could be a coincidence. Add up the totals for all three activities, and the result is quite striking. Sagittarius and Gemini score a whopping fifty-two! The average is only thirty-two, and the total for Cancer and Capricorn is only twenty. Mercury rules reading. Jupiter is audio - responsive, which is why natal Jupiter aspects are important for singers and composers. Look up the birth date of your favorite singer, and you should find that he or she significantly aspects your natal Jupiter. Moreover, many great writers have Pluto aspecting Jupiter or Mercury.

Because there are only ten "planets," each one has a wide variety of symbolic meanings. One thing that Jupiter denotes is athletics, presumably because sports are fun and wholesome. It therefore comes as no surprise that Jupiter won in the athletes' category. What <u>would</u> surprise astrologers, however, is that Pisces did better than Sagittarius! In fact, we have come to the conclusion that Pisces (Aug.-Sept.) is the best athlete in the zodiac. So many fascinating things can be learned about different kinds of people through astrological research! It seems a shame that so few people ever do any.

Please note that if one were to use Sun signs instead of Earth signs in tabulating all of the foregoing data, the results would make no sense. Venus would lead the way among military men, Mars would be first among artists, Jupiter among scientists, Mercury among athletes, the Moon among dictators and Saturn among talk show hosts – all of which flies in the face of what astrologers say about the significance of the planets. Either astrologers have been completely wrong in their claims, or they have been using the wrong zodiac. We vote for the latter, given the fact that there is a zodiac that does work.

SORTING OUT LIBRA TRAITS

Each zodiac sign is a confusing mixture of two different types of traits. These two types must be separated so that readers can understand where they came from and how they came to be associated with a given sign. One type of trait comes from astrologers' interpretation of the meaning of a sign and its ruling planet, based on traditions thousands of years old. The second type of trait results from actual observation of persons born in a particular month.

TYPE 1	TYPE 1	TYPE 2
artistic	diplomatic	energy
aesthetic	charming	vitality
cultured	affectionate	spirited
romantic	accommodating	dynamic
symmetry	negotiating	passionate
harmony	treaties	vehement
balance	agreements	alive
adjusting	partnering	vivacious

The Type 1 traits are associated with Libra because of the meaning of Venus. Unfortunately, astrologers failed to notice that, as our data show, these qualities are found in April, not October. The Type 2 traits were correctly observed among the April people—but astrologers, assuming them to be Aries, assigned energy to Mars. As the data show, actors are under Venus, planet of emotion. Why are actors interesting to watch? Precisely because of their powerful emotional energy (Venus). Mars, a masculine symbol, is less overtly emotional. No one thinks that Mars rules actors, yet many continue to believe that Mars – not Venus – is all about energy and vitality.

SORTING OUT ARIES TRAITS

Type 1: Rightly linked to Aries, wrongly linked to April
Type 2: Rightly linked to October, wrongly linked to Libra

Researchers have found that a lot of military men were born in September and October – the period tropical astrologers call Libra–even though soldiers are supposed to be under Aries! Paradoxes of this kind are common when the wrong zodiac is used.

TYPE 1	TYPE 1	TYPE 2
leader	origins	detached
zealous	beginnings	objective
crusading	childhood	just
pioneering	primitive	evaluating
progressive	military	comparing

Astrologers believed that leaders and crusaders were under Aries, even though actually there are few noted leaders to be found in April. They also thought that origins and a more or less primitive way of life should be under Aries, failing to notice that these concepts are evidenced in October.

The Type 2 qualities were correctly perceived to be possessed by the Fences. Since emotional Venus is necessarily subjective, it follows that its opposite, Mars, must be capable of objectivity. The Mars person is a realist who sees life as it is. He can see that there is much injustice in the world, so he crusades against it.

SORTING OUT SCORPIO TRAITS

Type 1: Rightly linked to Scorpio, wrongly linked to November
Type 2: Rightly linked to May, wrongly linked to Taurus

TYPE 1	TYPE 1	TYPE 2
destroying	drilling	constructive
causing rebirth	penetrating	causing growth
aggressive	probing	the future
despotic	incisive	

People always emphasize the negative side of Scorpio. It is indeed the sign of destruction, but it is also the sign of rebirth. Scorpio tears down the old in order to bring forth a new order that he believes will better society. His ideas may seem extreme, but he considers himself more constructive than destructive. Astrologers knew that Scorpio was supposed to possess these Type 1 traits, but they failed to notice that these qualities were on full display in May, not November. In fact, they imagined the Drills to be a conservative sign!

The Type 2 traits were correctly associated with May, which astrologers assumed to be Taurus. "Constructive" and "causing growth" are the positive side of radical reform. Scorpio is the sign that looks ahead to the future – not tradition-loving Taurus. When Mars, ruler of Scorpio, has strong aspects to Pluto and the Sun, that denotes a stubborn person. Venus aspects do not have this effect.

SORTING OUT TAURUS TRAITS

Type 1: Rightly linked to Taurus, wrongly linked to May
Type 2: Rightly linked to November, wrongly linked to Scorpio

TYPE 1	TYPE 1	TYPE 2
materiality	enduring	researching
tangible	stable	patient
sense of form	deliberative	persevering
artistic	plodding	thorough
lover of beauty	compiling	magnetic

Astrologers knew that Taurus, a Venus earthy sign, ought to make a good sculptor, so they assigned such artists to May. Alas, they soon discovered that November was full of sculptors! Seeking to explain this contradiction, they pointed out that Mars is said to rule sharp instruments, a dubious assertion. Artists don't sculpt because they like to use knives! They sculpt because they love beauty, form and creating art. You can sculpt in soft clay without using any cutting implement.

The Drills' love of radical reform can scarcely be depicted by such Taurus words as stable, enduring or plodding. Such similar traits as patient, persevering and thorough were observed in November and thus assigned to Scorpio. Compiling was assigned to May, while researching was given to November. The latter is correct, for what are researchers but compilers of data? The Rocks are the compilers.

Astrologers noticed that November people are often magnetic, so they assigned this trait to Scorpio. Yet Mars is not a magnet. Venus is the magnet. Mars repels; Venus attracts. Therefore, Taurus is the magnetic sign—not Scorpio. Judges, found in November more often than May, are deliberative Taureans.

SORTING OUT CAPRICORN TRAITS

Type 1: Rightly linked to Capricorn, wrongly linked to January
Type 2: Rightly linked to July, wrongly linked to Cancer

TYPE 1	TYPE 1	TYPE 2
status seeker	the Law	conservative *
ambitious	rules	prudent *
successful	authoritarian	thrifty *
businessman	dictatorial	security-loving
executive	dominating	possessive
pragmatic	controlling	fixed assets
prudent *	limiting	real estate
conservative *	suppressing	savings
thrifty *	disciplining	old age
miserly	strict	the grave

Notice that the three starred qualities are both TYPE 1 and TYPE 2. Because of the meaning of Saturn, astrologers correctly judged these traits to be Capricornian. However, they observed these qualities among July people, whom they assumed to be Cancer. They therefore assigned to supposedly opposite signs the very same traits! This kind of chaos is not good enough for the twenty-first century. Astrology must get its house in order.

The quality which we have called "constructing" is not mentioned on the lists because astrologers have not emphasized it. This is ironic because they know that Saturn rules structure, which comes from the same root. Because of the strict, exacting nature of this planet, Capricorns are very self-disciplined, meticulous, careful and precise in their work. They are natural craftsmen, which is why they make such good painters.

SORTING OUT CANCER TRAITS

Type 1: Rightly linked to Cancer, wrongly linked to July
Type 2: Rightly linked to January, wrongly linked to Capricorn

TYPE 1	TYPE 1	TYPE 2
tuned-in	motherly	politician
impressionable	protective	police
receptive	nurturing	great heights
sympathetic	changeful	farthest limits

Astrologers understand very well the receptive and nurturing qualities of Cancer and the Moon. It's a shame that they never figured out that, as our data show, it is the January people who possess these qualities – not the July people.

Astrologers know that a lot of politicians were born in January. They assumed that the Antennas were Capricorns; therefore, politicians became associated with that sign even though it really doesn't make much sense. All the literature asserts that Capricorns are comparatively introverted and uncommunicative – hardly a recipe for success in politics! Cancers, on the other hand, are very adept at dealing with the public (Moon).

One of the major misconceptions is that "climbing" Capricorn reaches for the farthest limits. Saturn is all about imposing limits – not surpassing them. Our data on people who stretch the boundaries of our awareness – as well as those who see visions – confirm that it is the Moon's children who push boundaries.

SORTING OUT LEO TRAITS

TYPE 1: Rightly linked to Leo, wrongly linked to August
TYPE 2: Rightly linked to February, wrongly linked to Aquarius

TYPE 1	TYPE 1	TYPE 2
leader	hosting	popular
confident	entertaining	charismatic
commanding	theatrical	friendly
organizing	warm	convivial
centralizing	sunny	social
inspirational	radiant	mixing
magnetic	vivifying	networking

Aside from baseball managers, there is hardly any leadership to be found in August. There are a few conquerors like Napoleon, Mussolini and Castro, but these dictator types are under oppressive Saturn. Leo gets elected to posts. They are extroverts (gabby Moon) who find it easy to charm the public (Moon) with their sparkling personalities. They use what appears in the middle column above to obtain what appears in the first column.

Astrologers couldn't help but notice how friendly and popular the February people, whom they believed to be Aquarius, are. They were also influenced by the meaning of the Eleventh House of Friends, not realizing that this is Leo's house. It's not unusual to find in the literature references to Aquarius as "detached" (Saturn), which seems in contradiction to terms like "friendly" and "popular." Astrology should not be full of contradictions, and it need not be.

SORTING OUT AQUARIUS TRAITS

Type 1: Rightly linked to Aquarius, wrongly linked to February
Type 2: Rightly linked to August, wrongly linked to Leo

TYPE 1	TYPE 2
visual art	amorous
designing	has affairs

There is hardly anything to sort out for this sign because, as we have seen, astrologers completely missed the boat when they assigned Aquarius to Uranus. There are a number of cases of Don Juans in August, such as Wilt Chamberlain, Magic Johnson and Bill Clinton. Also Mae West had the image of a femme fatale in her movies, and Mata Hari had many affairs. This trait might stem from the fact that Aquarius is one of the best-looking signs.

Sadly, the original meanings of Aquarius as a Saturn sign are lost to us. About the only trait that has survived the purge is designing, which several authors have mentioned. Saturn people are very good at visual art, whereas they seldom do much with music because its uplifting nature is rather incompatible with the thoroughly grounded Saturn.

SORTING OUT VIRGO TRAITS

Type 1: Rightly linked to Virgo, wrongly linked to September
Type 2: Rightly linked to March, wrongly linked to Pisces

TYPE 1	TYPE 1	TYPE 2
analytical	details	thrill seeking
splitting up	meticulous	addicted
efficient	systematic	psychic
practical	methodical	controversial

The Type 1 qualities are the traits of a scientist, and the Slingshots boast more famous scientists than any other sign. In addition to their analytical mind, there is the fact that Virgos, like many scientists, are rather introverted and thus temperamentally suited to studious pursuits.

People seem locked into the notion that thrill seeking, addiction and psychic ability are under Pisces, but the data make it clear that these traits are under Virgo. This sign is associated with pharmacies, and many celebrities become addicted to prescription drugs. Mercury people are very nervous and may find drugs calming. Years ago, many were probably chain smokers.

Although Virgos are not especially sociable, they are very articulate, thanks to their ruler. We see this in their penchant for demanding reforms and stirring up controversies. Pisces, on the other hand, is often described as inarticulate.

SORTING OUT PISCES TRAITS

Type 1: Rightly linked to Pisces, wrongly linked to March
Type 2: Rightly linked to September, wrongly linked to Virgo

TYPE 1	TYPE 1	TYPE 2
inarticulate	mystery	caretaking
withdrawn	enshrouded	medicine
solitary	secretive	anatomy
secluded	scandal	scholarly
confined		critics

Pisceans are always described as withdrawn and secretive, which could explain why they don't like to talk to press. Reporters can expose their secrets and foment scandal. Pisces prefers to be enshrouded in mystery rather than be subjected to criticism. Ironically, they may become critics themselves, but they don't attack people in a personal way. They only critique society at large or works of art, based on their expertise and scholarship. They are also knowledgeable about health and sickness. Pisces rules confinement (hospitals), which may manifest as a disability.

Pisces is always described as highly spiritual. We don't have proof of this in our data, but it's what astrologers believe. We don't think this would fit the March people very well at all. The Slingshots are heavily involved in science, which is very different from religion. The scientist focuses entirely on the material world of things he can quantify. The religious person focuses on spiritual things that cannot be measured or even proven. Sometimes science and religion are even in conflict, as in the evolution controversy. Richard Gere is one Tower who is very spiritual. Another was James Coburn.

SORTING OUT SAGITTARIUS TRAITS

Type 1: Rightly linked to Sagittarius, wrongly linked to December
Type 2: Rightly linked to June, wrongly linked to Gemini

TYPE 1	TYPE 1	TYPE 2
religious	joking	jack-of-all-trades
hopeful	grabs attention	master of none
confident	advertising	scattered
eminent	publishing	diffusive
respectable	reaching out	spreading news
sophisticated	cosmopolitan	avid shopper
prodigal	generalizing	

Our research shows that the Trumpets do a lot of performing, but that is not listed above because astrologers never mention it, although we do have "attention grabbing" on the list. We also have "joking," which is verified in the data by TV comedians. The word "jovial" comes from "Jove" (Jupiter).

We know of no important reason why Gemini would need to be a "jack-of-all-trades, master of none." We believe this trait was observed among the June people and results from Jupiter overexpansion. Gemini may well know the latest news, but spreading it (reporters) is a form of Jupiter expansiveness, along with advertising and publishing.

The Jupiter person is considered a big spender. Avid shopping was observed among the June people, whereas "prodigal," meaning much the same thing, was handed down to us from antiquity. The faith of religious people makes them more hopeful and confident than cynical nonbelievers. Sagittarius has always been considered sophisticated, cosmopolitan, and above all respectable – sometimes even eminent.

SORTING OUT GEMINI TRAITS

Type 1: Rightly linked to Gemini, wrongly linked to June
Type 2: Rightly linked to December, wrongly linked to Sagittarius

TYPE 1	TYPE 1	TYPE 2
clever	articulate	education
intellectual	fluent	quick
literary	talkative	witty
translating	irritable	impulsive
skilled	unstable	outspoken
knowledgeable	restless	tactless
well-read	traveling	shooting at

Astrological symbolism leaves no doubt that quick, clever Mercury is the planet of wit, which explains why we find so many witty people born in late fall. Being knowledgeable, literary, intellectual and educated all relate to brainy Mercury.

Gemini has always been considered a talker, although a Mercury sign cares more about the ideas conveyed, whereas a Lunar talker cares more about the companionship of the people with whom he converses and perhaps influences. The Lunar person wants to be popular. This does not particularly interest the Mercury person, which explains his lack of tact.

Not everyone knows that the Rapiers have the hottest temper in the zodiac. We found this out by keeping track of athletes who get into brawls. This lack of self-control stems from such Mercury traits as impulsive, unstable and irritable. This Gemini restlessness also causes them to want to travel.

THE MOON IN A CHART

The Moon in a sign means a number of things to astrologers that have nothing to do with occupation. Even so, we did find some interesting cases in which a high total in our data either agreed with other research in this book or else agreed with what astrologers customarily say about the signs. Here are examples of this:

Moon in Aries: leaders, violent types

Moon in Gemini: businessmen

Moon in Cancer: helpers

Moon in Leo: actors, leaders

Moon in Virgo: physical scientists, daredevils

Moon in Libra: artists, musicians, writers, actors

Moon in Sagittarius: athletes, daredevils

Moon in Aquarius: intellectuals, helpers

Moon in Pisces: life scientists, artists

The 250 helpers are 73 clergymen, 67 reformers, 34 educators, 32 astrologers, 23 missionaries and 21 psychics.

The 300 leaders are 60 politicians, 53 film directors, 50 generals, 39 quarterbacks, 37 conductors, 34 coaches and 27 baseball managers.

The 300 athletes are 55 basketball stars, 45 baseball .300 hitters, 44 runners, 42 home run sluggers, 39 quarterbacks, 25 offensive linemen, 25 defensive linemen and 25 boxers.

The 150 violent types are 50 murderers, 50 generals, 25 boxers and 25 defensive linemen.

The 200 daredevils are 40 jockeys, 39 quarterbacks, 35 astronauts, 35 miscellaneous daring people, 26 auto racers and 25 bullfighters.

The 150 businessmen are 72 executives, 37 tycoons, 27 showmen and 14 economists.

The 200 physical scientists are 63 physicists, 44 inventors, 41 engineers, 35 astronauts and 17 astronomers.

The 120 life scientists are 32 zoologists, 26 botanists, 24 miscellaneous doctors, 21 bacteriologists and 17 surgeons.

The 200 intellectuals are 51 columnists, 36 philosophers, 34 judges, 27 historians, 24 theologians, 17 economists and 11 anthropologists.

The 300 writers are 77 poets, 69 novelists, 51 columnists, 46 dramatists, 43 humorists and 14 critics.

The 250 actors are 96 dramatic actresses, 96 dramatic actors and 58 comedians.

The 300 musicians are 80 singers, 64 instrumental soloists, 53 composers, 37 conductors, 36 songwriters and 30 dancers.

The 200 artists are 61 painters, 34 miscellaneous artists, 32 sculptors, 28 architects, 27 cartoonists and 18 fashion designers.

PART THREE

RESEARCH ON PLANETARY ASPECTS

ASPECTS AND VOCATIONS

Signs are not the only thing to consider in astrology. Planetary aspects are important too. Aspects are the geometric angles that planets form with each other and with the Earth. There are seven important aspects: conjunction (zero degrees), opposition (180°), square (90°), semisquare (45°), sesquisquare (135°), trine (120°) and sextile (60°). The semisquare and the sesquisquare are sometimes called "minor" aspects, but there is nothing minor about them. They are just as important as the rest and should always be calculated. Aspects do not have to be exact as long as they are "within orb." We use an orb of seven degrees on all aspects.

Let's clarify with a couple of examples. Suppose Mars is in ten degrees of Aries and Venus is in ten Leo. This is an exact trine. There are 360 degrees in the circle of the sky, so each of the twelve signs contains thirty degrees. Going from Aries (the first sign) to Leo (the fifth sign) is a distance of four signs, and four times thirty equals 120 degrees. Now suppose Mars is in ten Aries and Pluto is in seventeen Leo. This is not an exact trine, but it still counts because it is within the seven-degree orb. The two planets are 127 degrees apart. If this sounds difficult, all you need is some practice. Soon you'll be computing aspects as easily as the pros. Now let's look at how various aspects impact vocational preference.

Visual Art: Saturn is the planet of painters, presumably because careful attention to detail is paramount. The common aspects are Saturn-Mars and Saturn-Mercury. Sculptors may have these aspects, but more common are Uranus-Mars and Uranus-Sun. Uranus is about spacial relations and visualization. Film directors and fashion designers often have Mars-Uranus. Cartoonists have patterns involving Neptune, Saturn and Mars.

Music: Composers have the Sun aspecting Mars, Jupiter or Neptune. Jupiter-Neptune is also very musical. Singers have these same aspects. Musicians (people who play an instrument) have Venus aspecting Mercury or Jupiter. Venus broadly represents the performing arts. Conductors may have the Moon (people) aspecting Venus (performing). Dancers often have Mercury aspecting Saturn because of the discipline and rigorous training required. They may also have aspects like athletes, such as Venus-Uranus.

Actors, if they're any good, have Venus aspecting the Sun, Mars or Pluto. Orators have these aspects too because they too are emoting forcefully. Comedians have Mercury aspecting Jupiter or Neptune, wherein the latter pair provide the humor and Mercury supplies the cleverness. Comedy isn't funny if it's not clever. People who are funny in real life have similar aspects. Pluto is the planet of writers, possibly because writers work alone and Pluto is a loner. Look for Pluto aspecting Mercury or Jupiter. Journalists often have Pluto-Moon, since interviewing people is part of their job. Occultists who write about what they know are apt to have Pluto-Saturn, where the latter shows deep thought. Inventors have aspects like writers: Pluto-Mercury and Pluto-Jupiter.

Scientists have practical Saturn aspecting Venus, Neptune or intellectual Mercury. Saturn and Mercury would be expected, but what do Venus and Neptune contribute? They could show the feeling of awe and wonder that scientists often experience, or they could be showing compassion for humanity. When Saturn aspects Jupiter, it shows that something deep and weighty must be pondered. You are apt to find this aspect in charts of psychologists, judges, theologians, etc. Philosophers, however, are ruled by Mars, probably because philosophy is all about arguments. Look for Mercury or Jupiter to aspect Mars.

Astrologers have Uranus aspecting Sun, Moon or Mars. Uranus is important because it shows the ability to understand the interrelationships among many parts of a whole. Look for Uranus-Mars in charts of chess masters, engineers, etc. The most common aspect we found for business tycoons was Mars-Neptune. In this case, Neptune is loosening or unleashing Mars, so that the person can be reckless or ruthless enough to take big risks when necessary. Some aspects to practical Saturn can help, but too many would make the businessman too cautious. When Saturn aspects the honorable Sun, that shows someone who can be given responsibility in the company.

Politicians have Jupiter aspecting the Moon or Mars.

Moon-Jupiter is a popularity aspect. Since philosophers often have Mars-Jupiter, it could show a leader who has a strong political philosophy by which he governs. Political reformers and other altruistic people often have Moon-Saturn, which denotes a social conscience. What sometimes happens is that the person is disappointed in his emotional life, so he redirects his love towards all of humanity. Clergymen usually have combinations involving Moon, Saturn and the Sun. Note that all three of these are parent symbols. Movie and TV producers, who sometimes have to make quick decisions, are apt to have Moon-Mercury. These quick-moving bodies reveal a quick thinker. Moon-Mars shows a guiding talker, like a talk-show host.

Aspects don't have to be "soft" (trines and sextiles) in order to be useful and beneficial. In fact, hard aspects are often preferable. Alcoholics are apt to have soft aspects involving Neptune, Jupiter and the Sun or Moon. Soft aspects make <u>you</u> soft: weak and self-indulgent. Richard Speck, the mass murderer, had a grand trine among three ominous planets. Murderers have aspect patterns involving Venus, Uranus, Neptune and Mars. We already have mentioned that Mars-Neptune can produce a reckless, ruthless person. This is the most common aspect in murderers' charts. By itself, Venus-Uranus can show someone who plays a violent sport. Generals have charts a lot like murderers.

Uranus is a very physical planet, often involved in sports. Athletes are apt to have Uranus aspecting Mercury or Venus, as though these fast-moving planets energize Uranus. Saturn aspecting this trio confers discipline. Mar-Pluto is a fierce competitor. Uranus-Jupiter indicates adventurers and daredevils. It's a gambler's aspect and can show a person who takes big, unnecessary risks. Uranus-Mercury occasionally shows an unbalanced person, but mental illness is more often a Neptune-Moon phenomenon (suggesting a fantasy world).

Sun-Mercury is a rare aspect because Mercury is moving fast when it conjoins the Sun, so that the conjunction doesn't last very long. This aspect shows someone who is an expert or an authority on some subject. Other people turn to him for information or advice. Sometimes he is a critic. Sun-Pluto is an aspect of extreme individuality. Often there is something physical that sets the person apart from the crowd and makes him distinctive. He could be a giant or a dwarf or a muscle-bound hulk or an extremely overweight individual.

Having now covered all combinations of planets except Uranus-Pluto and Neptune-Pluto (very slow-changing aspects), we turn your attention to a brief comparison between planets and signs. We said that Lunar aspects are about relating to people. Well, sure enough, the Lunar signs – Cancer and Leo – are the most successful at this. We said that Mercury represents cleverness in comedy. Sure enough, a Mercury sign – Gemini – produces the wittiest people. Venus is the planet of acting, and the Venus signs – Libra and Taurus – give us great actors. Mars is the planet of philosophy, and a Mars sign – Scorpio – provides us with the most great philosophers. Saturn is the planet of painting, and a Saturn sign – Capricorn – produces the most painters. Note that all of the above is according to Earth signs. If you use Sun Signs instead, you lose all of these correspondences between planets and signs–and they are important because astrology needs to be consistent. The research on signs and the research on aspects should support each other.

Everything we have said above about aspects was based on tabulations of what was actually found in charts. Some of what we learned does not agree with standard astrological texts. Isn't it very important and necessary that we base our beliefs on research rather than blind articles of faith? A typical student would look at a Venus-Neptune aspect and think that that person would make a great actor or a great musician, when actually this combination of planets is not helpful in either of these fields. Venus aspecting certain other planets is very useful for actors, and Neptune aspecting certain planets is helpful in composing, singing, and comedy acting. But the Venus-Neptune aspect means other things entirely. How many students would know that Pluto is the key planet for writing, or that Saturn is the key planet for painting? Only research can uncover these important realities.

Let us look at the actual numbers for some key activities. Of 70 murderers, 48 had Neptune-Mars and 46 had Neptune-Venus. Of 37 fighting men (soldiers and boxers): Venus-Uranus 27, Venus-Neptune 22, and Uranus-Neptune 21. Of 44 athletes: Uranus-Mercury 30, Venus-Saturn 28, Venus-Mercury 25. Of 29 businessmen: Mars-Neptune 23, Uranus-Sun 22. 60 statesmen: Jupiter-Moon 45, Jupiter-Mars 44.

41 top comedians: Mercury-Jupiter 33, Mercury-Neptune 25. 58 great actors: Venus-Mars 45, Venus-Sun 42, Venus-Pluto 42. 34 musical instrumentalists: Venus-Mercury 26, Venus-Jupiter 21. 32 composers: Jupiter-Neptune 24, Jupiter-Sun 21, Neptune-Sun 20.

29 painters: Saturn-Mercury 23, Saturn-Mars 20. 21 designers: Uranus-Mars 14, Uranus-Sun 12. 31 directors: Uranus-Mars 23, Uranus-Sun 23. 59 creative writers: Pluto-Jupiter 46, Pluto-Mercury 45. 31 philosophers: Mars-Mercury 26, Mars-Jupiter 21. 43 singers: Jupiter-Neptune 38. 40 astrologers: Uranus-Mars 30, Uranus-Sun 26, Uranus-Moon 24. 29 scientists: Saturn-Mercury 20, Saturn-Venus 20, Saturn-Neptune 18.

One of the problems with astrologers doing research is that some only test for what they expect to find. We tested all planetary combinations. Much research remains to be done, but beware of extremely large samples. A lot of people paint, but they don't paint like Rembrandt. If you can't find the relevant astrological significators among the most impressive and most celebrated, we don't know where else you would expect to find them. The greater the quantity of your sample, the lesser the quality.

If you're wondering what would be normal – what would occur by chance – the answer is fifty percent of your sample. We compute this as follows: There are twelve places from which a given point can be aspected: two squares, two semisquares, two sesquisquares, two trines, two sextiles, one conjuction and one opposition. If you use a seven-degree orb, there are fifteen degrees in each spot that would count as an aspect. Twelve spots times fifteen degrees in each equals 180 degrees, which is exactly half of the 360 degrees in the whole circle of the sky. Merely figuring the frequency of an aspect can be a little misleading, however. For example, if a comedian has the Mercury-Jupiter aspect, he doesn't need to have Mercury-Neptune. He only benefits from Mercury-Neptune if he doesn't have Mercury-Jupiter.

Authors are fond of saying that astrology is a "language" in which one simply learns the meaning of each "word," each symbol. We don't care for this formulation. It makes the planets sound like mere abstractions. It implies that a planet means what it means only because that meaning is in the mind of the astrologer. We believe that the meaning of each planet is something more intrinsic that arises from the relative speed of each sphere. If planets are mere words in a language, one ought to be able to combine these words and always form a tradition-confirming "sentence." Yet our research on aspects reveals that, in most cases, planets' meanings are a little different from what astrologers have described.

Let us now consider the orb on all these occupational aspects. We examined 809 aspects and tallied up the number having an orb between zero and seven degrees.

Here are the totals:

Zero	144	Two	156	Four	101	Six	74
One	123	Three	135	Five	86	Seven	62

The total for zero degrees was actually seventy-two, but we doubled that because there is only one way that an aspect can have a zero-degree orb, whereas there are two ways that the orb could be one degree, two degrees, etc. Notice that the close aspects (zero to three) add up to 558, while the wide aspects (four to seven) total just 323. This proves that a close aspect is more powerful and influential than a wide one. Any astrologer could tell you this, but the general public doesn't know things like that, which is why this book was written.

In the following pages, we present most of our evidence, showing examples of people who have the appropriate aspects. The 29 categories, in order of their appearance in these pages, are these:

1. Popular Celebrities
2. Statesmen
3. Altruists
4. Experts
5. Philosophers
6. Businessmen
7. Inventors
8. Astronauts
9. Psychologists
10. Scientists
11. Painters
12. Actors
13. Comedians

14. Instrumentalists
15. Singers
16. Composers
17. Creative Writers
18. Reporters
19. Athletes
20. Murderers
21. Fighting Men
22. Adventurers
23. Adventure Stars
24. Bank Robbers
25. Conductors
26. Cartoonists
27. Fashion Designers
28. Film Directors
29. Astrologers

JUPITER – MOON

Julie Andrews
Desi Arnaz
Lucille Ball
Brigitte Bardot
John Barrymore
David Cassidy
Farrah Fawcett
Ava Gardner
Cary Grant
Rita Hayworth
Katharine Hepburn
Carole Lombard
Sophia Loren
Myrna Loy
Paul McCartney
Marilyn Monroe

Paul Newman
Ginger Rogers
Frank Sinatra
Robert Taylor
Rudolph Valentino
John Wayne
Mae West
Natalie Wood
Robert Young
Steve Allen
Louis Armstrong
Neil Armstrong
Milton Berle
William F. Buckley
George Burns
Johnny Carson
Dick Cavett
Charlie Chaplin
Bill Cullen
Sammy Davis Jr.
Hugh Downs
Jimmy Durante
John Glenn
Merv Griffin
Joan of Arc
Emmet Kelly
Gypsy Rose Lee
Art Linkletter
Mickey Mantle
Willie Mays
Jack Paar
Michael Phelps
Will Rogers
Dick Van Dyke

JUPITER-MOON, JUPITER-MARS

John Quincy Adams
Konrad Adenauer
David Ben-Gurion
Otto von Bismarck
Willy Brandt
Leonid Brezhnev
George W. Bush
Wm. Jennings Bryan
Chiang Kai-Shek
Winston Churchill
Cicero
Georges Clemenceau
Grover Cleveland
Oliver Cromwell
Charles De Gaulle
Benjamin Disraeli
Stephen A. Douglas
Dwight Eisenhower
Elizabeth I
Francisco Franco
Mohandas Gandhi
Warren G. Harding
Benjamin Harrison
Henry VIII
Paul von Hindenburg
Adolf Hitler
Herbert Hoover
Andrew Jackson
Thomas Jefferson
Lyndon Johnson
John F. Kennedy
Martin Luther King
Vladimir Lenin
Abraham Lincoln

Huey Long
Mao Tse-Tung
Marcus Aurelius
Benito Mussolini
Napoleon I
Gamal Abdul Nasser
Richard Nixon
Barack Obama
James K. Polk
Ronald Reagan
Franklin Roosevelt
Joseph Stalin
Wm. Howard Taft
Margaret Thatcher
George Washington
Woodrow Wilson

MOON-SATURN

Susan Atkinson
Clara Barton
Daniel Berrigan
John Calvin
Tom Dooley
Bob Dylan
Bob Geldof
Billy Graham
Andrew Greeley
James Groppi
G. Manley Hopkins
Petra Karin Kelly
Martin Luther King
Abraham Lincoln
Karl Marx
Elmo Mays

Ralph Nader
Florence Nightingale
Norman Vincent Peale
Troy Perry
James Pike
Franklin Roosevelt
Pete Seeger
Brigham Young
Emile Zola

MERCURY-SUN

James Agee
Conrad Aiken
Mathew Arnold
Hugo Black
Marjorie Boulton
Joseph Campbell
Charles Goren
Samuel Johnson
Camille Jullian
Henry Kissinger
Charles Lamb
Ann Landers
Richard Lewis
Hugh MacLennon
William H. Masters
H. L. Mencken
Vance Packard
Edgar Allan Poe
Knute Rockne
Paul Valery
Abigail Van Buren
Gore Vidal
Earl Warren

Alan Watts
Theodore H. White

MARS-MER, MARS-JUP

St. Augustine
Francis Bacon
Rene Descartes
John Dewey
Ralph W. Emerson
Georg W. F. Hegel
Martin Heidegger
Thomas Hobbes
David Hume
William James
Immanuel Kant
Soren Kierkegaard
Niccolo Machiavelli
Karl Marx
John Stuart Mill
Friedrich Nietzsche
Blaise Pascal
Jean J. Rousseau
Bertrand Russell
Jean-Paul Sartre
Arthur Schopenhauer
Baruch de Spinoza
Emanuel Swedenborg
F. M. A. Voltaire
A. North Whitehead

MARS-NEP, URA-SUN

Elizabeth Arden
P. T. Barnum

August Belmont
Warren Buffett
Andrew Carnegie
Bennett Cerf
Walter P. Chrysler
Dick Clark
Walt Disney
Marshall Field
Henry Ford
William Clay Ford
Bill Gates
John Paul Getty
Jay Gould
Wm. Randolph Hearst
Conrad Hilton
Howard Hughes
Steve Jobs
Joseph P. Kennedy
Alfred Krupp
J. P. Morgan
Cecil Rhodes
John D. Rockefeller
Donald Trump

PLU-MER, PLU-JUP

John L. Baird
A. Graham Bell
Thomas Edison
Enrico Fermi
Leonardo da Vinci
Guglielmo Marconi
Michelangelo
Samuel Morse
Alfred Nobel

Auguste Piccard
Christopher Sholes
Charles Steinmetz
Nicola Tesla
Orville Wright
Wilbur Wright

PLU-MER, PLU-JUP

Buzz Aldrin
Neil Armstrong
Frank Borman
Roger B. Chaffee
L. Gordon Cooper
Don Eisele
Yuri Gagarin
John Glenn
Richard F. Gordon
Virgil Grissom
James Lovell
James McDivitt
Walter Schirra
David R. Scott
Edward White Jr.

SATURN-JUPITER

Alfred Adler
Anna Freud
Sigmund Freud
James Hillman
William James
Arthur Janov
Carl Jung
Rollo May

Fritz Perls
Ira Progoff
Wilhelm Reich
B. F. Skinner

SAT: MER, VEN, NEP

Johann Bode
Niels Bohr
Tycho Brahe
Alexis Carrel
Marie Curie
Charles Darwin
Rudolf Diesel
Thomas Edison
Albert Einstein
Camille Flammarion
Alexander Fleming
Benjamin Franklin
Galileo Galilei
Stephen Jay Gould
Edmund Halley
Julian Huxley
Thomas H. Huxley
Johannes Kepler
Joseph Lister
Isaac Newton
Alfred Nobel
J. Robert Oppenheimer
Paracelsus
Louis Pasteur
Albert Schweitzer

SAT-MER, SAT-MARS

Mary Cassatt
John Constable
Salvador Dali
Edgar Degas
Paul Gauguin
Francisco de Goya
Winslow Homer
Rockwell Kent
Paul Klee
Leonardo da Vinci
Edouard Manet
Michelangelo
Joan Miro
Claude Monet
Grandma Moses
Pablo Picasso
Jackson Pollock
Raphael
Rembrandt
Pierre Renoir
Norman Rockwell
Henri Rousseau
Georges Seurat
H. Toulouse-Lautrec
Vincent van Gogh

VENUS-MARS, VENUS-SUN, VENUS-PLUTO

Anne Bancroft
Ethel Barrymore
John Barrymore
Lionel Barrymore
Anne Baxter

Ingrid Bergman
Marlon Brando
Richard Burton
Julie Christie
Lee J. Cobb
Claudette Colbert
Gary Cooper
Bette Davis
Daniel Day-Lewis
Olivia de Havilland
Robert DeNiro
Marlene Dietrich
Sally Field
Jodie Foster
Greta Garbo
Helen Hayes
Susan Hayward
Audrey Hepburn
Katharine Hepburn
William Holden
Trevor Howard
James Earl Jones
Shirley Jones
Deborah Kerr
Angela Lansbury
Charles Laughton
Jack Lemmon
Shirley MacLaine
Fredric March
Ray Milland
Jack Nicholson
Peter O'Toole
Sean Penn
Anthony Quinn
Michael Redgrave
Vanessa Redgrave

Ralph Richardson
Jason Robards
Edward G. Robinson
George C. Scott
Sissy Spacek
Elizabeth Taylor
Spencer Tracy
Shelley Winters
Loretta Young

MER-JUP, MER-NEP

Woody Allen
Lucille Ball
Jack Benny
Victor Borge
George Burns
Johnny Carson
Dick Cavett
Charlie Chaplin
Phyllis Diller
W. C. Fields
Dick Gregory
Moss Hart
Bob Hope
Alan King
Stan Laurel
Jerry Lewis
Groucho Marx
Jim Nabors
Dorothy Parker
Carl Reiner
Peter Sellers
Neil Simon
Tom Smothers

Tracey Ullman
Mae West

VENUS-MERCURY

Cannonball Adderley
Herb Alpert
Wilhelm Backhaus
Julian Bream
Dave Brubeck
Pablo Casals
Eric Clapton
Pete Fountain
Errol Garner
Dizzy Gillespie
Buddy Guy
Jimi Hendrix
Al Hirt
Vladimir Horowitz
B. B. King
Liberace
Herbie Mann
Thelonious Monk
Peter Nero
I. J. Paderewski
Artur Rubinstein
Jimmy Smith
Isaac Stern
Sonny Terry
Fats Waller

JUP-NEP-SUN

Julie Andrews
Harry Belafonte

Tony Bennett
Pat Boone
Sarah Brightman
Enrico Caruso
Charlotte Church
Patsy Cline
Judy Collins
Perry Como
Doris Day
Celine Dion
Placido Domingo
Connie Francis
Judy Garland
Emmylou Harris
Billie Holiday
Julio Iglesias
Peggy Lee
Nellie Melba
Edith Piaf
Elvis Presley
Elizabeth Schwarzkopf
Dinah Shore
Frank Sinatra
Barbra Streisand
Sarah Vaughan
Andy Williams

JUP-NEP-SUN

Johann S. Bach
Irving Berlin
Frederic Chopin
George M. Cohan
John Denver
Antonin Dvorak

Bob Dylan
Stephen Foster
Joseph Haydn
Henry Mancini
Jules Massenet
Paul McCartney
Wolfgang A. Mozart
Tom Paxton
Sergei Rachmaninoff
Maurice Ravel
Richard Rodgers
Gioacchino Rossini
Franz Schubert
John Philip Sousa
Max Steiner
Johann Strauss
P. I. Tchaikovsky
Giuseppe Verdi
Richard Wagner

PLUTO-JUPITER, PLUTO-MERCURY

Sherwood Anderson
Jane Austen
C. Baudelaire
Charlotte Bronte
Elizabeth B. Browning
Robert Browning
Lord Byron
Lewis Carroll
M. de Cervantes
Joseph Conrad
J. Fenimore Cooper
John Dos Passos
Arthur Conan Doyle
Theodore Dreiser

Alexandre Dumas
T. S. Eliot
Robert Frost
Andre Gide
J. Goethe
Nikolai Gogol
Maxim Gorky
Thomas Hardy
Nathaniel Hawthorne
Ernest Hemingway
Henry James
James Joyce
Rudyard Kipling
Harper Lee
Sinclair Lewis
H. W. Longfellow
Arthur Miller
John Milton
Clifford Odets
Eugene O'Neill
Edgar Allan Poe
Carl Sandburg
Sir Walter Scott
W. Shakespeare
P. B. Shelley
John Steinbeck
Booth Tarkington
A. Lord Tennyson
W. M. Thackeray
Mark Twain
Jules Verne
Edith Wharton
Walt Whitman
Tennessee Williams
Wm. Wordsworth
Emile Zola

PLUTO-MOON

David Brinkley
Tom Brokaw
John Chancellor
Walter Cronkite
Lou Dobbs
Jeff Greenfield
Seymour Hersh
Megyn Kelly
Dorothy Kilgallen
Chris Matthews
Edward R. Murrow
Drew Pearson
Harry Reasoner
Geraldo Rivera
Morley Safer
Diane Sawyer
Bob Schieffer
Howard K. Smith
Lesley Stahl
Chuck Todd
Greta Van Susteren
Mike Wallace
Brian Williams
Walter Winchell
Bob Woodward

MER-URA-VEN-SAT

Henry Aaron
K. Abdul-Jabbar
Usain Bolt
Bjorn Borg
Tom Brady

Jim Brown
Wilt Chamberlain
Nadia Comaneci
Gertrude Ederle
Lou Gehrig
Red Grange
Mia Hamm
Eric Heiden
Sonja Henie
Gordie Howe
LeBron James
Nancy Kerrigan
Billie Jean King
Carl Lewis
Bob Mathias
Joe Namath
Jesse Owens
Michael Phelps
Jackie Robinson
Babe Ruth

NEP-MARS, NEP-VEN

Susan Atkins
David Berkowitz
Kenneth Bianchi
Ted Bundy
Mark Chapman
John N. Collins
Albert DeSalvo
Adolph Eickmann
John Wayne Gacy
Charlene Gallego
Gary Gilmore
Heinrich Himmler

Edmund Kemper
Werner Kniesek
Henri Landru
Charles Manson
Thomas Odle
Clifford Olson
Lee Harvey Oswald
Oscar Pistorius
Richard Ramirez
Richard Speck
Charles "Tex" Watson
Charles Whitman
Aileen Wuornos

VEN-URA-NEP

Muhammad Ali
Lt. William Calley
Jack Dempsey
James Doolittle
Wyatt Earp
Dwight Eisenhower
Francisco Franco
Joe Frazier
U. S. Grant
Wm. Henry Harrison
Paul von Hindenburg
Andrew Jackson
Stonewall Jackson
Robert E. Lee
Joe Louis
Douglas MacArthur
Rocky Marciano
Floyd Mayweather
Archie Moore

Napoleon I
George Patton
Erwin Rommel
Max Schmeling
Zachary Taylor
Duke of Wellington

URANUS - JUPITER

Buzz Aldrin
Neil Armstrong
Billy the Kid
Daniel Boone
Richard Burton
Richard E. Byrd
Casanova
James Cook
Davy Crockett
El Cordobes
John Glenn
Mata Hari
Thor Heyerdahl
Louis Joliet
Evel Knieval
T. E. Lawrence
Charles Lindbergh
David Livingstone
Robert E. Peary
Eddie Rickenbacker
Sally Ride
Ernest Shakelton
Jackie Stewart
Al Unser
Bobby Unser

URANUS - JUPITER

Jim Arness
Lex Barker
Richard Boone
William Boyd
Pierce Brosnan
James Cagney
Lynda Carter
Sean Connery
Chuck Connors
Michael Dudikoff
Errol Flynn
David Janssen
Michael Landon
Jack Lord
Steve McQueen
Tom Mix
Roger Moore
Hugh O'Brien
Roy Rogers
Randolph Scott
Sylvester Stallone
Kiefer Sutherland
Rudolph Valentino
John Wayne
Johnny Weissmuller

URANUS-JUPITER

Clyde Barrow
Bonnie Parker

MOON-VENUS

Count Basie
Ray Conniff
Tommy Dorsey
Nelson Eddy
Arthur Fiedler
Benny Goodman
Andre Kostelanetz
Erich Leinsdorf
Norman Luboff
Lorin Maazel
Mantovani
Glenn Miller
Mitch Miller
Eugene Ormandy
David Rose
Leopold Stokowski
George Szell
Rudy Vallee
Lawrence Welk

NEP-SAT-MARS

Ernie Bushmiller
Al Capp
Jules Feiffer
Chester Gould
Walt Kelly
Hank Ketchum
Ted Key
Bill Mauldin
Charles Schulz
James Thurber
Mort Walker

URA-MARS, URA-SUN

Giorgio Armani
Pierre Balmain
Bill Blass
Pierre Cardin
Coco Chanel
Christian Dior
Don Loper
Bob Mackie
Mary McFadden
Yves Saint Laurent

URA-MARS, URA-SUN

Woody Allen
Ingmar Bergman
Bernardo Bertolucci
James L. Brooks
Frank Capra
Kevin Costner
Clint Eastwood
Federico Fellini
John Ford
Milos Forman
Alfred Hitchcock
Elia Kazan
Stanley Kubrick
Akira Kurosawa
Ang Lee
Roman Polanski
Steven Spielberg
George Stevens
Oliver Stone
Francois Truffaut

Orson Welles
Billy Wilder
William Wyler
Robert Zemeckis
Fred Zinnemann

URA: MARS, SUN, MOON

Evangeline Adams
John Addey
Garth Allen
C. E. O. Carter
Wm. M. Davidson
Zipporah Dobyns
Llewellyn George
Bruno Huber
Louise Huber
Marc Edmund Jones
Karl Ernst Krafft
Alan Leo
William Lilly
R. J. Morrison
Sydney Omarr
A. J. Pearce
Raphael I
Carroll Righter
Vivian Robson
Lois M. Rodden
Dane Rudhyar
Sepharial
Ebenezer Sibly
Carl Payne Tobey
C. C. Zain

UNDERSTANDING URANUS

Of all planets in the sky, the one least understood is Uranus. Some people think that the Mercury-Uranus aspect indicates genius, but we found no evidence of that. Uranian ingenuity is best brought out by "enabling" bodies like Mars and the Sun, which lend impetus and motivation to the planets they aspect. Mercury-Uranus is too unstable.

Many astrologers think that Uranus stands for science and radical reform because it was discovered during the Industrial Revolution. This is a fallacy. Planets don't suddenly acquire extra power just because they got discovered! Their influence is the same every year and every century. This falsehood stems from a theory known as idealism. It holds that a tree crashing to the ground makes no sound unless someone hears it – that everything is only in your mind. We dare not guess what percentage of astrologers believe in this notion, but we guarantee that not a single scientist on the globe subscribes to it. Scientists know all about sound waves. In truth, Uranus represents neither science (Saturn) nor revolution (Mars, Pluto).

Do you recall those intelligence tests in which you had to look at little boxes and figure out how to wrap them? The Uranus in your chart is good at this kind of task. It is the power to visualize and to integrate the many parts of a whole. Sculptors, astrologers, directors, chess masters and businessmen all do this. Uranus gives us an expanded look so that we can see the way something is arranged. Under a Uranus transit, we rearrange or relocate ourselves. We change homes or change jobs. The new house may be decades old, but you weren't aware of it. The new job used to be done by someone else, so you weren't aware of it. Uranus extends our field of vision so that we can see new things, which we call surprises.

Physically, Uranus is a very athletic planet when configurated with Mercury or Venus. Most sports involve a lot of running around. Mercury and Venus, both swift planets, provide the speed of movement. As you run about, you continually relocate yourself. You are aware of where you are on the field and where your opponents are. Soccer, tennis, basketball – all are like this. Uranus represents the Xs and the Os of sports. When aspecting Jupiter, there is an expanded relocation, as with explorers, pilots and other adventurous people.

COMPARING SIMILAR PLANETS

Let us begin our discussion with Venus and Uranus, since we just spoke about the latter. These planets can be quite physical – even violent – when they aspect each other or Neptune. Uranus-Mercury is usually physical too, and so is Venus-Mercury in the sense that playing a musical instrument is a physical activity, one in which Mercury supplies dexterity and nimbleness.

Each planet has another side to it, however, that is not very similar to the other's. When aspecting Mars or the Sun, Uranus becomes a symbol of visualization – a mental faculty. When Venus aspects Mars or the Sun (or Pluto), it produces an actor or orator – an emotional activity. Thus, we may say that Venus is physical-emotional, while Uranus is physical-mental. We imagine that every planet actually has a mental, a physical, and an emotional side, but the emphases are different.

Jupiter and Neptune are the planets of relaxation, and people relax through music and laughter. When these planets aspect the Sun, the person is musically gifted. When they aspect Mercury, the person is gifted in comedy. Music is uplifting and exhilarating – an effect that drugs also can produce. This explains why so many musicians become addicted. Music and drugs are just opposite sides of the same Jupiter-Neptune coin.

The difference between these two planets is that benefic Jupiter, aside from alcohol, has no downside, whereas malefic Neptune does. Moon-Jupiter is a popular politician, but the Moon – Neptune person may have psychological disorders. Neptune aspects to Mars, Venus, and Uranus can be dangerously violent, whereas Jupiter aspects to these same planets are perfectly harmless. There is something wild, reckless, extremist, unprincipled about Neptune. Both he and Jupiter are expansive, but the Jupiter person always knows where the limits of responsible behavior are, while the Neptune person often does not (or doesn't care?).

Mars and Pluto are alike in their assertiveness, zeal, and drive, though Pluto is more anti-social. When they aspect each other, the result is a stubborn, contentious nature. John McEnroe had a powerful aspect between these bodies. Their dynamic influence on Venus or the Moon is not very different, yet their effects on some other planets disclose a subtle distinction between them. Mars is more grounded in practicality and realism, while Pluto is more abstract and imaginative.

When Mars aspects Mercury or Jupiter, it produces a philosopher. When Pluto aspects these same planets, it denotes poets and novelists – writers whose imaginations soar. Philosophers write too, of course, but they maintain a more logical and realistic view of the world than a creative writer requires. When Mars aspects Saturn, it brings out the latter's meticulous attention to detail, its practical ability to focus and construct – hence a painter. When the more abstract Pluto aspects Saturn, it brings out the latter's contemplative side, resulting in an occultist – someone who is not much interested in the material world. One might say that Mars holds a tighter rein on the mind, while Pluto gives it more freedom.

Mercury and Saturn are much alike in some respects. Both are intellectual, logical, rational. Aspects to Saturn show aptitude for science, and the Mercury sign of Virgo is the best scientist. Even so, there are differences between these two bodies.

When Saturn aspects the Moon, there is a deep concern for humanity. Mercury aspecting Luna is useful in illuminating the intellect, but there is not the same social conscience. It must be that Mercury is not very sympathetic, since the Moon is. A Saturn aspect to Uranus is beneficial in stabilizing the latter, but Mercury aspecting Uranus is destabilizing. When Saturn aspects Jupiter or Neptune, it deepens the mind for serious, scientific inquiry. Mercury aspecting these bodies merely tickles the funny bone, which seems frivolous by comparison. The Mercury signs – Virgo and Gemini – can be dangerously reckless. Saturn is cautious.

We may summarize the contrast by stating that Saturn is mature and responsible, while Mercury is immature and irresponsible. Mercury is always depicted as a young person, while Saturn is seen as a lot older. Mercury moves fast, like the young. Saturn is slow like the old. Mercury has knowledge; Saturn has wisdom. Perhaps that is why they complement each other so well.

What is the best way to think about aspects? We suggest you think about the planets in the order of their "dominance." Here is how we would rank them:

1. Uranus
2. Saturn
3. Venus
4. Mars
5. Neptune
6. Pluto
7. Moon
8. Jupiter
9. Mercury
10. Sun

A Saturn-Venus aspect is mostly about Saturn. A Venus-Mars aspect is mostly about Venus. A Mars-Neptune aspect seems mostly about Mars. A Neptune-Moon aspect seems mostly about Neptune, and so forth. The higher-ranked planet "dominates" the lower-ranked body. The latter should be viewed as "modifying" the former, the way an adjective modifies a noun.

Suppose, for example, that you want to know what the Jupiter-Saturn aspect means. The easier way, it seems to us, is to think first about Saturn as the planet of science. How would Jupiter modify it? Jupiter is extroverted and Saturn is introverted. Therefore, Jupiter's impact would be to make the person feel more at ease in dealing with people. As a result, the scientist becomes a psychiatrist or psychologist.

Suppose you don't know what the Moon-Jupiter aspect signifies. Think first about the Moon as the planet of conversation and dealing with people. How would Jupiter modify Luna? Since he always represents expansion, the effect would be to widen her circle of friends and acquaintances. The person becomes popular – perhaps even popular enough to succeed in politics.

KEYWORDS FOR THE PLANETS

Having examined the significance of the the planetary aspects, and having compared the most similar bodies, we now will try to encapsulate the meaning of each planet through the use of keywords. Here are the words we have chosen:

Sun.: Loftiness	Jupiter: Relaxation
Moon: Conversation	Saturn: Conscientiousness
Mercury: Nimbleness	Uranus: Orientation
Venus: Energy	Neptune: Exhilaration
Mars: Competition	Pluto: Writings

"Loftiness" implies something high, and the Sun is all about elevation. Great music (Sun-Jupiter, Sun-Neptune, Sun-Mars) has a grand and uplifting quality. Tycoons (Sun-Uranus) and clergy (Sun-Saturn, Sun-Moon) are looked up to and held in high esteem. "Oracles" (Sun-Mercury) are respected for their knowledge. A certain type of actor (Sun-Venus) struts about and takes command of the stage, while the audience watches in awe.

"Conversation" fits the Moon because virtually all her aspects are about interacting with people. Astrologers (Moon-Uranus) and clergy (Moon-Sun) counsel those who seek their help. Politicians (Moon-Jupiter) and altruistic reformers (Moon-Saturn) have to be able to communicate. So do reporters (Moon-Pluto), talk-show hosts (Moon-Mars) and producers (Moon-Mercury). Conductors (Moon-Venus) instruct the orchestra on how they want the music to be played.

"Nimbleness" is the best keyword for Mercury because it can be either mental or physical. Mentally, it applies to such brainy people as philosophers

(Mercury-Mars), scientists (Mercury-Saturn), critics (Mercury-Sun) and creative writers (Mercury-Pluto). Comedians (Mercury-Jupiter, Mercury-Neptune) cleverly make us laugh. On the physical level, we have nimble-fingered musicians (Mercury-Venus) and nimble-footed athletes (Mercury-Uranus).

"Energy" was chosen for Venus because it can mean either physical or emotional vigor. Physically, it is the rugged, even violent activity shown by Venus-Uranus or Venus-Neptune. Emotionally, we are mesmerized by vehement, intense actors (Venus-Sun, Venus-Mars, Venus-Pluto). Both emotionally and physically, we have musicians (Venus-Mercury, Venus-Jupiter), vigorously and passionately playing their instruments. Conductors (Venus-Moon) wave their arms frenetically in time to the music.

"Competition" describes Mars because, with this planet, there always must be conflict. Entrepreneurs (Mars-Neptune) compete against one another. Indeed, it may be said that Mars is well suited for business, even though his signs, Aries and Scorpio, are too liberal to be obsessed with profits. Capricorn is the sign of business and Saturn is the planet of acquisition–but remember that Mars is said to be exalted in Capricorn.

Philosophers (Mars-Mercury, Mars-Jupiter) forcefully argue in favor of theories that may well be in conflict with what others have written. The most competitive athletes are apt to have the Mars-Pluto aspect. Artists don't like to think of themselves as competing, but actually they do have to vie for the blessing of critics and for the opportunities that will aid their career. This is true of actors (Mars-Venus), painters (Mars-Saturn) and sculptors (Mars-Uranus). Each artist hopes to stand out from the rest, Mars ruling distinctiveness.

"Relaxation" describes the slow, easy, moderate pace of Jupiter's movement. It is slow enough to symbolize a relaxed state of mind, but not so slow as to denote a disgruntled plodder (Saturn). Just as you achieve success through meditation and slowing down your heart rate, Jupiter brings good luck by taking things slow and easy. This relaxed state shows that a Jupiter type of person is confident – not quick and nervous like Mercury. His confidence is attractive to others, making him popular enough to be a successful politician (Jupiter-Moon, Jupiter-Mars). It also gives him the courage to take risks and enjoy exciting adventures (Jupiter-Uranus). Relaxation often takes the form of music (Jupiter-Sun, Jupiter-Neptune,

Jupiter-Venus) or comedy (Jupiter-Mercury). When someone tells a joke, it breaks the ice and relaxes everyone.

"Conscientiousness" is the hallmark of the Saturn person. He takes the greatest pains to make sure that every last detail is exactly right. He double-checks and triple-checks his work. It takes extra time to be conscientious, Saturn being slow. This assiduous care is valuable in science (Saturn-Venus, Saturn-Jupiter), in art (Saturn-Mars), or in both (Saturn-Mercury, Saturn-Neptune). This type of person has a strong conscience, making him well suited for the clergy or other altruistic endeavors (Saturn-Moon, Saturn-Sun).

"Orientation" is the best word we could find to describe Uranus, which we have already discussed at length. Mental orientation involving visualization and spacial relations, as in sculpture and astrology, is represented by Uranus-Mars, Uranus-Sun and Uranus-Moon. More physical orientation, as is done in athletics, is shown by Uranus-Venus, Uranus-Mercury and Uranus-Saturn. Reorientation in the course of an adventure that may require travel is depicted by Uranus-Jupiter.

"Exhilaration" describes Neptune, which is like Jupiter on steroids. He is the ultimate thrill seeker who throws caution to the winds and cares not whether his cravings are sanctioned by society. Neptune -Venus, Neptune-Uranus and Neptune-Mars describe this tendency. Music is another source of exhilaration, as shown by Neptune-Sun and Neptune-Jupiter. Wild, crazy comedy is represented by Neptune-Mercury. Neptune-Moon depicts self-destructive pitfalls like drugs and bizarre delusions. At its best, Neptune-Moon describes a very convivial person, a party goer, a reveler.

"Writings" is the best keyword we could use for Pluto because it indicates printed material that is usually a book but does not have to be. Pluto-Venus, for example, denotes an actor: someone who is emoting from a script. Normally, however, Pluto aspects describe creative writing – novels, plays, poetry, etc. (Pluto-Mercury, Pluto-Jupiter). Other writings include books on the occult (Pluto-Saturn) and newspaper and magazine columns (Pluto-Moon, which is the signature of journalism). Does Pluto confer imagination? It could, since inventors have the same kind of Pluto aspects as authors. Solitude is a big factor in that inventors work alone, just as writers do.

It is unclear exactly what our survey of aspects is really measuring. Is it actual talent? Or is it qualities of temperament that make a person more suited to some endeavors than others? We would not be surprised if it is partly the former.

After discovering that 38 of 43 great singers had the Jupiter-Neptune aspect, we made a list of thirty-one vocalists who we thought did not have very good voices at all. They were all rock stars, ninety percent of whom, in our view, cannot really sing. In contrast, our forty-three had no rock in it at all except Elvis. We included him because of his fame and because he could sing gospel and tender ballads as well as rock, and his voice seemed respectable.

The result: our "control group" of thirty-one rockers did not do very well. Twenty-one had Neptune-Sun, but only fourteen had Jupiter-Neptune, and merely fifteen had Jupiter-Sun. This study suggests that possibly aspects can confer actual talent. It is interesting that Elton John, the most gifted person on the rockers' list because he's an excellent composer, did do well. He has all three of the above aspects, and his Jupiter-Neptune semisquare is the most powerful one. Even so, it surely must be possible to inherit a great talent regardless of the positions of the planets, or to be denied success because of a family tree bereft of talent.

The Moon and Pluto are uniquely opposite types. The Moon person is sociable and talkative. The Pluto person is withdrawn and would rather write than talk. These bodies are unique astronomically as well. The Moon is the only "planet" astrologers use that revolves around the Earth instead of the Sun. Pluto is the only one that has been demoted to the status of a dwarf planet. Let us set aside these two oddball planets and concentrate on the remaining eight. Draw a circle with a cross in it, and then bisect each quadrant so that you have a wheel with eight spokes.

Now let's place the planets outside the circle. Put Neptune above the top spoke. Then, continuing in a counterclockwise direction, put in Jupiter, the Sun, Mars, Saturn, Mercury, Uranus and Venus in that order. This circular continuum shows which planets are the most alike and which are the most different. Inside the circle, we will write in words that describe how adjacent planets are linked – what it is that they have in common.

Between Neptune and Jupiter write "rapture," for what they share is a love of melodious music that captivates and delights us (singers, composers) and a love of laughter and gaiety (comedians). Between Jupiter and the Sun write "elevation." Uplifting music continues to be a preoccupation, but for this pair of planets there is, in place of humor, a sense of importance. Jupiter, the giant of planets, produces statesmen, while the bright, spectacular Sun gives us people who are looked up to, such as tycoons, film directors, astrologers, critics, etc.

Between the Sun and Mars write "constructiveness" because these bodies provide impetus for creative effort in business, directing, designing and astrology. Between Mars and Saturn write "acuity" because there is a keenness of perception that is helpful visually for painting and intellectually for such pursuits as philosophy and science.

Between Saturn and Mercury write "precision." The meticulous Saturn person strives to be exactly right in all that he does, while the Mercury person can master details with pinpoint accuracy. Both science and painting require this type of precision and diligent effort. Between Mercury and Uranus write "ingenuity" because these spheres are the most useful intellectually. Mercury's cleverness spans philosophy, writing and wit, while Uranus confers the capacity to visualize in designing, directing and astrology. This ability to immediately understand a situation is also helpful in athletics.

Between Uranus and Venus write "physicality," whether or not it's in your dictionary. The high energy of Venus and the corporal side of Uranus are suited for athletics and especially physical combat. The vitality of Venus is also an essential quality for acting and playing music. Between Venus and Neptune write "precipitateness," for these planets are useful not only for combat but also for murder.

As you move your eyes counterclockwise around the wheel, you can see how the qualities of the spheres gradually change, starting with the most musical planets (music having a spiritual or soulful dimension) and ending with the most physical planets. Neptune is the gateway between the physical and the spiritual. Notice that, before you get to athletic Mercury, Uranus and Venus, you have Saturn, which is somewhat less athletic, but still physical in that it pertains to the tangible, material world of science and art.

Let us consult our wheel again, and you will see that the planets opposite each other are exactly what they ought to be. Jupiter (Sagittarius,

Pisces) is opposite Mercury (Gemini, Virgo). The Sun, often associated with Leo, is opposite Uranus, often linked to Aquarius. Mars (Aries, Scorpio) is opposite Venus (Taurus, Libra). The pair that are not usually mentioned as opposites – but actually are very opposite types indeed – are Saturn and Neptune. Saturn is practical, cautious and responsible, while Neptune is delusional, reckless and out-of-control. At its best, Neptune is spiritual, while Saturn is material.

In concluding our discussion of planets, we should point out that occasionally there is some difference between a planet in aspect and the signs it rules. For example, the Venus signs, the Bridges and the Rocks, seem to be good at almost any kind of art, but Venus aspects only pertain to the performing arts. The Mars signs, the Fences and Drills, make good soldiers, but Mars aspects are not useful for this profession. The Jupiter signs are good at sports, but Jupiter aspects are not helpful to athletes. The aspects of Mercury, Saturn and the Moon are more consistent with the attributes of the signs they rule.

Astrologers are fond of referring to outer planets as "octaves" of more inner planets. We don't care for the term "octave" because we think it implies greater similarity between a planet and its "octave" than really exists. We prefer the term "analog" and would describe the relationships between the planets as follows: Jupiter is the Sun's analog, Saturn is Mercury's analog, Uranus is Venus' analog, Neptune is the Moon's analog, Pluto is Mars' analog, and perhaps a faraway sphere is the analog of Ceres (a dwarf planet that orbits between Mars and Jupiter).

Before leaving the subject of planets, we would like to clarify the meanings of a few of them about whom there are some misconceptions. Some of the meanings attributed to Mars, for example, could more properly be listed under Venus or Mercury. Planetary aspects reveal that there is more energy, action and violence under Venus than under Mars. The older authors inaccurately describe Venus as passive, perhaps because, in olden times, women probably were perceived that way by men.

Another trait regularly associated with Mars is impulsiveness, but Mars is not quick enough to be as impulsive as the hasty, hurtling Mercury. Mars is a fighter (hence the word "martial"), but what is so impulsive about a soldier? He doesn't plunge willy-nilly into battle. He is disciplined, whereas an impulsive person lacks discipline. Neptune, while undisciplined, is not necessarily impulsive. The Neptune person's mind is in a fog. He doesn't think clearly enough to make prudent choices, so he blunders into ill-advised behavior.

If Mars is not about energy or violence or rashness, what is he all about? At his core, he is about identity and individualization. We find his aspects in the charts of various kinds of artists because he is striving, through his art, to be distinctive, different from the crowd, unique. He opposes and competes against his enemies because his opinions and goals are different from what they want. He thereby distinguishes himself from them.

Astrologers tend to associate all types of communication with Mercury, to the exclusion of other planets. This is a mistake. The evidence shows that the Moon is the primary ruler of conversation, given that most people like to talk because they crave companionship and an active social life, which are Lunar concerns. As for writing, Mercury probably does rule everyday matters like writing a letter or a paper for school. However, Pluto clearly is the planet of authors. Many writers who have families say that they have trouble finding enough time to be alone (Pluto).

PART FOUR

RESEARCH ON PHYSICAL APPEARANCE

PHYSICAL APPEARANCE

In addition to occupations, the physical appearance of persons is something that lends itself to objective study. It is widely believed in astrological circles that your rising sign (the sign on the eastern horizon at the time of day on which you were born) governs your appearance. We have never seen any study that proves this–and, frankly, we don't believe it. Science tells us that what we are destined to look like is determined at conception–not at the moment of birth. As far as we know, there is no connection between the hour of conception and the hour of birth. However, there is a connection between the date of conception and the date of birth, since most people are conceived nine months before they are born. Therefore, it is appropriate to look to the Sun sign (or better yet, the Earth sign) when we want to know about someone's appearance. The rising sign ought to be altogether irrelevant. If it's not, astrologers have certainly made a major discovery that the scientific world would like to know about!

Not everyone looks like his sign. Sometimes the inherited traits are so pronounced that the person just looks like the rest of his family. You can only look like your sign if your family tree makes it possible for you to inherit appropriate traits. Therefore, if you like to guess people's signs, don't expect always to be right. If you had, say, thirty photos of persons who all were born under the same sign, your chances of being correct would be better. The heredity factor would be neutralized, and the only resemblance recurring would be the astrological factor. Another experiment you might try is to examine a family portrait and note the deviations from the inherited norm. In the Kennedy family, for example, it would not be hard to pick out Ted as the Slingshot, JFK as the Trumpet, Rose as the Hammer, Joe Sr. as the Tower, and RFK as a Rapier type.

We have provided the reader with 180 examples of each sign. About one-third of them are women, good examples of whom are harder to find because makeup and hair styles can change appearance. Study each person carefully. If you don't know who some of them are, see if their picture is on the internet. Another good source is Current Biography, a new volume of which is published each year. Libraries have these volumes. Historical figures can be found in encyclopedias. For athletes, sports trading cards are a good source. You can also check out sports magazines. Soap opera magazines have good pictures of soap stars. Other actors can be found in Screen World and Theatre World, volumes of which many libraries carry.

Remarkably, astrology even transcends race! Black folks born in a given month look more like white folks born in that same month than like black folks born in other months! Check the 180 examples and see for yourself.

THE RAPIERS

The typical Rapier has a narrow, somewhat diamond-shaped face with a narrow, pointed chin and pointed features. The nose is slender, with a narrow bridge and a pointed tip. The teeth are long and narrow. Sometimes even a child, whose adult face is not yet formed, can be seen to have long front teeth. Rapiers have small, peering, shrewd-looking eyes that are almost diamond-shaped because the corners are pointed. The face of the Rapier has all of its detail sharply etched, like a fine piece of sculpture. If you know your astrology, you know that the face we have been describing is that of Gemini. The sharp detail and the narrowness are associated with Mercury, symbol of details and slenderness.

We attempted to place in the same column people that we thought resembled one another in some way. We put the subjects with the narrowest noses in the first column. Some Rapiers have rather a long head as viewed from the side; we put these types in the second column. William F. Buckley, John Kennedy Jr., Eric Sevareid, Efrem Zimbalist Jr., Andy Williams, John Cassavetes, Douglas Fairbanks Jr., Frank Sinatra and Dick Van Dyke all have this look. In the third column are people with sharp-angled faces. Jeff Chandler and Dewey Martin have the same facial construction – sort of a fox-faced look.

Rapiers with wider faces are in the fourth column, where you will find many examples of the remarkable, diamond-shaped eyes. Howard Duff, Treat Williams, Lee J. Cobb, Van Heflin and Lauralee Bell are some examples. More typical, narrow faces are in the fifth column, but some of them don't have much of the usual pointedness. The sixth column contains two classes. One type has the keen, peering eyes of Gemini. These include Judy Woodruff, Lucy Liu, Ron Raines, Brian Orser and many others. The other type has a longer nose than you usually find: Prince Charles, Eli Wallach, Woody Allen, Kirk Douglas, Ted Cruz and various others.

We did not usually have exactly 25 examples of a particular type. Sometimes we had more; sometimes we had less. We had to divide up the 180 people as best we could, so occasionally you will come across a person that you might think would more logically belong in a different column. This is true for all the signs.

RAPIERS – 1

11/20 Jeff Locke
11/21 Rib Hillis
11/24 Rudy Tomjanovich
11/25 Noel Neill
11/26 Jan Stenerud
11/27 Marshall Thompson
11/29 Paola Turbay
11/30 Richard Crenna
12/02 Julie Harris
12/02 Zeke Moore
12/06 Kin Shriner
12/08 William S. Hart
12/08 David Carradine
12/11 Donna Mills
12/13 Karen Witter
12/14 Bridget Hall
12/14 Jennifer Hilary
12/15 Helen Slater
12/16 Lesley Stahl
12/16 Liv Ulmann
12/18 Shawn Christian
12/18 Keith Richard
12/20 Irene Dunne
12/21 Jane Fonda
12/24 John D'Acquisto

RAPIERS - 2

11/16 Joanna Pettit
11/17 Lauren Hutton
11/20 Robert Lipton
11/21 Joseph Campanella
11/22 Robert Vaughn
11/24 William F. Buckley
11/25 John F. Kennedy Jr.
11/26 Eric Sevareid
11/27 Eddie Rabbitt
11/28 Jon Stewart
11/30 Efrem Zimbalist Jr.
12/02 Jonathan Frid
12/03 Nicolas Coster
12/03 Andy Williams
12/04 Patricia Wettig
12/05 Sen. Strom Thurmond
12/08 Sammy Davis Jr.
12/09 John Cassavetes
12/09 Douglas Fairbanks Jr.
12/10 William Lloyd Garrison
12/12 Frank Sinatra
12/13 Dick Van Dyke
12/17 Bill Pullman
12/18 Gladys Cooper
12/20 Martha Galphin

RAPIERS – 3

11/22 Don Zimmerman
11/23 Maxwell Caulfield
11/25 Jill Hennessy

11/26 Tina Turner
11/27 Jim Price
11/28 Hope Lange
11/28 Sen. Gary Hart
11/29 Andrew McCarthy
12/01 Lee Trevino
12/02 Steven Bauer
12/03 Gilbert Stuart
12/05 Joseph Barbara
12/08 Dewey Martin
12/08 Tim Foli
12/09 Del Unser
12/09 Joe Lando
12/09 Frances Reid
12/09 Michael Nouri
12/11 Sally Eilers
12/12 Tracy Austin
12/15 Felicity LaFortune
12/15 Jeff Chandler
12/16 Thaao Penghlis
12/19 Walt Williams
12/22 Barbara Billingsley

RAPIERS – 4

11/17 Gordon Lightfoot
11/18 Owen Wilson
11/20 V.P. Joe Biden
11/20 Sen. Robert Kennedy
11/21 Stan Musial
11/22 Mariel Hemingway
11/24 Howard Duff

11/25 Jessie Royce Landis
11/27 Michael Vartan
11/30 Rex Reason
12/01 Treat Williams
12/04 Horst Buchholz
12/04 Jeff Bridges
12/08 Lee J. Cobb
12/10 Gloria Loring
12/10 Grady Alderman
12/11 Gilbert Rowland
12/12 Rich Coady
12/13 Van Heflin
12/13 Larry Parks
12/13 Mark Stevens
12/13 Sgt. Alvin York
12/14 Patty Duke
12/19 Tim Reid
12/22 Lauralee Bell

RAPIERS – 5

11/18 Alan Shepard Jr.
11/18 Andrea Marcovicci
11/20 Dick Smothers
11/23 Pres. Franklin Pierce
11/25 Ricardo Montalban
11/28 Alexander Godunov
11/29 Mayor Raum Emanuel
11/29 Don Cheadle
11/30 Robert Guillaume
11/30 Paul Westphal
12/01 Sarah Silverman

12/01 Richard Pryor
12/03 Daryl Hannah
12/03 Sen. Asa Hutchinson
12/08 Ann Coulter
12/08 Jim Morrison
12/09 Felicity Huffman
12/09 John Malkovich
12/11 Bess Armstrong
12/11 Ben Browder
12/13 Christopher Plummer
12/15 Don Johnson
12/18 Brad Pitt
12/22 Elizabeth Hubbard
12/25 Rod Serling

RAPIERS – 6

11/14 Prince Charles
11/18 Kevin Nealon
11/20 Judy Woodruff
11/23 Franco Nero
11/24 Pres. Zachary Taylor
11/29 Kim Delaney
12/01 Woody Allen
12/02 Warren William
12/02 Lucy Liu
12/02 Ron Raines
12/05 Peter Hansen
12/05 Morgan Brittany
12/06 Janine Turner
12/06 Richard Speck
12/07 Eli Wallach

12/08 Ian Somerhalder
12/09 Margaret Hamilton
12/09 Kirk Douglas
12/12 Mayor Ed Koch
12/12 Jennifer Connelly
12/14 Lee Remick
12/18 Steven Spielberg
12/18 Brian Orser
12/19 Alice Barrett
12/22 Sen. Ted Cruz

THIRTY MORE RAPIERS

11/14 Jerry Simmons
11/16 Paul Foytack
11/20 Kenesaw Landis
11/25 Portland Mason
11/26 Jorge Orta
11/27 Catherine Bigalow
11/27 Carol Roux
11/29 Frank Reynolds
12/03 Rep. Charles Wiggins
12/05 Art Monk
12/06 James Naughton
12/06 Dwight Stone
12/08 Michael Levin
12/10 Jeff Fager
12/10 Ted Martinez
12/10 Tisha Sterling
12/10 Daniel Markel
12/11 Elizabeth Bauer
12/11 Tom Fuccello

12/12 Holly Gagnier
12/13 Lemar Parrish
12/14 Jack Cafferty
12/15 Nick Buoniconte
12/17 Erskine Caldwell
12/17 David Rudisha
12/19 Malachi Throne
12/20 Tom Ferguson
12/21 Nate Wright
12/25 Howard Twilley
12/25 Chris Fletcher

THE TRUMPETS

It is sometimes claimed that, if you are a "Moon Child," you will have a "moon face." This is one of the silliest myths in all astrology. The planets are just as round as the Moon. As a matter of fact, neither the Antennas (Earth in Cancer) nor the Hammers (Sun in Cancer) have round faces at all. Jupiter rules roundness because it is the opposite of Mercury. Whereas the latter symbolizes precise little details, Jupiter rules that which is rounded off, estimated, generalized. Therefore, it is the Trumpets who have round faces and rounded features that are "estimates" of a face not too sharply defined. Noses are short but wider than Venus noses and not sharply pointed. Chins are not pointed either.

We put typically round faces in the first three columns of data. Of course, some people have round faces because they are overweight, but such examples still count because Jupiter rules weight gain. Although the Trumpets' broad, open faces are usually round, occasionally you'll see one with more of a square shape. The fourth column shows you how these square-faced types look. Female Trumpets often have short necks.

Some Sagittarians have faces that are between round and square. We put these broad faces in the fifth column. Some Trumpets have quite a "short" face: the distance between the eyes and the lips is short. Some examples are Michael Sarrazin, Phillipe Entremont, Larry Demery, Lydell Mitchell, Bob Cummings, Stan Laurel, Newt Gingrich and Lela Ivey. Long-faced Trumpets are rare, but we include a few in the sixth column, such as Scott Valentine, Victoria Wyndham, Prince and Carson Daly. Notice that all four of them have quite round eyes that give away their sign. Others with remarkably round eyes include Robert Morse, Bud Grant, Raymond Burr, Bob Hope, Tom Irwin, Judy Garland, Judy Holliday and Susan Strasberg.

TRUMPETS – 1

5/21 Robert Montgomery
5/22 Beau Kayzer
5/23 Herbert Marshall
5/24 John C. Reilly
5/26 Peggy Lee
5/26 Charles Winninger
5/27 Sam Snead
5/30 Michael J. Pollard
6/01 Lisa Hartman
6/01 Joan Caulfield
6/02 Wayne Brady
6/04 Horatio Sanz
6/04 Rosalind Russell
6/05 John Garlington
6/08 Barbara Bush
6/08 Kim Clijsters
6/09 Mona Freeman
6/11 Joshua Jackson
6/12 Alan Dysert
6/13 Shirl Conway
6/13 Ben Johnson
6/14 Burl Ives
6/15 Courteney Cox
6/18 Paul McCartney
6/22 Cyndi Lauper

TRUMPETS – 2

5/14 Amber Tamblyn
5/17 Maureen O'Sullivan
5/21 Dennis Day

5/24 Rep. Wilbur Mills
5/29 Blue Moon Odom
5/29 Al Unser
5/29 John Hinckley
6/03 Tony Curtis
6/05 William Boyd
6/06 Maria Montez
6/07 Diana Millay
6/08 James Darren
6/08 Rep. Gabrielle Giffords
6/09 Cole Porter
6/10 Hattie McDaniel
6/10 Sen. Harry Byrd Sr.
6/10 Doug McKeon
6/13 Ali Khan
6/14 Yasmine Bleeth
6/14 Will Patton
6/17 Joe Piscopo
6/20 Brian Wilson
6/20 Audie Murphy
6/21 Meredith Baxter
6/22 Billy Wilder

TRUMPETS – 3

5/17 Bill Paxton
5/17 Paige Turco
5/21 Mr. T
5/23 Joan Collins
5/25 Ethan Suplee
5/26 Margaret Colin
5/27 Ramsey Lewis

5/28 Sen. Marco Rubio
5/28 Jerry West
5/29 Annette Bening
5/29 Bob Logan
5/30 Gale Sayers
5/31 Norman Vincent Peale
6/01 Edward Woodward
6/01 Marilyn Monroe
6/01 Pat Boone
6/02 Jerry Mathers
6/05 Mark Wahlberg
6/11 Vince Lombardi
6/11 Jane Bryan
6/12 Vic Damone
6/13 Ralph Edwards
6/19 Jerry Reuss
6/19 Kathleen Turner
6/22 Sen. Elizabeth Warren

TRUMPETS – 4

5/18 Reggie Jackson
5/20 David Hedison
5/22 Morrissey
5/24 Priscilla Presley
5/24 Steve Cochran
5/25 Dixie Carter
5/27 Lucille Watson
5/28 Dan Pastorini
5/28 Carroll Baker
5/31 Sharon Gless
5/31 Brooke Shields

5/31 Colin Farrell
6/08 Alexis Smith
6/09 Michael J. Fox
6/09 Natalie Portman
6/09 Johnny Depp
6/10 June Haver
6/12 William Lundigan
6/13 Ally Sheedy
6/15 Neil Patrick Harris
6/16 Joan Van Ark
6/17 Jason Patric
6/20 John Goodman
6/21 Jane Russell
6/22 Sen. Dianne Feinstein

TRUMPETS – 5

5/18 Frank Capra
5/21 Al Franken
5/22 Michael Sarrazin
5/23 Drew Carey
5/24 Gary Burghoff
5/25 Karen Valentine
5/25 Octavia Spencer
5/27 Frank Thomas
5/27 V.P. Hubert Humphrey
5/29 La Toya Jackson
5/30 Lydell Mitchell
5/31 Jim Hutton
6/01 Robin Mattson
6/04 Larry Demery
6/07 Phillipe Entremont

6/08 Robert Preston
6/09 Robert McNamara
6/09 Robert Cummings
6/11 Chad Everett
6/14 Dorothy McGuire
6/16 Stan Laurel
6/17 Rep. Newt Gingrich
6/18 Roger Ebert
6/19 Gena Rowlands
6/23 Lela Ivey

TRUMPETS – 6

5/18 Robert Morse
5/18 Dwayne Hickman
5/20 Bud Grant
5/21 Raymond Burr
5/22 Apolo Ohno
5/22 Susan Strasberg
5/22 Victoria Wyndham
5/26 Philip Michael Thomas
5/26 Stevie Nicks
5/29 Anthony Geary
5/29 Bob Hope
6/01 Tom Irwin
6/01 Alanis Morissette
6/01 William Sloane Coffin
6/03 Allen Ginsberg
6/03 Sen. Karl Mundt
6/03 Scott Valentine
6/07 Prince
6/07 Bill Hader

6/10 Judy Garland
6/16 Faith Domergue
6/18 Michael Sutton
6/20 John McCook
6/21 Judy Holliday
6/22 Carson Daly

THIRTY MORE TRUMPETS

5/15 Gaye Huston
5/17 Pat Toomay
5/19 Marilyn Chris
5/21 Leo Sayer
5/22 Michael Constantine
5/22 Peter Nero
5/22 Jim Colborn
5/22 Barbara Parkins
5/22 Dick Benjamin
5/25 Bennett Cerf
5/26 Helena Bonham Carter
5/27 Bruce Weitz
5/27 Jim Holt
5/30 Christine Jorgensen
5/30 Mike Sadek
5/31 Jackie Brown
6/01 Joan Copeland
6/01 Antony Ponzini
6/02 Stacy Keach
6/02 Pat Hughes
6/03 Maurice Evans
6/05 Bill Moyers
6/05 Bill Hayes

6/06 Merv Rettenmund
6/09 Jim Bailey (football)
6/11 Joey Dee
6/13 Lesli Kay
6/14 Rosa Langschwadt
6/19 Malcolm McDowell
6/20 Brett Halsey

THE TOWERS

Like the Trumpets, the Towers are ruled by Jupiter and therefore typically have round faces. Their foreheads are not very high, which gives the impression that their heads are not tall enough in proportion to their faces. Their eyes are smaller than those of the Trumpets, and their lips are thicker. Unusually large ears are common. Their noses are hardly ever too long, but they're not well-chiseled. The bridge is low and often fleshy, which gives an indistinct look to the face. It is a perfect depiction of Pisces vagueness–that unique fogginess that makes these people seem so mysterious to the rest of us. The first column shows examples of these indistinct faces.

In the second column, we put notably round-headed Towers. Many persons in the other columns have round heads too, but we think these are the best examples. What we thought were the best-looking Towers are in the third list. They still look like their sign – only cuter. The fourth column shows that Pisces can symbolize not only indistinctness but also indistinctiveness. How do you describe the people on this list? There's nothing wrong with their appearance – it's just not very interesting. Their faces are less round, but they are curved. One is tempted to call these people "potato heads."

Many Towers, though not the majority, have nose oddities. Sometimes the bridge of the nose looks squashed. You'll find some examples of this in the fifth and sixth columns, such as Ben Gazzara and Frank Robinson. Another rather common problem is that there is too much width at the base of the nose. Nearly everyone in the fifth column has this difficulty. Larger than usual noses are in the sixth column. Sometimes nostrils of these people look large even when the nose is not. There is often an unusually large space between the nose and the mouth. Barbara Bain, Kim Cattrall and Jane Greer are pretty enough for the third column, but we put them in the sixth because they share this trait with John Houseman, Wendy Hiller and some others. When you see some Towers in profile, you will notice that the lower part of the face is quite a bit in advance of the forehead: Paul Muni, Raymond Massey, Julie Kavner, Anne Seymour. Many Towers have a curiously convex look, like your reflection in a Christmas bauble or the back of a spoon.

TOWERS – 1

8/17 Mae West
8/22 Cindy Williams
8/23 Gene Kelly
8/25 Graham Jarvis
8/28 Peggy Ryan
8/28 LeAnn Rimes
8/30 Shirley Booth
8/30 Roy Wilkins
8/30 Gov. Huey Long
8/30 Fred MacMurray
9/02 Michael Dante
9/02 Marge Champion
9/03 Hank Thompson
9/06 Jo Anne Worley
9/10 Charles Kuralt
9/10 Zaida Coles
9/10 Joe Bravo
9/11 Kristy McNichol
9/13 Mel Torme
9/14 Michelle Stafford
9/16 Anne Francis
9/20 Kristen Johnston
9/22 Debby Boone
9/23 Mary Kay Place
9/25 Anson Williams

TOWERS – 2

8/18 Martin Mull
8/25 Regis Philbin
8/25 Rachael Ray
8/26 Chris Burke
8/27 Sam Goldwyn
8/28 John Demarie
8/30 Michael Chiklis
8/31 Arthur Godfrey
8/31 Roger Newman
9/01 Conway Twitty
9/02 Jimmy Connors
9/02 Chuck McCann
9/07 Bud Delp
9/08 Sen. Robert A. Taft
9/08 Patsy Cline
9/09 Michael Keaton
9/10 Arnold Palmer
9/15 Oliver Stone
9/15 Ted Tinling
9/16 Mark McKewen
9/18 Robert Blake
9/19 Paul Williams
9/22 Bonnie Hunt
9/23 Mickey Rooney
9/24 Lou Dobbs

TOWERS – 3

8/21 Tammy Amerson
8/23 Nicole Bobek
8/25 Sean Connery

8/28 Emma Samms
8/31 Van Morrison
8/31 Carole Wells
9/02 Linda Purl
9/03 Alan Ladd
9/07 June Harding
9/07 Peggy Noonan
9/09 Cliff Robertson
9/09 Michelle Williams
9/10 Barbara Treutelaar
9/12 Peter Scolari
9/13 Claudette Colbert
9/14 Kimberly Williams
9/14 Joey Heatherton
9/14 Faith Ford
9/17 Kyle Chandler
9/20 Debbi Morgan
9/20 Mandy Bruno
9/21 Larry Hagman
9/22 Ingemar Johansson
9/23 Romy Schneider
9/25 Catherine Zeta-Jones

TOWERS – 4

8/20 Norma Connolly
8/22 Gen. Norman Schwarzkopf
8/24 Dennis James
8/24 Preston Foster
8/24 Gov. Mike Huckabee
8/25 Don De Fore
8/25 Van Johnson

8/26 Gov. Tom Ridge
8/29 Isabel Sanford
8/29 Robin Leach
8/31 Ramon Hernandez
8/31 Buddy Hackett
9/01 Walter Reuther
9/01 Johnny Mack Brown
9/01 Dr. Phil McGraw
9/04 Mitzi Gaynor
9/12 Anne Helm
9/14 Bud Palmer
9/15 Merlin Olsen
9/15 Don Carrithers
9/15 Fay Wray
9/16 Susan Ruttan
9/16 Allen Funt
9/18 James Gandolfini
9/20 Sister Elizabeth Kenny

TOWERS – 5

8/24 Yasser Arafat
8/25 Gov. George Wallace
8/27 Martha Rae
8/28 Simon Oakland
8/31 Frank Robinson
8/31 Carl Garrett
9/01 Yvonne De Carlo
9/01 Alan Dershowitz
9/02 Richard Neal
9/04 Richard Castellano
9/04 Danny Ponce

9/05 Rosie Perez
9/10 Bill O'Reilly
9/10 Edmond O'Brien
9/12 Mickey Lolich
9/13 Michael Johnson
9/13 Nell Carter
9/13 Reta Shaw
9/14 Jack Hawkins
9/16 Richard Perle
9/19 Larry Brown
9/20 Rachel Roberts
9/22 Abe Gibron
9/23 Walter Lippmann
9/24 Jim McKay

TOWERS – 6

8/15 Wendy Hiller
8/20 Jim Reeves
8/21 Kim Cattrall
8/25 Charlie Sanders
8/28 Ben Gazzara
8/29 Dick O'Neill
8/30 Raymond Massey
8/30 William G. Schilling
8/31 Edward Lee Thorndike
8/31 Warren Berlinger
9/01 Gloria Estefan
9/03 Helen Wagner
9/03 Eileen Brennan
9/07 Julie Kavner
9/09 Jane Greer

9/11 Anne Seymour
9/12 Jennifer Hudson
9/13 Ben Savage
9/13 Barbara Bain
9/15 Jackie Cooper
9/15 Kate Mansi
9/16 Mike Garman
9/22 Paul Muni
9/22 John Houseman
9/23 Elizabeth Pena

THIRTY MORE TOWERS

8/15 Georgann Johnson
8/17 Boog Powell
8/19 Molly Bee
8/19 Bill Shoemaker
8/21 Jack Weston
8/22 Cecil Kellaway
8/23 Gene Kennedy
8/24 Hugh Franklin
8/24 Gerry Mullins
8/25 Tom Skerritt
8/29 Willard Waterman
8/30 Tug McGraw
8/30 Johnny Mann
9/02 Jimmy Clanton
9/03 Carla Suarez Navarro
9/03 Bob Ussery
9/05 Jerry Le Vias
9/05 Jack Valenti
9/09 Billy Preston

9/13	Jean Smart
9/15	Pres. Wm. Howard Taft
9/15	Tawny Schneider
9/16	Rogelio Moret
9/18	Patricia Roe
9/18	Billy Champion
9/19	Joe Morgan
9/19	Mario Batali
9/20	Tom Tresh
9/23	Oscar Zamora
9/25	Catherine Burns

THE SLINGSHOTS

The Slingshots typically have rather a heart-shaped face with neat, precise, birdlike features crowded in the middle of it. It is a perfect depiction of the Virgo habit of zeroing in on the trees (the details of the face) while ignoring the forest (the border of the face). The forehead is rounded, and there is a forward rounding of the cheeks. The face seems to converge toward a point midway between the small, close-set, peering, shrewd-looking eyes. This intelligent look, which they share with the Rapiers, is related to Mercury, their ruler. The nose is apt to be pointed and often reminds one of a bird's beak. Many Slingshots have an arched upper lip that exposes the top of their teeth, especially when they smile. We put typical, generic Slingshots on the first two columns. The third column has more long-headed types. Some of the more birdlike examples would include Edward Arnold, Thorsten Kaye and Edward Everett Horton.

It is not necessary to possess all of the Slingshot traits in order to have enough of their special look to make their sign identity clear to the observer. In the fourth column, we find people whose eyes are not so close-set. We actually think these Virgos look the best because the crowded effect does not happen to appeal to us, though perhaps some people like it. Even so, we find on this list a lot of neat, precise features and shrewd eyes. The fifth column shows persons with quite close-set eyes, but their faces are lean and lack the typical shape. On the sixth list, we have people who do possess the rounded cheeks and forehead but may lack the usual crowded eyes.

SLINGSHOTS - 1

2/13 Bess Truman

2/14 Stu Erwin

2/17 Kathleen Freeman
2/18 Adolphe Menjou
2/18 Edward Arnold
2/22 Sybil Leek
2/22 Robert Young
2/22 Rachel Dratch
2/25 Myra Hess
2/26 Fats Domino
3/01 Judge Robert Bork
3/02 Desi Arnaz
3/02 Al Waxman
3/04 Knute Rockne
3/05 Kimberly McCullough
3/06 Shaquille O'Neal
3/07 Mary Beth Evans
3/07 Jenna Fischer
3/10 Curley Culp
3/11 PM Harold Wilson
3/11 Lawrence Welk
3/13 Neil Sadaka
3/15 Rev. Jimmy Swaggart
3/20 Carl Reiner
3/21 Edgar Buchanan

SLINGSHOTS – 2

2/14 Johnny Longden
2/15 John Hadl
2/17 Roger Craig
2/18 Molly Ringwald
2/19 Carlyn Glynn
2/20 John Daly

2/20 Sandy Duncan
2/21 Jennifer Love Hewitt
2/24 Bud Collins
2/25 Denny Lemaster
2/25 Tony Lema
2/25 Jim Backus
2/26 Tom Kennedy
2/27 Franchot Tone
2/27 Chelsea Clinton
2/27 Josh Groban
3/01 Cesare Danova
3/03 Jessica Biel
3/04 Chas Bono
3/06 John Smith
3/11 Albert Salmi
3/13 L. Ron Hubbard
3/14 Tim Rossovich
3/16 Stephanie Gatschet
3/17 Casey Siemaszko

SLINGSHOTS – 3

2/14 Lionel Aldridge
2/16 Sonny Bono
2/18 Burt Mustin
2/19 Cedric Hardwicke
2/20 Malcolm Atterbury
2/20 W. H. Auden
2/21 William Baldwin
2/22 Thorsten Kaye
2/23 Sheldon Leonard
2/25 Bobby Riggs

2/25 Sally Jessy Raphael
2/26 Doris Belack
2/26 Clarice Blackburn
2/27 Reginald Gardiner
2/27 Justice Hugo Black
3/05 Pete Rozelle
3/05 Rev. Joel Osteen
3/06 Rob Reiner
3/07 Wanda Sykes
3/09 Bobby Walden
3/12 Gordon MacRae
3/12 Mandel Kramer
3/15 Judd Hirsch
3/18 Edward Everett Horton
3/20 Michael Redgrave

SLINGSHOTS – 4

2/17 Paris Hilton
2/17 Wayne Morris
2/22 John Mills
2/22 Sen. Ted Kennedy
2/24 Barry Bostwick
2/25 Tea Leoni
2/25 George Harrison
2/25 Diane Baker
2/25 Ron Santo
2/26 Tony Randall
2/26 Johnny Cash
2/27 Elizabeth Taylor
3/01 David Niven
3/02 Daniel Craig

3/02 Barbara Luna
3/04 John Garfield
3/05 Marsha Warfield
3/07 Ivan Lendl
3/08 Cyd Charisse
3/08 Aidan Quinn
3/10 James Earl Ray
3/10 Chuck Norris
3/13 Robert S. Woods
3/17 Mercedes McCambridge
3/19 Patrick McGoohan

SLINGSHOTS - 5

2/10 Laura Dern
2/14 Gregory Hines
2/18 John Travolta
2/19 Merle Oberon
2/19 Jeff Daniels
2/20 Justin Verlander
2/21 Alan Rickman
2/24 Edward James Olmos
2/24 Fred Biletnikov
2/24 Marjorie Main
2/24 James Farentino
2/26 Margaret Leighton
2/27 Howard Hesseman
3/05 Rex Harrison
3/06 Eduardo Rodriguez
3/07 Anna Magnani
3/09 Marty Ingels
3/09 Brittany Snow

3/11 Jeffrey Nordling
3/14 Rita Tushingham
3/14 Albert Einstein
3/18 George Plimpton
3/19 Jeff Mullins
3/19 Glenn Close
3/20 Ted Bessell

SLINGSHOTS - 6

2/14 Hugh Downs
2/20 Aleksei Kosygen
2/21 Trisha Nixon Cox
2/21 Tyne Daly
2/21 Rep. Barbara Jordan
2/21 Ann Sheridan
2/21 Christine Ebersol
2/22 Drew Barrymore
2/26 William Frawley
2/26 Jackie Gleason
2/27 Joan Bennett
2/27 Joanne Woodward
2/28 Charles Durning
2/29 Sharon Hugueny
3/02 Jennifer Jones
3/03 Jean Harlow
3/06 Bob Trumpy
3/06 Guy Kibbee
3/07 Tammy Faye Messner
3/08 Claire Trevor
3/08 Camryn Manheim
3/13 Dana Delany

3/16 Sen. Daniel Moynihan
3/18 Queen Latifah
3/20 Lauritz Melchior

THIRTY MORE SLINGSHOTS

2/13 Tenn. Ernie Ford
2/15 Harvey Korman
2/16 Jeffrey Lynn
2/19 Carson McCullers
2/20 Amanda Blake
2/21 Zachary Scott
2/24 Billy Zane
2/25 Jim Tyrer
2/25 Danny Cater
2/26 Jim Bertelson
2/27 Charlie Edge
2/28 John Turturro
2/28 Zero Mostel
2/28 Ilene Graf
2/28 John Pitts
2/28 Bubba Smith
2/29 John Niland
3/03 Larry Pine
3/05 Charles Dudley
3/06 Willie Stargell
3/07 John Heard
3/07 Michael Eisner
3/08 Meredith Scott Lynn
3/14 Garry Puetz
3/15 Macdonald Carey
3/17 Pat Crowley

3/19 Shelly Burch
3/20 Wendell Corey
3/20 Jack Barry
3/21 Kathleen Widdoes

THE BRIDGES

The Bridges are among the very best-looking people in the zodiac – and this should not surprise us because their ruler is Venus, the goddess of beauty. They have a tall, well-shaped head that is in good proportion (Libra symbolizes balance) to their face. Although the forehead is high and spacious, the chin is narrow, which produces a slightly triangular face. Their large eyes have a star-like beauty. We all remember the song "Bette Davis Eyes," but Bette was not the only Bridge with great eyes. Check out Catherine Spaak or Paulina Porizkova. Libras have a small, well-chiseled nose – often upturned–an impish grin, and all of their features in good proportion to one another. Please note that, if you insist on using Sun signs instead of Earth signs, Aries becomes better-looking than Libra, which is certainly not what we were taught.

There is very little variation in the Bridges' appearance except, of course, among those who don't look like their sign. It therefore didn't matter much how we listed our 180 examples. We elected to put what we thought were the wider faces on the first two columns, and the seemingly longer faces on the second two columns. On the third two columns, we placed people for whom we couldn't decide whether their face should be considered wide or long. Some readers might well disagree with some of our decisions on length and width. In the second column, we threw in a few people – Pete Rose, General Westmoreland–who demonstrate that you can be a little less good-looking than most Libras and still resemble your sign. Bridges tend to be tall-waisted; that is, they have a long back and long arms.

BRIDGES – 1

3/12 Barbara Feldon
3/22 Brian Farrell
3/22 Reese Witherspoon
3/23 Keri Russell
3/26 Diana Ross
3/27 David Janssen
3/29 Dennis McLain
4/01 Carol White
4/02 Aiden Turner
4/03 Jan Sterling
4/05 David Winters
4/05 Bette Davis
4/05 Michael Moriarty
4/08 John Schneider
4/09 Keesha Knight Pulliam
4/10 Omar Sharif
4/12 Virginia Cherrill
4/12 Hardy Kruger
4/12 Nicholas Brendon
4/12 Shannen Doherty
4/16 Barry Nelson
4/17 Lon McCallister
4/19 Keith Ericson
4/20 Joey Lawrence
4/22 Glen Campbell

BRIDGES – 2

3/14 Billy Crystal
3/21 Kassie DePaiva
3/24 Kirk Geiger

3/25 Gloria Steinem
3/25 Elton John
3/25 Danica Patrick
3/26 Gen. Wm. Westmoreland
3/27 Mariah Carey
3/30 Mark Consuelos
4/01 Debbie Reynolds
4/01 Ali MacGraw
4/02 Reggie Smith
4/02 Buddy Ebsen
4/04 James Roday
4/04 Gary Geiger
4/05 Frank Gorshin
4/09 Kristen Stewart
4/10 Peter MacNicol
4/13 Rick Schroder
4/13 Jean Carol
4/14 Pete Rose
4/16 Bobby Vinton
4/17 Kimberly Elise
4/17 Jo-Wilfried Tsonga
4/22 Jack Nicholson

BRIDGES – 3

3/12 John-Paul Lavoisier
3/20 Murray Bartlett
3/21 David Eisenhower
3/23 Joan Crawford
3/23 Craig Breedlove
3/26 Rep. Nancy Pelosi
3/30 Warren Beatty

4/02 Rita Gam
4/04 Heath Ledger
4/06 Merle Haggard
4/12 David Letterman
4/13 Kelli Giddish
4/13 Jonathan Brandis
4/14 Anthony Michael Hall
4/14 Bradford Dillman
4/14 Anthony Perkins
4/17 Charles Frank
4/17 William Holden
4/17 Victoria Beckham
4/17 Jennifer Garner
4/19 James Franco
4/20 Johnny Tillotson
4/20 Brody Hutzler
4/22 Peter Frampton
4/22 Joseph Bottoms

BRIDGES -- 4

3/13 Christopher Collet
3/17 Patrick Duffy
3/17 Rob Lowe
3/17 Rudolf Nureyev
3/22 Virginia Grey
3/22 Dax Griffin
3/22 Veleka Gray
3/26 Billy Warlock
3/27 Chris McCarron
3/30 Jerry Lucas
3/31 Ewan McGregor

4/02 Keren Woodward
4/02 Emmylou Harris
4/04 Sarah Michelle Gellar
4/04 Dylann Roof
4/07 Bobby Bare
4/08 Robin Wright
4/09 Jean-Paul Belmondo
4/09 Paulina Porizkova
4/15 Bessie Smith
4/15 Robert Walker Jr.
4/15 Emma Watson
4/16 Kareem Abdul-Jabbar
4/18 Eric McCormack
4/23 Gail Goodrich

BRIDGES – 5

3/21 Francoise Dorleac
3/23 David Tom
3/24 Steve McQueen
3/26 Keira Knightley
3/28 Dirk Bogarde
3/29 Terence Hill
3/31 William McNamara
3/31 Shirley Jones
4/02 Brian Goodell
4/04 Luke Halpin
4/04 Robert Downey Jr.
4/04 Catherine Spaak
4/06 Judith McConnell
4/09 Brandon De Wilde
4/13 Tony Dow

4/14 Julie Christie
4/14 Bobbie Nichols
4/15 Claudia Cardinale
4/16 Edie Adams
4/17 Boomer Esiason
4/17 Teri Austin
4/18 Robert Kelker-Kelly
4/18 Bryce Johnson
4/20 Shemar Moore
4/23 Craig Sheffer

BRIDGES – 6

3/15 Rick Volk
3/17 Justin Bieber
3/21 Tommy Davis
3/21 Matthew Broderick
3/22 Bob Costas
3/24 Kim Johnston Ulrich
3/26 Amy Smart
3/29 Dianne Kaye
3/29 Kurt Thomas
3/31 Melissa Ordway
4/02 Bethany Joy Lenz
4/03 Tommy Haas
4/03 Marlon Brando
4/04 Christine Lahti
4/07 Wayne Rogers
4/07 James Garner
4/08 John Gavin
4/09 Taylor Kitsch
4/13 Lyle Waggoner

4/13 Pres. Thomas Jefferson
4/15 Evelyn Ashford
4/16 Isaac Murphy
4/19 Dick Sargent
4/20 Ryan O'Neal
4/23 David Birney

THIRTY MORE BRIDGES

3/16 Ted Marcoux
3/17 Lesley-Anne Down
3/19 Louis Hayward
3/20 Ozzie Nelson
3/20 Don Briscoe
3/21 Bill Plummer
3/26 Joby Baker
3/26 Robert Frost
3/28 Richard Backus
3/28 Janice Lynde
3/28 Rudolph Serkin
4/02 Kevin Bernhardt
4/03 Gregg Marx
4/03 Wally Moon
4/03 Tim Bassett
4/06 Janet Lynn
4/07 John Oates
4/08 Jim Lampley
4/09 Hugh Hefner
4/12 Louise Lasser
4/13 Wayne Colman
4/14 Neil Johnson
4/15 Annie Farge'

4/16 Tom Nardini
4/16 Bill Boland
4/17 Lindsay Hartley
4/18 Lori Martin
4/18 Cindy Pickett
4/19 Hayden Christensen
4/22 English Gardner

THE FENCES

Unlike most signs, the Fences come in two distinct types. One kind has a tough, pugilistic look (Mars) caused by a strong, wide, prominent jaw that sometimes produces a flat-looking face when seen from the side. Fences of this strong-jawed type are found in the first three columns. Some of them look a little like Cro-Magnon Man, Aries being the sign of origins. In the first column are Fences who have more of a flat look. The second list shows people with very strong jaws, headed by George Zimmerman, Mike Singletary, Angus T. Jones, and Brad Maule. There is more subtlety in the third list. We even threw in a few examples of Fences who do not have a heavy jaw at all, but have a flat-looking smile. These include Julie Andrews, Maury Wills and a few others.

The second type of Aries has a narrow forehead and chin, but a prominence at the cheekbones that pulls the face into an oval or egg shape. The last three columns show examples of this type. On the fourth list, we placed those whose cheekbones jut out rather sharply. In the fifth column, the prominence produces more of a roundedness at the cheekbones. The sixth list shows people with smoothly oval faces with little or no protuberance.

Why are there two different kinds of Fences? These two types are merely two versions of the same principle: the principle of distortion. Since Venus rules balance and proportion, it follows that its opposite, Mars, must rule imbalance and disproportion. Fortunately, these facial distortions do not spoil one's appearance much, if at all. Fences evidently have very short eyelashes; it's not unusual to see men whose lashes are all but invisible. Has anyone ever found Chris Wallace's missing eyelashes? The women, of course, paint their lashes or wear false ones. Since the Fences are ruled by the red planet, Mars, it should not surprise us that there are more redheads born under this sign than any other.

FENCES – 1

9/16 Amy Poehler
9/18 Fred Willard
9/20 Tommy Nobis
9/24 Paul Hamm
9/26 Lynn Anderson
9/26 Donna Douglas
9/30 Marcia McClain
10/01 Mark McGwire
10/01 Chief Justice Rehnquist
10/04 Lori Saunders
10/04 Alicia Silverstone
10/07 Christopher Norris
10/07 Vaughn Monroe
10/07 Evan Longoria
10/12 Dick Cunningham
10/13 Dick Pole
10/13 Burr Tillstrom
10/16 Angela Lansbury
10/17 Marsha Hunt
10/18 Mike Ditka
10/19 John Lithgow
10/21 Ken Watanabe
10/23 Augusta Dabney
10/23 Lilyan Tashman
10/23 Nancy Grace

FENCES – 2

9/20 Dennis Wirgowski
9/21 Stephen King
9/25 John Ericson

9/27 Sen. Charles Percy
9/29 Erika Eleniak
9/29 Greer Garson
9/30 Robin Roberts (baseball)
10/01 Randy Quaid
10/02 Lani O'Grady
10/04 Liev Schreiber
10/05 Nancy Barrett
10/05 George Zimmerman
10/08 Danny Murtaugh
10/09 Mike Singletary
10/09 Angus T. Jones
10/09 Lila Kedrova
10/11 Brad Maule
10/13 Bob Bailey
10/13 Pamela Tiffin
10/14 Usher
10/15 Emeril Lagasse
10/19 Emile Gilels
10/19 Grover Norquist
10/20 Will Rogers Jr.
10/23 Frank Sutton

FENCES – 3

9/19 Trisha Yearwood
9/19 Alison Sweeney
9/24 Phil Hartman
9/25 Tate Donovan
9/29 Rep. Paul McCloskey
9/29 Lizabeth Scott
10/01 Julie Andrews

10/02 Maury Wills
10/05 Kate Winslet
10/06 Carole Lombard
10/07 June Allyson
10/09 Sharon Osbourne
10/09 Sen. Trent Lott
10/09 PM David Cameron
10/10 Mario Lopez
10/13 Cliff Gorman
10/13 Laraine Day
10/14 Greg Evigan
10/14 Isaac Mizrahi
10/16 Noah Webster
10/16 Tim Robbins
10/17 George Wendt
10/19 Kathie Browne
10/20 Alfredo Campoli
10/22 Tony Roberts

FENCES – 4

9/23 Paul Petersen
9/23 Bruce Springsteen
9/25 Scotty Pippin
9/25 Christopher Reeve
9/25 Will Smith
9/25 Josh Taylor
9/26 Serena Williams
9/29 Jerry Lee Lewis
9/29 Drake Hogestyn
9/29 Robert Gentry
10/02 Mohandas Gandhi

10/06 Gary Gentry
10/10 Roger Metzger
10/10 Conrad Dobler
10/13 Nancy Kerrigan
10/13 PM Margaret Thatcher
10/15 Penny Marshall
10/16 Irene Demich
10/17 Beverly Garland
10/18 Erin Moran
10/18 Mark LaMura
10/19 Michael Steele
10/20 Snoop Dogg
10/22 Jeff Goldblum
10/22 Joan Fontaine

FENCES – 5

9/17 Tomas Berdych
9/21 Ricki Lake
9/22 Rob Stone
9/24 Ed Bryce
9/24 Alan Colmes
9/24 Don Porter
9/24 Jacqueline Courtney
9/25 Juliet Prowse
9/28 Arnold Stang
9/28 Ed Sullivan
10/01 Stanley Holloway
10/02 Groucho Marx
10/03 Clive Owen
10/03 Chubby Checker
10/07 Melba Rae

10/08 Paul Hogan
10/09 Edward Andrews
10/10 Adlai Stevenson III
10/13 Ives Montand
10/14 John Wooden
10/15 Robert Trout
10/18 Lee Harvey Oswald
10/18 Bobby Troup
10/21 Skip Butler
10/21 Jeremy Miller

FENCES – 6

9/18 Holly Robinson Peete
9/26 Patrick O'Neal
9/26 Pope Paul VI
9/27 Gwyneth Paltrow
9/27 Claude Jarman Jr.
9/27 Jenna Elfman
9/30 Lacey Chabert
9/30 Fran Drescher
10/07 PM Vladimir Putin
10/08 Chevy Chase
10/08 Garbine Muguruza
10/14 Charlie Joiner
10/14 Stephen A. Smith
10/15 Renee Jones
10/15 Vanessa Marcil
10/16 Suzanne Somers
10/16 Arthur Schleshinger Jr.
10/17 Arthur Miller
10/17 Irene Ryan

10/19 Chris Kattan
10/20 Michael Dunn
10/21 PM Benjamin Netanyahu
10/23 Johnny Carson
10/26 Keith Urban
10/26 Dylan McDermott

THIRTY MORE FENCES

9/19 Duke Snider
9/24 Anthony Newley
9/27 Ken Ellis
9/27 Kathy Nolan
9/27 Randy Bachman
9/29 Altie Taylor
9/29 Steve Busby
10/08 Derk Cheetwood
10/14 Sheila Young
10/14 Lillian Gish
10/19 Jack Anderson
10/19 Bill Melchionni
9/19 Ray Danton
9/19 Justice Lewis Powell
9/27 Jayne Meadows
9/30 Tony Hale
9/30 Jody Powell
10/01 Mayor Sam Yorty
10/02 Darren Cahill
10/03 Gore Vidal
10/05 Shell Kepler
10/07 Elijah Muhammad
10/09 Scott Baluka

10/10 Ben Vereen
9/24 Mean Joe Greene
9/29 Dave Wilcox
10/01 Tom Bosley
10/04 Cedrick Hardman
10/14 Bob Kuechenberg
10/22 Wilbur Wood

THE DRILLS

The Drills – just like the other Mars sign, the Fences–come in two distinct types. One type has considerable width across the cheekbones, producing a kite-shaped face. There is often protrusion on the sides of the face, which makes this type look something like the oval-faced Fences. The first three columns are devoted to this kite-shaped type. The comparative narrowness of the top and bottom of the face symbolizes Mars imbalance. Ears that stick out are more common here than in other signs. The most beautiful kite-shaped faces belong to Katharine Hepburn and Judy Collins, mostly because their eyes are larger and more spectacular than would be normal for this sign.

The second type of Scorpio has quite a long face. The last three columns show examples of this type. The fact that the length is so much greater than the width is another form of Mars imbalance. It is quite a contrast with their opposites, the Rocks, who typically have wide faces. Many Drills have high, handsome cheekbones, which is perhaps most evident in the fifth column. On the sixth list, you will notice quite a few large noses, but in most cases this doesn't seem to spoil the appearance. John Beradino had a big nose, but he was considered a nice-looking man anyway. Among the women, the largest nose belongs to Beulah Bondi, but she had a sweet, motherly look that was not at all unpleasant. The most impressive long-faced Drill was Audrey Hepburn, but her delicate, Rapier-like beauty is not very typical of her sign. Even so, she looks a little like Roberta Peters and Margot Fonteyn.

DRILLS – 1

4/15 Emma Thompson

4/18 James Drury

4/19 May Robson
4/22 Spencer Haywood
4/23 Timothy McVeigh
4/27 Nick Kyrgios
4/27 George Gervin
4/27 Michael Lipton (soaps)
4/29 Jim Ryun
4/29 Rod McKuen
5/02 Bing Crosby
5/06 Stewart Granger
5/08 Lex Barker
5/09 Gregory Beecroft
5/12 Lindsay Crouse
5/12 Florence Nightingale
5/12 Wilfred Hyde-White
5/13 Juan Beniquez
5/13 John Roseboro
5/16 Margaret Sullavan
5/16 Billy Martin
5/17 Dennis Hopper
5/18 Bill Macy
5/20 Toussaint L'Ouverture
5/23 Mary Fickett

DRILLS – 2

4/11 Bill Irwin
4/12 Ed O'Neill
4/15 Ted Kwalick
4/16 Anatole France
4/16 John Hodiak
4/25 Paul Mazursky

4/28 Sidney Toler
4/28 Lionel Barrymore
4/29 Carnie Wilson
4/29 Uma Thurman
5/01 Bob Allietta
5/01 Judy Collins
5/03 William Shakespeare
5/03 Greg Gumbel
5/05 Tammy Wynette
5/07 Johnny Unitas
5/09 Albert Finney
5/12 Katharine Hepburn
5/12 Bruce Boxleitner
5/13 Empress Maria Theresa
5/15 Jamie-Lynn Sigler
5/17 Danny Manning
5/17 Ruth Donnelly
5/18 Brooks Robinson
5/19 Johns Hopkins

DRILLS – 3

4/16 Peter Ustinov
4/20 Adolf Hitler
4/21 Gov. Pat Brown
4/23 Michael Moore
4/23 Roy Orbison
4/25 Jack E. Leonard
4/27 Gary Huff
4/30 Kirsten Dunst
5/01 Frank Beard
5/01 Kate Smith

5/02 Theodore Bikel
5/02 Hedda Hopper
5/03 Walter Slezak
5/03 Mary Hopkin
5/09 Alley Mills
5/12 Beth Maitland
5/15 Trini Lopez
5/15 Mayor Richard J. Daley
5/16 Liberace
5/16 Lainie Kazan
5/18 Perry Como
5/18 Meredith Willson
5/21 Peggy Cass
5/23 Jewel
5/24 Jean Paul Marat

DRILLS – 4

4/18 Tamara Braun
4/21 Patti Lupone
4/21 Anthony Quinn
4/21 Elaine May
4/25 Talia Shire
4/25 Guglielmo Marconi
4/26 Carol Burnett
4/29 Jerry Seinfeld
4/30 Jill Clayburgh
4/30 Eve Arden
5/02 Christine Baranski
5/02 Dr. Benjamin Spock
5/03 Alex Cord
5/08 Fernandel

5/08 Bishop Fulton J. Sheen
5/10 Nancy Walker
5/11 Margaret Rutherford
5/11 Phil Silvers
5/12 Yogi Berra
5/16 Tori Spelling
5/17 Horace McMahon
5/18 Ann Williams
5/18 Polina Edmunds
5/20 Ron Reagan
5/20 James Stewart

DRILLS – 5

4/16 Ron Bolton
4/19 Don Adams
4/22 Jason Miller
4/23 Joe Ferguson
4/23 Melina Kanakaredes
4/24 J. D. Cannon
4/25 Edward R. Murrow
4/27 Mack Alston
4/28 Pres. James Monroe
4/28 Nancy Grahn
5/01 Barry Clemens
5/03 Pete Seeger
5/06 PM Tony Blair
5/06 Rudolph Valentino
5/12 Jason Biggs
5/13 Dennis Rodman
5/14 Patrice Munsel
5/14 Tim Roth

5/15 John Smoltz
5/16 Megan Fox
5/20 Bronson Pinchot
5/20 James Douglas
5/20 Cher
5/21 Rick Jason
5/22 Novak Djokovic

DRILLS – 6

4/20 Mayor Robert F. Wagner
4/21 Queen Elizabeth II
4/21 Andie MacDowell
4/21 Tony Danza
4/23 Warren Spahn
4/23 Dan Frischman
4/24 Barbra Streisand
4/25 Al Pacino
4/27 Sheena Easton
4/27 Jack Klugman
4/28 Justice Elena Kagan
4/29 Daniel Day-Lewis
5/01 John Beradino
5/02 "The Rock" Johnson
5/03 Beulah Bondi
5/04 Roberta Peters
5/04 Audrey Hepburn
5/07 Gary Cooper
5/10 Fred Astaire
5/12 Gabriel Byrne
5/14 Richard Deacon
5/14 Cate Blanchett

5/17 Bob Saget
5/18 Margot Fonteyn
5/24 Bob Dylan

THIRTY MORE DRILLS

4/12 Jerry Tagge
4/22 Phil Smith
4/22 Yehudi Menhuin
4/22 J. Robert Oppenheimer
4/22 Hal March
4/24 Carroll Dale
4/27 Doug Buffone
4/28 Madge Sinclair
4/30 Isiah Thomas
4/30 Dan Goich
5/01 Wes Welker
5/01 Farrah Fath
5/01 Steve Cauthen
5/02 Leslie Gore
5/05 Wayne Mulligan
5/06 Raymond Bailey
5/07 Robin Strasser
5/08 Mike Cuellar
5/10 Mike Souchak
5/10 Sen. Rick Santorum
5/11 Mort Sahl
5/11 Salvador Dali
5/13 Lena Dunham
5/14 Tony Perez
5/14 Dave LaRoche
5/15 Don Nelson

5/17	Birgit Nilsson
5/20	Stan Mikita
5/20	George Gobel
5/24	Clint Jones

THE ROCKS

The Rocks have a very square jaw and a high, broad forehead, giving the face a square shape and a firm, solid look that symbolize Taurus stability. Although their faces are wider than those of the Bridges, their Venus-ruled features are much the same: nice eyes, small noses, winning smiles. Their eyes are their best feature. They are more deep-set than those of any other sign, and often their gaze can be quite hypnotic. Sometimes the space between the nose and the mouth is bigger than normal. Some Rocks have rather heavy lips, but not unattractively so. Notice that the picture we are painting–broad face, short nose–is much the way Taurus has always been described, whereas the Drills seem nothing like how Taurus is supposed to look.

We put the squarest heads we could find in the first column. On the second list, we placed the most interesting eyes we could find. Notice how, even in rare cases in which the person is not very attractive (Marie Dressler, Ruth Gordon), the face still has an intense, compelling look. Of all the twelve visages of the zodiac, we suspect that a sculptor would rather carve a Taurus face than any other. The third column is composed of two types of Rocks: those with unusually wide faces, and those with more of a triangular shape than you usually see. The fourth and fifth columns are not very different except that we think the faces on the fourth list are squarer. The sixth column shows you what Rocks look like if they inherit an atypically narrow face. The Rocks are usually tall-waisted like the Bridges.

ROCKS -1

10/26 Pat Sajak
10/28 Lauren Holly

10/28 Bruce Jenner
10/29 Akim Tamiroff
10/31 Larry Mullen Jr.
10/31 Dan Rather
11/01 Bill Anderson
11/02 Rachel Ames
11/04 Martin Balsam
11/04 Gig Young
11/07 Christopher Knight
11/08 Bonnie Raitt
11/08 Courtney Thorne-Smith
11/11 Sen. William Proxmire
11/11 Demi Moore
11/11 Leonardo DiCaprio
11/14 Johnny Desmond
11/14 Rosemary De Camp
11/14 Sen. Joseph McCarthy
11/14 McLean Stevenson
11/17 Rock Hudson
11/18 Linda Evans
11/19 Ted Turner
11/20 Norman Thomas
11/21 Marlo Thomas

ROCKS -2

10/25 Pablo Picasso
10/25 Dave Collins
10/26 Sasha Cohen
10/28 Jane Alexander
10/29 Winona Ryder
10/30 Louis Malle

10/30 Ruth Gordon
10/31 Dave Freisleben
11/02 Larry Little
11/02 Burt Lancaster
11/02 Pres. James K. Polk
11/04 Peter Boynton
11/06 Ethan Hawke
11/07 Rev. Billy Graham
11/09 Marie Dressler
11/11 Sen. Barbara Boxer
11/12 Charles Manson
11/13 Oskar Werner
11/15 Judith Chapman
11/16 Lisa Bonet
11/17 Gov. Howard Dean
11/20 Sean Young
11/21 Gov. Scott Walker
11/22 Marvin Upshaw
11/23 Boris Karloff

ROCKS - 3

10/15 Sarah Ferguson
10/25 Tom Eplin
10/28 Mark Derwin
11/01 Jeff Probst
11/03 Dennis Miller
11/04 Art Carney
11/05 Peter Noone
11/05 Natalie Schafer
11/06 Sally Field
11/06 Maria Shriver

11/07 Mark Philippoussis
11/10 Ellen Demming
11/10 Miranda Lambert
11/13 Tracy Scoggins
11/13 Madeleine Sherwood
11/14 Laura San Giacomo
11/14 Condoleezza Rice
11/14 Don Stewart
11/17 Bob Mathias
11/18 David Hemmings
11/19 Nancy Carroll
11/19 Jodie Foster
11/21 Ken Doll Sr.
11/21 Goldie Hawn
11/21 Ken Griffey Jr.

ROCKS - 4

10/16 Tim McCarver
10/18 Andy Hassler
10/18 Bill Russell (baseball)
10/19 Tom Domres
10/26 Jaclyn Smith
10/28 Joaquin Phoenix
11/01 Penn Badgley
11/01 Betsy Palmer
11/01 Mags Furuholmen
11/03 Mike Evans
11/06 Judy Lewis
11/07 Lawrence O'Donnell
11/12 Steve Bartkowski
11/13 Daniel Pilon

11/13 Dack Rambo
11/14 Fred Haise
11/15 Sen. Howard Baker
11/16 Jay Hammer
11/16 Jo Jo White
11/17 Dylan Walsh
11/18 Rev. Billy Sunday
11/21 Robert Drivas
11/22 Billie Jean King
11/22 Jack Reynolds
11/22 Michael Callan

ROCKS - 5

10/18 Zac Efron
10/25 Christopher Sean
10/25 Ruby Dee
11/02 Johnny Vander Meer
11/03 Lois Smith
11/03 Wanda Hendrix
11/04 Heather Tom
11/04 Eric Karros
11/05 Bob Kowalkowski
11/06 Brad Davis
11/06 Lance Kerwin
11/07 Jeremy London
11/07 Madame Marie Curie
11/09 Eric Dane
11/09 Tom Weiskopf
11/10 Sinbad
11/12 Neil Young
11/12 Nadia Comaneci

11/14 Liz Keifer
11/15 Beverly D'Angelo
11/17 William R. Moses
11/20 Jason Thompson
11/21 Vivian Blaine
11/22 Geraldine Page
11/22 Burt Douglas

ROCKS - 6

10/17 Howard E. Rollins
10/23 Ryan Reynolds
10/27 Eddie Alderson
10/29 Kate Jackson
10/29 Ed Kemmer
10/30 Harry Hamlin
10/31 Vanila Ice
11/01 Jeff Richards
11/01 Ted Hendricks
11/01 Michael Zaslow
11/05 Bryan Adams
11/06 Ernest Thompson
11/07 Todd McKee
11/08 Parker Posey
11/08 Morley Safer
11/11 Robert Ryan
11/12 Ann Flood
11/14 Josh Duhamel
11/15 Petula Clark
11/15 Lewis Stone
11/16 Guy Stockwell
11/16 Marg Helgenberger

11/19 Clifton Webb
11/21 Laurence Luckinbill
11/22 Brian Robbins

THIRTY MORE ROCKS

10/15 Milt Moran
10/24 Rawley Eastwick
10/24 John Didion
10/24 Chester Marcol
10/25 Lisa Trusel
10/27 Dylan Thomas
10/29 Grayson McCouch
10/29 Rian Garrick
10/31 Dave McNally
11/02 Alice Brady
11/03 Timothy Patrick Murphy
11/03 Kate Capshaw
11/03 Dwight Evans
11/08 Larry Casey
11/08 Alain Delon
11/10 Dave Loggins
11/12 Dale Schlueter
11/13 Robert Sterling
11/16 Alexa Havins
11/17 Mitch Williams
11/17 Dean Paul Martin
11/19 Ahmad Rashad
11/19 Sen. Tom Harkin
11/20 Fran Allison
11/20 Estelle Parsons
11/21 Troy Aikman

11/21 Ralph Meeker
11/22 Lew Burdette
11/22 Staughton Lynd
11/24 John LaGioia

THE ANTENNAS

The head of the Antennas has a curiously compressed look. It is as if something were tugging at the sides of the face, jerking them upward, pinching the crown together. This squeezed look symbolizes the fact that the Antenna period is squeezed into just forty-two days, the least of any sign. This look is caused by the extremely high cheekbones. The flat ears have a pinned-back look: their tops seem to point inward, toward the head. The nose is usually heavy-bridged and often quite long. Usually it does not project outward much, but droops downward. No other sign offers such an epidemic of large noses. The largest on record were placed in the first column. With each successive list, the noses get a little smaller–yet, even on the fourth list, the noses are longer than some people prefer.

Cancer is kinder to women because their noses are not as big as men's. There are no women in columns one and two, and two-thirds of them are in columns five and six. The best-looking Antennas are in the fifth column. Here we find such outstanding beauties as Loretta Young, Luise Rainer, Capucine, Eden Riegel, Susan Lucci and Ava Gardner. You might not even guess short-nosed Val Kilmer to be an Antenna unless you spotted the telltale tilt of his ears. On the sixth list, you will notice some faces that have a puffiness at the cheekbones that is not unusual for Cancer. Sometimes the person is considered nice-looking anyway, as was Elvis Presley, but on the whole we don't think this look is desirable. Moose Skowran, Jo Van Fleet, J. Edgar Hoover, Camilo Pascual, Stalin and Fellini all look as if they smell something bad. This look is not attractive either.

ANTENNAS – 1

12/14 Theo Goetz
12/16 Leonid Brezhnev
12/19 Fritz Reiner
12/21 Frank Zappa
12/22 Laurence Hugo
12/25 Frank Ferguson
12/25 Ken Harvey
12/29 PM William Gladstone
1/01 Xavier Cugat
1/01 David Nalbandian
1/02 Premier Joseph Stalin
1/02 Rep. Dan Rostenkowski
1/03 Hank Stram
1/03 Victor Borge
1/06 Danny Thomas
1/08 Ron Moody
1/08 Jose Ferrer
1/10 Jim Croce
1/15 Pres. Gamal Abdul Nasser
1/17 Naveen Andrews
1/18 Danny Kaye
1/19 Robert MacNeil
1/20 Bill Maher
1/20 Federico Fellini
1/21 Placido Domingo

ANTENNAS – 2

12/17 William Safire
12/21 Kurt Waldheim
12/21 Larry Bryggman

12/21 Joe Paterno
12/23 Jose Greco
12/25 Gary Sandy
12/29 Laffit Pincay, Jr.
12/30 Noel Paul Stookey
12/31 Ben Kingsley
1/04 Sterling Holloway
1/05 Sen. Walter Mondale
1/06 Vic Tayback
1/06 Shug McGaughey
1/06 Early Wynn
1/07 Alvin Dark
1/08 Soupy Sales
1/10 Ray Bolger
1/10 Rod Stewart
1/13 Charles Nelson Reilly
1/14 Dr. Albert Schweitzer
1/14 William Bendix
1/15 Edward Teller
1/17 Maury Povich
1/21 Mac Davis
1/23 Franklin Pangborn

ANTENNAS – 3

12/14 Morey Amsterdam
12/17 Dave Madden
12/20 Albert Dekker
12/22 Lady Bird Johnson
12/22 Paul Wolfowitz
12/27 Gerard Depardieu
12/29 Mike Lucci

12/30 Sandy Koufax
1/01 J. D. Salinger
1/01 Billy Parks
1/03 Josephine Hull
1/05 Charlie Hough
1/07 Jack Greene
1/08 Genevieve Cortese
1/10 Willie McCovey
1/11 Veda Ann Borg
1/12 Randy Jones
1/12 Ray Price
1/13 Gwen Verdon
1/14 Nina Totenberg
1/15 Mary Pierce
1/19 Drea de Matteo
1/19 Jean Stapleton
1/20 Arte Johnson
1/20 DeForest Kelley

ANTENNAS – 4

12/14 James Horan
12/22 Ralph Fiennes
12/22 Ruth Roman
12/24 Pres. Hamid Karzai
12/25 Annie Lennox
12/26 Steve Allen
12/27 Sydney Greenstreet
12/28 John Milner
12/28 Patrick Rafter
12/30 Matt Lauer
12/30 Bernard Barrow

12/30 Tracey Ullman
12/31 Paul Casanova
1/01 Don Parish
1/02 Anna Lee
1/04 Rosemary Prinz
1/07 Vincent Gardenia
1/07 Shirley Ross
1/07 Sen. Rand Paul
1/11 Stanley Tucci
1/11 Mary J. Blige
1/15 Lloyd Bridges
1/16 Alexander Knox
1/21 Telly Savalas
1/23 Humphrey Bogart

ANTENNAS – 5

12/21 Florence Griffith Joyner
12/23 Susan Lucci
12/24 Ava Gardner
12/29 Viveca Lindfors
12/29 Inga Swenson
12/31 Val Kilmer
1/01 Eden Riegel
1/02 Gabrielle Carteris
1/03 Eli Manning
1/05 Bradley Cooper
1/05 Jean Pierre Aumont
1/06 Capucine
1/06 Loretta Young
1/07 Nicolas Cage
1/07 Diane Rousseau

1/10 Sal Mineo
1/10 Paul Henreid
1/11 Rod Taylor
1/11 Luise Rainer
1/12 Patsy Kelly
1/13 Robert Stack
1/13 Patrick Dempsey
1/15 Andrea Martin
1/18 Jesse L. Martin
1/18 Kevin Costner

ANTENNAS – 6

12/18 Moose Skowran
12/18 Betty Grable
12/19 Al Kaline
12/19 Tony Taylor
12/20 Audrey Totter
12/23 Elizabeth Hartman
12/26 Chm. Mao Tse-Tung
12/27 Marlene Dietrich
12/30 Dennis Morgan
12/30 Jo Van Fleet
12/31 Odetta
1/01 J. Edgar Hoover
1/03 Dabney Coleman
1/04 Jane Wyman
1/05 Raisa Gorbachev
1/08 Lydia Bruce
1/08 Elvis Presley
1/09 Gracie Fields
1/11 Eva LeGallienne

1/12 James Farmer
1/15 Martin Luther King Jr.
1/16 Ethel Merman
1/16 Katy Jurado
1/17 Jane Elliot
1/20 Camilo Pascual

THIRTY MORE ANTENNAS

12/17 Tommy Steele
12/21 Dave Kingman
12/22 Gene Rayburn
12/24 John Cardinal Cody
12/25 Barton MacLane
12/25 Tony Martin
12/25 Francoise Durr
12/26 Larry Reynolds
12/28 Len Wayland
1/02 Christy Turlington
1/02 Pat Fischer
1/03 Stephen Stills
1/05 Jim Otto
1/07 Pres. Millard Fillmore
1/07 Joe Ponazeki
1/09 Gypsy Rose Lee
1/09 Bart Starr
1/10 Pat Benatar
1/11 Gary Brokaw
1/12 Ray Brown
1/12 Tex Ritter
1/13 Sophie Tucker
1/15 Bobby Grich

1/16 Sade
1/16 Kate Moss
1/16 Julian Sands
1/18 Myron Pottios
1/19 Ron Behagen
1/19 Terry Hanratty
1/20 Leon Ames

THE HAMMERS

Capricorn is the hardest sign to recognize and the hardest to describe because the characteristics are more subtle than those of other signs. Triangular faces are common, but so are rectangles. There are even some squares, mostly in the second column, but you almost never find a round face. Usually the Hammer faces have considerable length. Their noses tend to be on the long side too, but often there also is considerable width at the base. There is apt to be a short space between the nose and the mouth – and then a long chin. These people would look better if the mouth were placed lower on the face. Then both the nose and the chin would look shorter.

The eyes are near-slits. Often they seem to stretch out into horizontal lines. This "stretched" look symbolizes the fact that the Hammer period is stretched out over forty-five days, the most of any sign. (The Earth is moving its slowest then, thus requiring extra time to pass through this twelfth of the sky.) These people appear to be perpetually squinting. They actually <u>can</u> open their eyes wider if the want to, but they hardly ever do. Examples of these unusual eyes can be found on the first two columns.

The lips also have a stretched look in the sense that they are typically quite thin. Sometimes the upper lip is all but invisible. Occasionally the combination of a wide nose, thin lips and a short space between them–plus the squinty eyes–can give the person a mean look. You can capture that look yourself by standing in front of a mirror and making a mean face. The Capricorn mouth is somewhat like that of the Slingshots in that you can see a lot of their teeth when they talk. Examples of this unusual mouth are found on the next two columns. The fifth column shows the thin, narrow faces that one often sees. The sixth list combines two types: those with the longest noses and some with wider faces, usually V-shaped.

If the foregoing account of the Hammers does not sound so auspicious, remember that it is possible to be good-looking under any sign. We believe the best-looking Hammer is Eleanor Parker.

HAMMERS – 1

6/14	Donald Trump
6/15	Helen Hunt
6/19	Jim Slaton
6/22	Meryl Streep
6/22	Bobby Douglass
6/23	Francesca Schiavone
6/24	Billy Casper
6/26	Eleanor Parker
6/28	Raymond Chester
6/28	Lester Flatt
7/04	Mitch Miller
7/04	Floyd Little
7/05	Garry Matthews
7/05	David Farragut
7/06	Burt Ward
7/07	Robin Weigert
7/08	Nelson Rockefeller
7/10	Jeff Donnell
7/12	Ken Curtis
7/13	Robert Forster
7/13	Dan Abramowicz
7/13	Patrick Stewart
7/14	Ingmar Bergman
7/18	Harriet Nelson
7/22	Bobby Sherman

HAMMERS – 2

06/16 Ian Buchanan
6/18 Eddie Cibrian
6/19 Dame May Whitty
6/28 Don Nottingham
6/29 Maria Conchita Alonso
6/30 Mike Tyson
7/04 Virginia Graham
7/05 Milburn Stone
7/07 Bill Melton
7/08 Eugene Pallette
7/08 Gov. George Romney
7/09 Donald Rumsfeld
7/10 David Brinkley
7/10 James A. Whistler
7/11 Ron McAnally
7/12 Paul Silas
7/13 Bob Crane
7/13 Sidney Blackmer
7/14 George Tobias
7/14 Bob Purkey
7/15 Jan-Michael Vincent
7/16 Jerry Sisemore
7/18 John Glenn
7/18 Jerome Barkum
7/20 K. T. Stevens

HAMMERS – 3

6/14 Marla Gibbs
6/15 Wade Boggs
6/16 John Cho

6/17 Dean Martin
6/21 Derrick Coleman
6/21 Michael Gross
6/26 Babe Didrikson
6/30 Michael Phelps
7/02 Richard Petty
7/02 Dan Rowan
7/04 Geraldo Rivera
7/05 Cecil Rhodes
7/06 Mowry twins
7/06 Geoffrey Rush
7/07 Ringo Starr
7/08 Jeffrey Tambor
7/09 Fred Savage
7/12 Bill Cosby
7/13 Dave Garroway
7/15 Arianna Huffington
7/18 Dick Button
7/19 Sen. George McGovern
7/22 Don Henley
7/23 Nomar Garciaparra
7/25 Fred Scherman

HAMMERS – 4

6/13 Paul Lynde
6/25 Sidney Lumet
6/25 Ricky Gervais
6/29 Gary Busey
7/01 Constance Ford
7/01 Missy Elliott
7/02 Gov. John Sununu

7/07 Vonda Shepard
7/09 Spike Jones (football)
7/09 Brian Dennehy
7/12 Milton Berle
7/12 Kristi Yamaguchi
7/15 Ken Kercheval
7/17 Bob Warren
7/17 Phyllis Diller
7/17 Art Linkletter
7/18 Red Skelton
7/18 Darlene Conley
7/18 Dion
7/19 Patricia Medina
7/21 Robin Williams
7/22 Rose Kennedy
7/22 Ron Turcotte
7/23 Woody Harrelson
7/24 John Aniston

HAMMERS – 5

6/15 Tim Lincecum
6/18 Robin Christopher
6/20 Michael Corbett
6/20 Lillian Hellman
6/21 Daniel Carter Beard
6/25 Anne Revere
6/30 Nancy Dussault
7/03 Montel Williams
7/03 George Sanders
7/06 Merv Griffin
7/07 Doc Severinsen

7/08 John D. Rockefeller
7/08 Anjelica Huston
7/09 Nikola Tesla
7/10 Virginia Wade
7/14 Matthew Fox
7/14 Jane Lynch
7/19 Helen Gallagher
7/20 Sandra Oh
7/21 Edward Herrmann
7/21 Patricia Elliott
7/22 Sparky Lyle
7/22 Jennifer Bassey
7/22 David Spade
7/26 Helen Mirren

HAMMERS – 6

6/13 Mary Wickes
6/14 Steffi Graf
6/18 Richard Boone
6/19 Nancy Marchand
6/25 Charlotte Greenwood
6/27 Svetlana Kuznetsova
6/27 Ross Perot
6/28 Maxine Stuart
7/01 Florence Stanley
7/02 Ron Silver
7/03 Sen. Lamar Alexander
7/04 George Steinbrenner
7/04 Pres. Calvin Coolidge
7/06 LaVerne Andrews
7/09 PM Edward Heath

7/10 Nick Adams
7/14 Jules Mazarin
7/14 Gloria Stuart
7/15 Roy Winston
7/16 Barbara Stanwyck
7/16 Margaret Court
7/18 Chill Wills
7/22 Amy Vanderbilt
7/23 Michael Wilding
7/23 Coby Dietrick

THIRTY MORE HAMMERS

6/14 Tom Matte
6/14 Nat Polen
6/24 Ken Reitz
6/26 Bill Robinson (baseball)
6/26 Hal Greer
6/26 Edith Pearlman
6/28 Chris Speier
6/29 Harmon Killebrew
6/29 Richard Lewis
7/01 Rick Cash
7/01 William Wyler
7/03 Leon Errol
7/04 Eric Fleming
7/04 Sidney Coleman
7/05 Sam Davis
7/05 John McKay
7/05 Paul Carpinelli
7/06 Terry Owens
7/06 Dorothy Kirsten

7/07	Craig Cotton
7/07	Jim Barnett
7/07	Jerry Sherk
7/12	Timon Kyle Durrett
7/12	Andrew Wyeth
7/14	Woody Guthrie
7/14	Dale Robertson
7/19	Pat Hingle
7/19	Jamie Fields
7/20	Judy Greer
7/23	Steve Tannen

THE PATTERNS

The Patterns are better-looking than the other Saturn sign, the Hammers, perhaps because Aquarius has a softening influence on the traits of its ruler, Saturn, that Capricorn lacks. The typical Pattern has a tall head. The face has a lot of what we shall call "tapering." The cheeks are finely molded, the result of a very graceful, tapered transition from a high, broad forehead to a narrow chin. Between the cheeks and the chin, there is a becoming indentation that few signs have. The lips are nicely tapered, and the nose is well-chiseled and a little longer than the noses of the Venus signs. The first column lists an assortment of typical, generic Patterns. The second column shows Patterns who did not inherit such a tall head, but still resemble their sign in other respects. Some of the them have very long faces that may make the forehead seem lower than it really is.

Some Patterns have very slender noses that make them resemble Rapiers, while others have shorter noses that make them look like Bridges. All three of these signs have narrow chins. The Patterns are a happy medium between the Rapiers and the Bridges, signs with which they form a harmonious "grand trine" aspect. Fifty Aquarians who look like Gemini are shown on columns three and four, while Aquarians who resemble Libra are on columns five and six. Readers who are unsure what we mean by "tapering" may want to study the faces in the fourth column because we think that they have the most tapering. As we saw earlier in this book, there are many Aquarius models, which is not surprising because Patterns have the type of face that modeling agencies are seeking.

PATTERNS – 1

7/22 Camila Banus
7/23 Daniel Radcliffe
7/24 Gloria Hoye
7/26 George Bernard Shaw
7/27 Lenore Kasdorf
7/30 Arnold Schwarzenegger
8/02 Beatrice Straight
8/04 Dallas Green
8/04 Crystal Chappell
8/06 Grant Aleksander
8/06 Lucille Ball
8/07 B. J. Thomas
8/08 Connie Stevens
8/08 Roger Federer
8/11 Millette Alexander
8/15 T. E. Lawrence
8/16 Madonna
8/16 Robert Culp
8/18 Patrick Swayze
8/18 Roberto Clemente
8/18 Robert Redford
8/18 Grant Williams
8/19 Pres. Bill Clinton
8/19 Kyra Sedwick
8/20 Joan Allen

PATTERNS – 2

7/24 Jennifer Lopez
7/24 Chris Sarandon
7/26 Mick Jagger

7/26 Jason Robards
7/27 Alex Rodriguez
7/28 Doug Collins
7/29 Peter Jennings
7/30 Hilary Swank
7/30 Ken Olin
7/30 Edd Byrnes
8/02 Marci Miller
8/02 Peter O'Toole
8/03 Dolores Del Rio
8/03 Lance Alworth
8/04 Pres. Barack Obama
8/05 John Huston
8/05 Gov. Brian Sandoval
8/13 John Beal
8/15 Ben Affleck
8/17 Guillermo Vilas
8/20 Rep. Ron Paul
8/21 John Derek
8/21 Wilt Chamberlain
8/21 Princess Margaret
8/23 Rick Springfield

PATTERN – 3

7/15 Willie Aames
7/22 Rob Estes
7/23 Ronnie Cox
7/26 Nicholas Walker
7/27 Dennis Ralston
7/29 Robert Horton
7/30 Peter Bogdanovich

8/1 Pete Mackanin
8/1 Arthur Hill
8/2 Edward Furlong
8/6 Jan Clayton
8/8 Keith Carradine
8/8 Brooke Bundy
8/11 Amber Brkich Mariano
8/12 Bruce Greenwood
8/12 Roy Wary
8/14 Halle Berry
8/15 Zeljko Ivanek
8/15 Debra Messing
8/15 Tess Harper
8/19 David A. Gregory
8/19 Jill St. John
8/21 Mitchell Anderson
8/23 Shelley Long
8/25 Mel Ferrer

PATTERNS – 4

7/23 Beth Ehlers
7/24 Robert Hays
7/25 Linsey Godfrey
7/27 Nicolai Coster – Waldace
7/27 Peggy Fleming
7/30 Simon Baker
7/30 Ralph Taeger
7/31 Susan Flannery
8/3 Jay North
8/3 Bethel Leslie
8/8 Richard Anderson

8/8 Jayne Bentzen
8/9 Paul Kelly
8/9 Michael Storm
8/10 Rosanna Arquette
8/10 Norma Shearer
8/14 Christopher Gorham
8/15 Abby Dalton
8/18 Denis Leary
8/18 Maureen Garrett
8/19 Frank Telfer
8/19 Diana Muldaur
8/22 Elena Goode
8/22 Diana Sands
8/26 Deborah Hobart

PATTERNS – 5

7/15 Leonard Stabb
7/20 Erik Howell
7/20 Lola Albright
7/20 Natalie Wood
7/20 Diana Rigg
7/21 Josh Hartnett
7/23 Stephen Martines
7/26 Kathryn Hays
7/27 Eric Martsolf
7/31 Don Murray
8/1 Brian Patrick Clarke
8/7 Charlize Theron
8/12 Peter Krause
8/12 Stephen Brooks
8/16 Timothy Hutton

8/16 Josh Casaubon
8/16 Kevin Dillon
8/17 Christian Laettner
8/18 Madeleine Stowe
8/19 Bobby Richardson
8/19 Mary Joe Fernandez
8/22 John Lupton
8/22 Valerie Harper
8/23 Tony Bill
8/25 Morgan Englund

PATTERNS – 6

7/19 Jerry Smith
7/22 Terence Stamp
7/22 John Leguizamo
7/24 Mark Goddard
7/25 Matt LeBlanc
7/29 Stephen Dorff
7/30 Anita Hill
8/1 Terry Kiser
8/3 Tom Brady
8/4 Jeff Gordon
8/5 Neil Armstrong
8/16 Malcolm Groome
8/17 Julia Marlowe
8/18 Trey Ames
8/18 Christopher Jones
8/19 John Stamos
8/19 Matthew Perry
8/21 Jim McMahon
8/23 Natalie Coughlin

8/25 Claudia Schiffer
8/25 Blair Underwood
8/26 Chris Pine

THIRTY MORE PATTERNS

7/17 Richard Bekins
7/23 Lute Proctor
7/24 Pam Tillis
7/24 Anna Paquin
7/24 Sam Behrens
7/25 Janet Margolin
7/29 Kevin Spirtas
7/30 Ben Jorgensen
7/31 Gerald Anthony
8/1 Jill Trenary
8/2 Mary-Louise Parker
8/4 John Riggins
8/5 Patrick Ewing
8/7 Anjanette Comer
8/9 Clint Ritchie
8/10 Jane Wyatt
8/10 Daniel Hugh – Kelly
8/12 Roy Hay
8/13 Zooey Hall
8/13 Kevin Tighe
8/15 Eugene Upshaw
8/16 Julie Newmar
8/16 Frank Gifford
8/19 Peter Gallagher
8/19 Adam Arkin
8/20 Sam Melville

8/20	Theresa Saldana
8/20	Peter Davies
8/22	Delles Howell
8/24	David Gregory

THE LIGHTS

Whereas the appearance of the Patterns emphasizes the top of the head, their opposites, the Lights, accentuate the bottom. They have a strong, assertive chin that gives them a proud, majestic look that we might well expect of Leo. The Lights have a long, rectangular face, the sides of which are quite flat planes. You can virtually draw a straight vertical line from the cheekbone to the jawbone. Whereas the Patterns' faces have a lot of curves, the Lights' faces can be reduced to a few simple straight lines. Their features are nicely constructed and in good proportion. The Lights have the kind of face that would look good on Mount Rushmore. In fact, one of them–Abraham Lincoln–is already there!

There is hardly any variation in the face of the Lights, which made it difficult to decide how to list them. We put what we thought were the strongest-looking chins on Columns One and Two. The longest faces are in the third column, and the widest faces are in the fourth column (to the extent that Leo faces are ever wide at all). Columns Five and Six have fifty typical Lights, organized in no particular way. The Lights are one of five signs that are apt to be considered nice-looking. The others are the Bridges, Rocks, Patterns and Rapiers. It's possible to be good-looking under any of the other seven signs, but that would be an exception rather than the rule.

In our data, there were many more blondes born in fire and air signs than in earth and water signs, by a ratio of five to three. Leo had the most blondes, and Scorpio had the fewest.

LIGHTS - 1

1/19 Fritz Weaver

1/19 Gen. Robert E. Lee

1/21 Ann Wedgeworth
1/22 John Wesley Shipp
1/23 Justice Potter Stewart
1/26 Gen. Douglas MacArthur
1/27 James Cromwell
1/27 Bridget Fonda
1/28 Harley Kozak
1/29 Judy Norton Taylor
1/30 Vanessa Redgrave
1/30 Katharine Ross
1/30 Pres. Franklin Roosevelt
1/31 James Franciscus
2/04 Charles Lindbergh
2/05 Charlotte Rampling
2/05 Barbara Hershey
2/09 Janet Suzman
2/09 Peggy Wood
2/12 Cliff De Young
2/12 Josh Brolin
2/13 Carol Lynley
2/15 Kevin McCarthy
2/18 Cybill Shepherd
2/18 Matt Dillon

LIGHTS - 2

1/14 Julian Bond
1/14 Tom Tryon
1/21 Steve Reeves
1/25 Don Maynard
1/26 Jack Youngblood
1/27 Chief Justice Roberts

1/28 John Beck
1/29 Germaine Greer
1/30 Tammy Grimes
1/30 Dorothy Malone
1/31 Harry Wayne Casey
1/31 Jessica Walter
1/31 Joanne Dru
2/05 David Selby
2/06 Gayle Hunnicutt
2/07 Ashton Kutcher
2/07 Chris Rock
2/08 Joshua Morrow
2/09 Judith Light
2/11 Gov. Sarah Palin
2/11 Ben Oglivie
2/12 Pres. Abraham Lincoln
2/13 Sharon Wyatt
2/18 Billy De Wolfe
2/21 Kelsey Grammer

LIGHTS – 3

1/17 Angelique Kerber
1/19 Guy Madison
1/20 Countess Sophie
1/20 Lorenzo Lamas
1/21 Robby Benson
1/21 Paul Scofield
1/23 Dan Duryea
1/29 Matthew Ashford
1/30 Hugh Marlowe
1/30 John Ireland

2/01 Billy Mumy
2/03 Morgan Fairchild
2/04 Steve O'Neal
2/05 Roger Staubach
2/05 John Carradine
2/06 Jon Walmsley
2/09 Colin Egglesfield
2/11 Bradley Cole
2/14 Bart Matson
2/16 Hugh Beaumont
2/17 Dave Roberts (Padres)
2/17 Don Scardino
2/17 Zina Bethune
2/20 Andrew Shue
2/22 Van Arsdale twins

LIGHTS - 4

1/14 LL Cool J
1/16 Chandler Hill Harben
1/20 Carol Heiss
1/20 Gov. Nikki Haley
1/21 Geena Davis
1/23 Mariska Hargitay
1/24 Michael Ontkean
1/27 Donna Reed
1/27 Joe Dawkins
1/27 Mikhail Baryshnikov
1/29 John Forsythe
1/31 Mario Lanza
2/03 Thomas Calabro
2/04 Cheryl Miller

2/04 Clint Black
2/04 Lawrence Taylor
2/05 Jennifer Jason Leigh
2/05 Roberto Alomar
2/06 Chip Myrtle
2/06 Ramon Navarro
2/07 Jason Gedrick
2/10 Leontyne Price
2/12 Maud Adams
2/14 Rob Thomas
2/16 LeVar Burton

LIGHTS - 5

1/15 Maria Schell
1/18 Gov. Martin O'Malley
1/19 Stefan Edberg
1/21 Misha Barton
1/23 Randolph Scott
1/27 Ingrid Thulin
1/27 Migi Drummond
1/28 Bill White
1/28 Justin Hartley
1/29 Marc Singer
2/01 Sherman Hemsley
2/02 Farrah Fawcett
2/05 Val Dufour
2/06 Nick Zito
2/06 Mike Farrell
2/08 James Dean
2/08 Nick Nolte
2/10 Billy O'Dell

2/11 Catherine Hickland
2/12 Joanna Kerns
2/13 Kim Novak
2/16 William Katt
2/17 Luc Robitaille
2/18 Vanna White
2/20 Rihanna

LIGHTS – 6

1/11 Mitchell Ryan
1/14 Holland Taylor
1/15 Mario Van Peebles
1/25 Dean Jones
1/25 Gene Washington
1/28 Sarah McLachlan
1/30 Charley Neal
1/31 Carol Channing
2/01 David Knight
2/01 Michael C. Hall
2/02 Michael T. Weiss
2/02 Tom Smothers
2/03 Janet Grey
2/03 Blythe Danner
2/04 V.P. Dan Quayle
2/07 Jason Adams
2/08 Willie Rodgers
2/09 JM J. Bullock
2/09 Mia Farrow
2/11 Carey Lowell
2/14 Zach Galligan
2/14 Ken Wahl

2/16 Gretchen Wyler
2/17 Arthur Kennedy
2/19 Margaux Hemingway

THIRTY MORE LIGHTS

1/14 Barry Jenner
1/15 Wes Chesson
1/16 Harry Carey
1/18 Mark Messier
1/20 Dorothy Provine
1/24 Estelle Winwood
1/25 Leigh Taylor-Young
1/25 Mildred Dunnock
1/26 Walt Willey
1/28 Susan Howard
1/30 Glenn Doughty
1/31 John Agar
2/01 Pauly Shore
2/02 James Joyce
2/02 Dale Murray
2/02 Bo Hopkins
2/04 Michael Beck
2/05 Eddie Belmonte
2/07 Buster Crabbe
2/09 Alejandro Rey
2/11 Matthew Lawrence
2/12 Charles Van Doren
2/12 Wallace Ford
2/13 George Segal
2/14 Jay Hebert
2/14 Fred Carter

2/15 Melissa Manchester
2/15 Geoff Edwards
2/16 Hunt Block
2/17 Jeremy Slate

FURTHER REFLECTIONS

In the foregoing pages, we have shown two important things to be true. First, we have demonstrated that each of the twelve signs has its own distinctive look that is different from the other signs. Secondly, we showed that the appearance of each sign is exactly what it <u>ought</u> to be, based on the symbolism of that sign and its ruling planet.

Now draw a horoscope wheel with its customary twelve spokes, and write in the signs in their proper order, going in a counterclockwise direction as always. You will notice that Aries and Cancer form the sides of an arrowhead that points at the middle of Scorpio. Similarly, Libra and Capricorn form the sides of an arrowhead that points to Taurus. In the same manner, you will see that a Gemini-Capricorn arrow points to Virgo, while a Sagittarius-Cancer arrow points to Pisces. Now let's apply this to physical appearance.

We have already seen how the Scorpio face is somewhat like the Aries face. However, the cheekbones are higher and the nose is larger. Couldn't these differences indicate an influence coming from Cancer, sign of high cheekbones and large noses? Similarly, we have seen how the Taurus face is like the Libra face, since both are ruled by Venus. Yet the Taurus head is wider. That could be interpreted as a "stretching out" (Capricorn) of the Libra head to form Taurus.

Virgo has shrewd, peering eyes like Gemini, but it also has a mouth much like Capricorn, as though it is a composite of these two signs. Pisces has a round, Jupiter face like Sagittarius, but it has nose problems and an inadequate head–just like Cancer! You can apply this same logic to the more abstract characteristics of the signs, as shown below. Let's take these "composite signs" in the same sequence as before: first Scorpio, then Taurus, then Virgo, then Pisces.

Aries is supposed to represent aggression, and Cancer is said to symbolize containment and indeed all containers. Thus, in Scorpio we have "contained aggression," like a quiet volcano. Libra is supposed to indicate weighing and balancing on an intellectual level. However, Capricorn-Saturn represents something more concrete and tangible. Therefore, Taurus, a sign associated with money, symbolizes the tangible thing weighed, which used to be gold. Capricorn represents organized structure, and Gemini denotes connecting things together, as in reasoning. Therefore, the Virgoan is very orderly, seeking to connect each item to its proper place in an organized system. Cancer is said to be the great protector, the Mother Principle. But Sagittarius-Jupiter represents expansion and the broadening of one's perspective. Therefore, in Pisces we have an expanded protectiveness. Sympathetic Pisces wants to take care of the whole world – not just those in our own family or our own country.

All of the above provides interesting food for thought and for future study. There is always something new to be discovered! That is why some people have said, "It takes more than one lifetime to learn astrology."

Before we leave for good the subject of how to recognize the signs, we might mention that physical appearance is not the only clue you have. A person's voice can be significant too because the voice reflects the personality. This observer has noticed that positive signs (fire and air signs) have a different sound than negative signs (water and earthy signs). We suspect that a person could learn to tell whether a speaker is positive or negative, just by listening to the voice. The Hammers often have deep voices. Towers often speak slowly.

PART FIVE

MEGASIGNS: A NEW CONCEPT

THE FOUR MEGASIGNS

The tropical zodiac is supposed to be based on the seasons, but in some ways it doesn't conform to them very well. For example, in nature, April is surely more like May than like December. Yet, in tropical astrology, April is more like December because Aries (Apr.) and Sagittarius (Dec.) are both fire signs, whereas Taurus (May) is of the element earth. Similarly, we may say that April is more like January than May because Capricorn (Jan.) and Aries are both cardinal, whereas Taurus is of the fixed mode of action.

When you do research, you don't always find in the data a strong emphasis on just one sign. Sometimes a whole cluster of signs is accented. This led us to identify four "megasigns," one for each season. These megasigns span about five months, so that the dates of one megasign overlap on to the dates of the next one. We are used to the equinox and solstice points marking the commencement of each season, but in the megasign system, these points are near the center of each season. Here are the names and dates for the four megasigns:

Jan. 15-June 18: The Innovators (spring)
Apr. 18-Sept. 19: The Individualists (summer)
July 20-Dec. 21: The Preservers (fall)
Oct. 17-Mar. 20: The Friends (winter)

Notice how the type of person born in each season reflects the general character of that season. In the spring, innovation seems very appropriate because it is the time of nature's renewal. In the fall, you try to preserve whatever you can salvage. Squirrels store away nuts, and farmers harvest their crops. Summer marks the time of year when nature is in its glory. All of God's creatures are thriving and living it up. Everything in nature is flourishing. Food is abundant, and each animal grabs as much as he can. In the winter, when food is scarce, some creatures band together to help one another survive. The Pilgrims and other early settlers did much the same thing. Notice also that opposite seasons (those that are six months apart) produce opposite types of people. Because of the overlapping of the dates, about two-thirds of people are a mixture of two seasons.

The center of each megasign is as follows: Innovators, April 2; Individualists, July 4; Preservers, Oct. 5; and Friends, Jan. 2. The Innovators include the Lights, Slingshots, Bridges, Drills and Trumpets. The Individualists include the Drills, Trumpets, Hammers, Patterns and Towers. The Preservers include the Patterns, Towers, Fences, Rocks and Rapiers. The Friends include the Rocks, Rapiers, Antennas, Lights and Slingshots. Because of the way each megasign blends into the next one, we have a gradual change of season that accurately reflects nature – not the jarring contrasts from month to month that the tropical zodiac provides.

FILM ACTRESSES

1/20 Patricia Neal
1/21 Geena Davis
1/27 Donna Reed
1/30 Dorothy Malone
1/30 Vanessa Redgrave
2/08 Lana Turner
2/15 Gale Sondergaard
2/17 Brenda Fricker
2/27 Elizabeth Taylor
2/27 Joanne Woodward
2/28 Mercedes Ruehl
3/02 Jennifer Jones
3/03 Jean Harlow
3/07 Anna Magnani
3/08 Claire Trevor
3/12 Liza Minnelli
3/17 Mercedes McCambridge

3/20 Holly Hunter
3/22 Reese Witherspoon
3/23 Joan Crawford
3/25 Simone Signoret
3/28 Dianne Wiest
3/29 Eileen Heckart
3/31 Shirley Jones
4/02 Linda Hunt
4/03 Miyoshi Umeki
4/05 Bette Davis
4/08 Mary Pickford
4/08 Patricia Arquette
4/14 Julie Christie
4/15 Emma Thompson
4/20 Jessica Lange
4/24 Shirley MacLaine
4/24 Barbra Streisand
4/25 Renee Zellwegger
4/27 Sandy Dennis
4/29 Celeste Holm
4/30 Cloris Leachman
5/03 Mary Astor
5/04 Audrey Hepburn
5/07 Anne Baxter
5/09 Glenda Jackson
5/11 Margaret Rutherford
5/12 Katharine Hepburn
5/14 Cate Blanchett
5/20 Cher
6/01 Marilyn Monroe
6/04 Angelina Jolie
6/07 Jessica Tandy
6/15 Helen Hunt

FINE ACTING ON TV

1/17 James Earl Jones
1/21 Telly Savalas
1/25 Diana Hyland
1/25 Leigh Taylor-Young
1/29 Tom Selleck
1/31 Jessica Walter
1/31 Stuart Margolin
2/05 Barbara Hershey
2/10 Judith Anderson
2/11 Kim Stanley
2/15 Jane Seymour
2/17 Hal Holbrook
2/21 Tyne Daly
2/21 Larry Drake
2/22 Robert Young
2/24 Edward James Olmos
2/27 Barbara Babcock
3/06 Joanna Miles
3/07 Daniel J. Travanti
3/08 Susan Clark
3/09 Carl Betz
3/09 Will Geer
3/13 Dana Delany
3/19 Bruce Willis
3/23 Amanda Plummer
3/30 Richard Dysart
3/31 William Daniels
3/31 Richard Kiley
4/04 Christine Lahti
4/05 Michael Moriarty
4/07 James Garner

4/09 Michael Learned
4/18 James Woods
4/18 Barbara Hale
4/28 Madge Sinclair
5/03 Beulah Bondi
5/06 Mare Winningham
5/12 Susan Hampshire
5/13 Zohra Lampert
5/21 Raymond Burr
5/27 Bruce Weitz
5/28 John Karlen
5/31 Sharon Gless
6/03 Ellen Corby
6/03 Colleen Dewhurst
6/04 Dennis Weaver
6/08 Kathy Baker
6/12 Timothy Busfield
6/13 Richard Thomas
6/18 E. G. Marshall

MISCELLANEOUS FINE SINGING

1/28 Sarah McLachlan
2/09 Peggy Wood
2/09 Kathryn Grayson
2/10 Roberta Flack
2/14 Florence Henderson
2/21 Charlotte Church
2/22 Marni Nixon
2/23 Regina Crespine
2/24 Renata Scotto
2/25 Enrico Caruso

2/26 Emmy Destinn
2/27 Mirella Freni
2/27 Josh Groban
2/27 Marian Anderson
2/27 Lotte Lehmann
2/28 Geraldine Ferrar
3/01 Harry Belafonte
3/06 Kiri Te Kanawa
3/10 Carrie Underwood
3/12 Gordon MacRae
3/20 Lauritz Melchior
3/25 Anita Bryant
3/30 Celine Dion
3/31 Shirley Jones
4/01 Jane Powell
4/01 Susan Boyle
4/02 Emmylou Harris
4/08 John Reardon
4/08 Franco Corelli
4/09 Paul Robeson
4/09 Jackie Evancho
4/11 Paul Byrom
4/12 Lily Pons
4/12 Vince Gill
4/13 Howard Keel
4/21 Leonard Warren
4/24 Kelly Clarkson
5/01 Judy Collins
5/04 Roberta Peters
5/14 Patrice Munsel
5/17 Enya
5/17 Birgit Nilsson
5/18 Ezio Pinza

5/21 Dennis Day
5/25 Dixie Carter
5/30 George London
6/04 Robert Merrill
6/11 Rise Stevens
6/12 Jim Nabors
6/18 Jeanette MacDonald

COMPOSERS-CLASSICAL

1/27 Wolfgang A. Mozart
1/31 Franz Schubert
2/02 Fritz Kreisler
2/03 Felix Mendelssohn
2/22 Frederic Chopin
2/29 Gioacchino Rossini
3/04 Antonio Vivaldi
3/05 George F. Handel
3/07 Maurice Ravel
3/18 N. Rimsky-Korsakov
3/21 Modest Moussorgsky
3/31 Joseph Haydn
3/31 Johann Sebastian Bach
4/01 Sergei Rachmaninoff
4/23 Sergei Prokofiev
5/02 Alessandro Scarlatti
5/07 Johannes Brahms
5/07 Peter I. Tchaikovsky
5/12 Jules Massenet
5/22 Richard Wagner
6/02 Edward Elgar
6/08 Robert Schumann

6/11 Richard Strauss
6/15 Edvard Grieg
6/17 Charles Gounod

MISC. TOP MUSICIANS

1/31 Philip Glass
2/03 Sidney Lanier
2/10 Larry Adler
2/18 Andres Segovia
3/13 Tessie O'Shea
3/30 Eric Clapton
3/31 Herb Alpert
4/06 Carlos Salzado
4/07 Ravi Shankar
4/25 Albert King
5/21 Heinz Holliger
6/05 Kenny G.
6/08 Paula Robeson

UNINHIBITED

2/06 Nick Zito
2/16 John McEnroe
3/01 Harry Caray
3/07 Tammy Faye Bakker
3/15 Jimmy Swaggart
3/19 Wm. Jennings Bryan
3/28 Edmund Muskie
5/01 Jack Paar

ASTROLOGERS

1/18 John Partridge
1/22 Rupert Gleadow
1/24 Louis De Wohl
1/25 Johann Schoner
1/28 A. E. Partridge
1/30 Lorne E. Johndro
1/31 Charles E. O. Carter
1/31 Marguerite Carter
2/01 Jayj Jacobs
2/02 Carroll Righter
2/07 Joan McEvers
2/08 Evangeline Adams
2/10 Marion March
2/10 Wynn
2/13 M. Paul Choisnard
2/16 Reinhold Ebertin
2/23 Jean-Baptiste Morin
3/02 Alfred Witte
3/03 Donald Jacobs
3/04 Nicholas Campion
3/19 Raphael I
3/20 Sepharial
3/23 Dane Rudhyar
4/04 Doris Chase Doane
4/13 Tycho Brahe
4/13 Ivy G. Jacobson
4/20 Luke Broughton
4/20 Paul Grell
4/27 Carl Payne Tobey
5/01 David Cochrane
5/01 William Lilly

5/06 J. Claude Weiss
5/10 Louise Huber
5/10 Karl Krafft
5/11 Neil Michelson
5/16 Garth Allen
5/16 Jeff Jawer
5/21 Maritha Pottenger
5/22 Cyril Fagan
5/22 Marcia Moore 1928
5/22 Lois M. Rodden 1928
5/23 Alexander Ruperti
5/26 Vivian Robson
6/04 Ernest Grant
6/05 Jim Lewis
6/06 Dorothy Hughes
6/06 J. M. Regiomontanus
6/08 Grant Lewi
6/15 John Addey
6/15 R. J. Morrison

PLAYED MISFIT LONERS

8/18 Christian Slater
9/25 Catherine Burns
10/10 Kellie Martin
10/17 Montgomery Clift
11/15 John Kerr
11/22 Brian Robbins

TV REPERTORY ACTORS

7/29 Lloyd Bochner
8/03 Bethel Leslie
8/08 Ford Rainey
9/07 June Harding
9/09 Cliff Robertson
9/11 Anne Seymour
9/18 Robert Blake
10/02 Charles Drake
10/15 Jan Miner
10/23 Augusta Dabney
11/02 Warren Stevens
11/16 Guy Stockwell
11/23 John Newland
12/01 Mary K. Wells
12/05 Margaret Hayes

SEPARATE FROM GROUP

10/09 Alfred Dreyfuss
10/12 Scott O'Grady
10/15 John Dean
10/20 Wayne Morse
10/21 Patti Davis
10/27 Terry Anderson

WORKING-CLASS ROLE

7/28 Sally Struthers
8/09 Melanie Griffith
8/17 Mae West

8/18 Shelley Winters
8/22 Cindy Williams
8/30 Shirley Booth
9/30 Fran Drescher
10/15 Jane Darwell
10/15 Penny Marshall
10/15 Linda Lavin
10/17 Jean Arthur
11/03 Roseanne Barr
11/06 Sally Field
11/29 Diana Ladd
12/07 Ellen Burstyn

JUDGERS AND INTERPRETERS OF SPORTS

7/27 Peggy Fleming
7/31 Curt Gowdy
8/16 Frank Gifford
8/16 Tony Trabert
8/21 Chris Schenkel
8/28 Scott Hamilton
8/29 Jerry Bailey
9/02 Jimmy Connors
9/03 Bill Flemming
9/08 Duffy Daugherty
9/09 Jimmy the Greek
9/09 Clem McCarthy
9/09 Joe Theismann
9/11 Marty Liquori
9/12 Terry Bradshaw
9/12 John B. Campbell
9/14 Bud Palmer

9/15 Merlin Olsen
9/19 Joe Morgan
9/21 Shorty Ray
9/24 Jim McKay
9/25 Phil Rizzuto
9/25 Red Smith
9/28 Tom Harmon
10/02 Maury Wills
10/02 Darren Cahill
10/10 Bruce Devlin
10/11 Walter Vosburgh
10/12 Tony Kubek
10/14 Stephen A. Smith
10/15 Jim Palmer
10/16 Tim McCarver
10/18 Mike Ditka
10/18 Keith Jackson
10/18 Joe H. Palmer
10/21 Bob Rosburg
10/27 Ralph Kiner
10/28 Bruce Jenner
11/01 Grantland Rice
11/03 Nat Fleischer
11/03 Phil Simms
11/04 Walter Okeson
11/05 Bill Walton
11/07 Jim Kaat
11/12 Al Michaels
11/18 Lynn St. John
11/19 Ahmad Rashad
11/23 Oswald Tower
11/29 Vin Scully
12/12 Tracy Austin

PROPRIETY STANDARDS

7/22 Amy Vanderbilt
8/03 Martha Stewart
9/13 Judith Martin
10/02 Lord Chesterfield
10/27 Emily Post

CULTURAL STANDARDS

7/22 Bob Dole
7/26 Estes Kefauver
7/31 William Bennett
8/05 Richard Heffner
8/07 Alan Keyes
8/19 Tipper Gore
9/05 Jack Valenti
9/30 Bernhard Rust
9/30 Girolamo Savonarola
10/11 Nikolai Mikhailov
10/14 Joseph I. Breen
10/18 Jesse Helms
10/28 Jane Alexander
11/05 Will Hays
11/29 Paul Simon (Sen.)
12/15 Archbishop McNichols

ADVOCATED SOBRIETY

7/29 F. Scott McBride
7/30 Henry Ford
8/05 John Bidwell

8/08 Robert Holbrook Smith
8/26 Annie Wittenmyer
9/12 Joshua Levering
9/23 James Black
9/24 Joseph Kennedy Jr.
9/27 George Cruikshank
9/28 Frances Willard
10/31 Andrew Volstead
11/19 Billy Sunday
11/25 Carrie Nation
11/26 Wm. Griffith Wilson
12/08 Clinton B. Fisk

DOLL COLLECTORS

10/13 Marie Osmond
10/15 Penny Marshall
11/03 Roseanne Barr
11/11 Demi Moore
11/13 Whoopi Goldberg
12/19 Alyssa Milano

AMER. GRAFFITY NOSTALGIA

8/22 Cindy Williams
9/22 Paul LeMat
10/16 Suzanne Somers
10/29 Richard Dreyfuss
10/30 Charles Martin Smith
11/10 Mackenzie Phillips

MARY POPPINS MAGIC

7/23 Arthur Treacher
8/05 Reginald Owen
9/13 Reta Shaw
10/01 Julie Andrews
10/05 Glynis Johns
10/15 Jane Darwell
11/09 Ed Wynn
11/13 Hermione Baddeley
12/13 Dick Van Dyke

NIXED HONORS

10/01 Julie Andrews
10/18 George C. Scott

NAIVE, CHILDLIKE ROLE

8/04 Billy Bob Thornton
8/08 Dustin Hoffman
8/26 Chris Burke
9/09 Cliff Robertson
9/13 Jean Smart
9/23 Mickey Rooney
9/26 Edmund Gwenn
9/28 Joel Higgins
10/14 Harry Anderson
11/11 Leonardo DiCaprio
12/01 Treat Williams
12/06 Tom Hulce
12/09 John Malkovich

MARK TWAIN NOSTALGIA

7/25 Brad Renfro
8/28 Donald O'Connor
9/08 Jonathan Taylor Thomas
9/23 Mickey Rooney
10/26 Jackie Coogan
10/27 Jeff East
11/04 Michael Shea
12/13 Johnnie Whitaker

WARTIME MEMORIES

7/22 Willem Dafoe
8/02 Myrna Loy
8/12 George Hamilton
8/30 Timothy Bottoms
8/31 Fredric March
9/03 Charlie Sheen
9/15 Oliver Stone
9/23 Walter Pidgeon
9/27 Stephen Caffrey
9/29 Greer Garson
9/29 Stanley Kramer
10/01 Tim O'Brien
10/01 George Peppard
10/07 Helmut Dantine
10/08 Matt Damon
10/17 Montgomery Clift
10/18 George C. Scott
10/27 Teresa Wright
10/31 Robin Moore
11/02 Burt Lancaster

11/12 Richard Ney
12/08 Maximilian Schell
12/16 Noel Coward
12/16 Terence Knox
12/18 Steven Spielberg

HORSE RACING TRADITION

8/10 John W. Galbreath
8/13 Fred Capossela
8/16 Jack Price
8/17 John Hay Whitney
8/23 Harry F. Guggenheim
8/28 Jack Dreyfus
9/11 Daniel Wildenstein
9/16 Christopher T. Chenery
9/18 Ogden Mills Phipps
9/22 Alfred G. Vanderbilt
9/24 Jim McKay
9/25 Warren Wright
10/01 Jimmy Carter
10/04 Damon Runyon
10/06 Fred W. Hooper
10/16 Ernie Samuel
10/18 Willis Sharpe Kilmer
10/22 Leslie Combs II
11/15 Rex Ellsworth
11/22 John R. Gaines
11/26 Ogden Phipps
11/30 Olin Gentry
12/11 Adm. Gene Markey

12/12 Col. E. R. Bradley
12/14 Lucille Markey

HAPPY DAYS NOSTALGIA

8/08 Donny Most
9/02 Linda Purl
9/22 Scott Baio
9/25 Anson Williams
10/01 Tom Bosley
10/18 Erin Moran
10/25 Marion Ross
10/30 Henry Winkler

HISTORIANS, BIOGRAPHERS

7/26 Andre Maurois
8/01 Paul Horgan
8/03 James MacGregor Burns
8/06 Richard Hofstadter
8/27 Antonia Fraser
9/10 Bernard Bailyn
9/10 Carl Van Doren
9/13 John J. Pershing
9/15 Heinrich von Treitschke
9/16 Francis Parkman
9/19 Oscar Handlin
9/21 H. G. Wells
9/27 Alfred T. Mahan
9/27 Catherine Marshall
9/28 Prosper Merimee
10/01 Daniel Boorstin

10/03 George Bancroft
10/09 Bruce Catton
10/15 Arthur Schleshinger, Jr.
10/18 James Truslow Adams
10/25 Henry Steele Commager
10/25 Thomas Macaulay
10/28 George Dangerfield
10/29 James Boswell
11/05 Will Durant
11/05 Ida Tarbell
11/07 Margaret Leech
11/13 C. Vann Woodward
11/14 Frederick Jackson Turner
11/28 Nancy Mitford
11/30 Winston Churchill
12/02 Joseph P. Lash
12/04 Thomas Carlyle
12/08 Burton J. Hendrick

CARED ABOUT THE PAST

7/26 Carl Jung
7/28 Jacqueline Onassis
7/29 Ken Burns
7/30 Peter Bogdanovich
8/15 Joseph Scaliger
8/23 Edgar Lee Masters
8/25 Johann von Herder
8/27 James H. Breasted
9/03 Bessie Delany
9/07 Michael Feinstein
9/15 Oliver Stone

9/17 Dorothy Loudon
9/17 Roddy McDowall
9/18 Bud Greenspan
9/19 Paul H. Helms
9/19 James Van Alen
9/19 Sadie Delany
9/26 James F. Dobie
10/06 Thor Heyerdahl
10/07 Joanne Koch
10/13 Virgil
10/16 John A. Willis
11/13 Henri Langlois
11/14 Prince Charles
11/17 Martin Scorcese

COMIC BOOK ROLE

7/24 Lynda Carter
7/31 Dean Cain
9/09 Michael Keaton
9/19 Adam West
9/25 Christopher Reeve
10/17 Margot Kidder
12/08 Teri Hatcher
12/14 Helen Slater

COMIC STRIP ROLE

8/03 Jay North
9/15 Penny Singleton
10/01 Walter Matthau
11/05 Andrea McArdle

HAWAIIAN POLITICIANS

9/07 Daniel Inouye
9/11 Daniel K. Akaka
10/01 Hiram Fong
10/08 Spark Matsunaga
11/14 Ben Cayetano

ISRAELI LEADERS

8/02 Shimon Peres
8/16 Menachem Begin
9/17 Chaim Herzog
9/30 Ehud Olmert
10/15 Moshe Sharett
10/16 David Ben-Gurion
10/21 Benjamin Netanyahu
10/25 Levi Eshkol
11/03 Yitzhak Shamir
11/27 Chaim Weizmann
12/07 Moshe Arens

MISC. ETHNIC CHARM

8/28 Charles Boyer
9/12 Maurice Chevalier
9/18 Greta Garbo
9/18 Rossano Brazzi
9/28 Marcello Mastroianni
10/03 Gertrude Berg
10/08 Paul Hogan
11/13 Oskar Werner

11/25 Ricardo Montalban

12/03 Katarina Witt

REGIONAL OR ETHNIC FOCUS

7/31 Evonne Goolagong

8/28 Virginia Dare

9/03 Sarah Jewitt

9/06 Rosie Perez

9/06 Dolores O'Riordin

9/18 James Gandolfini

9/22 Ingemar Johansson

9/27 A. Martinez

9/28 Max Schmeling

9/30 Elie Wiesel

10/04 Frederic Remington

10/06 Jenny Lind

10/07 James Whitcomb Riley

10/14 Hannah Arendt

10/15 Mario Puzo

10/18 Martina Navratilova

10/23 Chi Chi Rodriguez

11/10 Russell Means

11/14 King Hussein

11/20 Wilfred Laurier

11/22 Boris Becker

12/08 Sinead O'Connor

12/10 Nelly Sachs

12/17 Mary Queen of Scots

12/18 Steven Spielberg

BLACK HIGH ACHIEVERS

8/02 James Baldwin
8/04 Barack Obama
8/11 Alex Haley
8/25 Althea Gibson
9/04 Richard Wright
9/05 Frank Yerby
9/07 Jacob Lawrence
9/16 B. B. King
9/16 James Alan McPherson
9/21 Melvin Van Peebles
10/02 Johnnie Cochrane
10/07 Imamu Baraka
10/09 Leopold Senghor
10/12 Charles Gordone
10/21 Dizzy Gillespie
10/26 Mahalia Jackson
10/31 Ethel Waters
11/09 Benjamin Banneker
11/13 Whoopi Goldberg
11/16 W. C. Handy
11/24 Scott Joplin
11/26 Art Shell
12/05 James Cleveland
12/18 Ossie Davis
12/19 Cicely Tyson

WATERGATE

7/26 James McCord, Jr.
8/08 Patrick McCarran
9/05 John Mitchell

9/13 Kenneth Parkinson
10/09 E. Howard Hunt
10/15 John Dean
10/16 Charles Colson
10/23 Robert C. Mardian
10/27 H. R. Haldeman
11/05 Jeb Stuart Magruder
11/30 G. Gordon Liddy

ANTI-COMMUNISM

8/12 John Poindexter
8/12 Cecil B. DeMille
9/07 Elia Kazan
9/28 Ed Sullivan
10/07 Oliver North
11/05 Martin Dies
11/14 Joseph McCarthy
12/01 Robert Welch
12/05 Walt Disney
12/20 John Birch

SEEMED BIGOTED

7/23 Don Imus
7/24 Michael Richards
8/01 Alfonse D'Amato
8/03 Isaiah Washington
8/04 Helen Thomas
8/11 Hulk Hogan
8/18 Marge Schott
8/25 George Wallace

8/25 Elvis Costello
8/26 Off. Lawrence Powell
8/29 Slobodan Milosevic
8/31 Eldridge Cleaver
9/01 Tim Hardaway
9/08 Hendrik Verwoerd
9/09 Jimmy the Greek
9/12 H. L. Mencken
9/14 Margaret Sanger
9/15 Prince Harry
9/24 Lou Dobbs
9/26 Martin Heidegger
9/26 Jan Brewer
9/30 Lester Maddox
10/01 William Rehnquist
10/07 Heinrich Himmler
10/07 Vladimir Putin
10/08 Jesse Jackson
10/09 Trent Lott
10/11 George Preston Marshall
10/12 Kirk Cameron
10/13 Theodore Bilbo
10/16 Louise Day Hicks
10/17 John Rocker
10/17 Eminem
10/18 Jesse Helms
10/23 Frank Rizzo
10/24 Karl Lueger
10/25 Father Charles Coughlin
10/28 Mahmoud Ahmadinejad
10/29 P. Joseph Goebbels
10/30 Clement Haynsworth
11/02 Al Campanis

11/02 Pat Buchanan
11/03 Roseanne
11/11 Fuzzy Zoeller
11/20 Kenesaw Landis
11/23 Sgt. Stacey Koon
11/27 Steve Bannon
12/05 Strom Thurmond
12/18 Ty Cobb
12/19 Reggie White
12/20 Tom Tancredo

SOUTHERN GOVERNORS

8/19 Bill Clinton
8/20 Terry Sanford
8/25 George Wallace
8/30 Huey Long
9/03 Ann Richards
9/11 Reubin Askew
9/30 Lester Maddox
10/01 Jimmy Carter

THE CARTER TEAM

7/22 Bob Bergland
7/30 Moon Landrieu
8/15 Lillian Carter
8/18 Rosalynn Carter
8/18 Jeff Carter
8/22 F. Ray Marshall
8/24 Shirley Hufstedler
8/25 Cecil Andrus

9/09 Charles Duncan Jr.
9/19 Harold Brown
9/21 Hamilton Jordan
9/30 Jody Powell
10/01 Jimmy Carter
10/13 Donald McHenry
10/19 Amy Carter
10/27 Warren Christopher
10/31 Griffin Bell

FOND OF FISHING

7/25 Walter Payton
7/31 Curt Gowdy
8/09 Deion Sanders
8/10 Herbert Hoover
8/18 Robert Redford
8/19 Izaac Walton
8/30 Ted Williams
9/08 Heather Thomas
9/21 Larry Hagman
10/01 Jimmy Carter
10/01 Walter Matthau
10/04 Charlton Heston
10/14 Dwight D. Eisenhower
10/30 Harry Hamlin
10/31 Dan Rather
11/30 Mark Twain
12/15 Don Johnson

COUNTRY-WESTERN MUSIC: PEACEFUL, TRADITIONAL

7/29 Martina McBride
8/08 Webb Pierce
8/08 Mel Tillis
8/10 Jimmy Dean
8/12 Buck Owens
8/12 Porter Wagoner
8/14 Connie Smith
8/20 Jim Reeves
8/21 Kenny Rogers
8/25 Billy Ray Cyrus
8/28 LeAnn Rimes
8/28 Shania Twain
8/30 Kitty Wells
9/01 Conway Twitty
9/08 Patsy Cline
9/08 Jimmie Rodgers (b. 1897)
9/12 George Jones
9/13 Bill Monroe
9/15 Roy Acuff
9/17 Hank Williams
9/18 Jimmy Rodgers (b. 1933)
9/19 Trisha Yearwood
9/21 Faith Hill
9/26 Lynn Anderson
9/26 Marty Robbins
9/29 Gene Autry
10/04 Leroy Van Dyke
10/10 Tanya Tucker
10/11 Dottie West
10/17 Alan Jackson
10/19 Jeannie C. Riley

10/20 Wanda Jackson
10/22 Shelby Lynne
10/23 Dwight Yoakam
10/25 Minnie Pearl
10/26 Keith Urban
10/27 Lee Greenwood
10/28 Brad Paisley
10/28 Charlie Daniels
11/01 Bill Anderson
11/01 Lyle Lovett
11/02 k. d. lang
11/05 Roy Rogers
11/08 Patti Page
11/10 Donna Fargo
11/10 Miranda Lambert
11/29 Merle Travis
12/13 Taylor Swift
12/14 Charlie Rich
12/15 A. P. Carter

THE INNOVATORS

I. EMOTING

- A. Film Actors Ω
- B. Film Actresses
- C. Fine Acting on TV
- D. Actors in Sci-Fi Shows
- E. Juvenile Actors Ω
- F. Former Teen Idols
- G. Emotionally Uninhibited Persons

II. MUSIC

- A. Classical Composers
- B. Composers of Film Scores
- C. Conductors Ω
- D. Pianists Ω
- E. Misc. Top Musicians
- F. Jazz Musicians
- G. Singers of Jazz, Blues and Soul Ω
- H. Opera Singers
- I. Misc. Fine Singers
- J. Choral Directors

III. ARTISTIC PURSUITS

- A. Painters and Sculptors Ω
- B. Horticulturists Ω
- C. Creative Writers Ω

IV. WISDOM

A. Philosophers
B. Astrologers
C. Mystics
D. Psychics

V. SHREWD MANEUVERING

A. Chess Masters and War Strategists
B. Negotiators

VI. SCIENCE AND MACHINES

A. Inventors
B. Physicists and Mathematicians ♍
C. Astronauts ♍

VII. DARING

A. Astronauts ♍
B. Bullfighters ♍
C. Auto Racers ♍
D. Controversy Sparkers ♍
E. Actors Who Played Gays ♍
F. Defiant Mavericks

VIII. LEFT-WING BELIEFS

A. Liberals in Government ♏
B. Liberal Celebrities ♏
C. Reformers
D. Misc. Radicals ♏
E. Revolutionaries ♏
F. Marxists

THE PRESERVERS

I. LONER TYPES

- A. Reserved, Private or Shy People
- B. Actors Who Played Misfit Loners
- C. Actors Who Wore Masks ♓
- D. Unmasked Victims of Scandal ♓
- E. Those Who Resented the Press ♓
- F. Those Separated from Their Group
- G. Isolationists ♓

II. SCHOLARSHIP, EXPERTISE

- A. Linguists and Lexicographers
- B. Librarians
- C. Data Compilers

III. JUDGING AND CRITICIZING

- A. Critics
- B. Columnists
- C. Judges
- D. Judgers of Sports
- E. Those Who Seemed Bigoted

IV. BEHAVIOR STANDARDS

- A. High-Achieving Athletes
- B. Advocates of Cultural Standards
- C. Advocates of Propriety

D. Sobriety Advocates
E. Peace Advocates

V. LABOR
A. Advocates for Workers' Rights ♉
B. Actresses in Blue-Collar Roles

VI. RURAL LIFE AND THE SOUTH
A. Actors Who Co-Starred with Animals ♈
B. Animal Rights Advocates ♈
C. Actors and Authors Presenting Rural Life ♈
D. Country Music Singers
E. Those Who Enjoyed Fishing
F. Southern Senators
G. Southern Governors
H. President Carter's team

VII. PATRIOTIC ZEAL
A. Nationalists and Patriots
B. Key Figures in Watergate
C. Anti-Communists

VIII. ROOTS AND DISTINCTIVENESS
A. Regional or Ethnic Focus
B. Regional or Ethnic Music
C. Regional or Ethnic Actors' Roles ♈
D. Misc. Ethnic Charmers
E. British Charmers ♈
F. Black High Achievers
G. Civil Rights Advocates ♈
H. Israeli Leaders
I. Hawaiian Politicians
J. Asians in the Arts

- K. Foreign-Born Beauties ♈
- L. Actors Playing Aliens or Their Co-stars ♈

IX. THE PAST
- A. Historians and Biographers
- B. Historical Novelists
- C. Misc. Others Who Cared about the Past
- D. Actors in American Graffiti
- E. Actors in Happy Days
- F. Actors in Films about the War
- G. Those Comprising Horse Racing Tradition

X. CHILDHOOD
- A. Actors Playing Naive, Childlike Role
- B. Actors in Comic Strip Role
- C. Actors in Comic Book Role
- D. Actors in Mary Poppins
- E. Actors in Mark Twain stories
- F. Doll Collectors

XI. LAUGHTER
- A. Humorists and Satirists ♊
- B. Cartoonists
- C. Puppeteers

XII. THEATRE
- A. Playwrights ♊
- B. Stage Actors
- C. Actor-Singers in Musicals
- D. TV Repertory Actors

XIII. THREE-DIMENSIONAL ART

- A. Sculptors ♉
- B. Fashion Designers
- C. Cosmetologists

XIV. BEAUTIFUL PEOPLE

- A. Screen Beauties ♒
- B. Foreign-Born Beauties
- C. Models
- D. Bodybuilders

XV. LIFE SCIENCE

- A. Doctors and Nurses ♓
- B. Zoologists and Naturalists ♓

Innovators	vs.	Preservers
Reforms		Traditions, Precedents
Artists		Critics
Experimentation		Nostalgia
Philosophy		History
New Machines		The Human Body
Negotiation		Isolation
Screen Acting (intimate)		Stage Acting (distanced)
Revolution		Peace, Decorum
Orchestras		Libraries
Freedom		Standards
Logic		Empiricism
Rashness		Circumspection
Emotion		Reserve
Progress		Continuity
The International		The Regional
Teen Rebellion		Young Childhood

Similes, Metaphors	Distinctions
Classical Music	Country Music
Plants	Animals

PLAYED STRICT PARENTS

4/22 Eddie Albert
5/14 Richard Deacon
5/25 Claude Akins
6/14 Burl Ives
6/14 Dorothy McGuire
7/01 Charles Laughton
7/11 Yul Brynner
7/19 Pat Hingle
7/28 Ann Doran
8/02 Carroll O'Connor
8/15 Ethel Barrymore
8/18 Shelley Winters
8/29 James Coburn
8/30 Raymond Massey

ACTUAL STRICT PARENTS

5/02 Bing Crosby
6/01 Pat Boone
6/10 Prince Philip
6/27 Ross Perot
7/06 Nancy Reagan
8/06 Lucille Ball
9/06 Joe Kennedy

RACEHORSE TRAINERS

4/21 H. Allen Jerkins
5/08 Laz Barrera
5/16 Sam Hildreth
5/22 H. Graham Motion
5/24 Doug O'Neill
5/30 Scotty Schulhofer
6/07 Jack Van Berg
6/07 Patrick Biancone
6/16 Gary Jones
6/18 Jerry Hollendorfer
6/26 Todd Pletcher
6/27 John Veitch
7/09 Bobby Frankel
7/11 Ron McAnally
7/13 Max Hirsch
7/23 James Fitzsimmons
7/25 Stanley Dancer
7/29 Bill Mott
7/29 Dermot Weld
7/30 John Sadler
8/07 Eddie Gregson
8/29 Carl Nafzger
9/01 Woody Stephens
9/02 D. Wayne Lukas
9/07 Bud Delp

MODERN BRITISH ROYALTY

4/21 Queen Elizabeth II
6/10 Prince Philip
6/19 Duchess of Windsor

6/21 Prince William
6/23 Duke of Windsor
7/01 Princess Diana
7/17 Duchess of Cornwall
8/04 The Queen Mother
8/15 Princess Anne
8/21 Princess Margaret
9/15 Prince Harry

THE ROCKEFELLER DYNASTY

5/01 Winthrop Rockefeller
5/26 Laurence Rockefeller
5/30 Nelson Rockefeller Jr.
5/31 William Rockefeller
6/09 Happy Rockefeller
6/12 David Rockefeller
6/18 Jay Rockefeller
7/08 Nelson Rockefeller
7/09 John D. Rockefeller
8/31 Edith Rockefeller

PORTRAYED ROYALTY

5/04 Audrey Hepburn
5/09 Glenda Jackson
5/12 Katharine Hepburn
5/14 Cate Blanchett
5/22 Laurence Olivier
7/01 Charles Laughton
7/01 Genevieve Bujold
7/11 Yul Brynner

8/02 Peter O'Toole
8/09 Robert Shaw
8/10 Norma Shearer

THE KENNEDY DYNASTY

5/29 John F. Kennedy
7/04 Kathleen Kennedy
7/10 Eunice Kennedy Shriver
7/22 Rose Kennedy
7/28 Jackie Kennedy Onassis
9/04 William Kennedy Smith
9/05 Joan Kennedy
9/06 Joe Kennedy Sr.
9/07 Peter Lawford
9/13 Rosemary Kennedy

CELEBRITIES WHO PAINTED

4/20 Adolf Hitler
4/21 Anthony Quinn
4/29 Duke Ellington
5/01 Sarah Armstrong-Jones
5/01 Jack Paar
5/09 Candice Bergen
5/12 Katharine Hepburn
5/16 Henry Fonda
5/17 Dennis Hopper
5/26 Peggy Lee
5/26 Jack Kevorkian
6/03 Tony Curtis
6/09 Mona Freeman

6/10 Leelee Sobieski
6/18 Paul McCartney
6/21 Leigh McCloskey
7/06 George W. Bush
7/06 James Kiberd
7/06 Sylvester Stallone
7/06 Judith Barcroft
7/14 Nick Benedict
7/17 Phyllis Diller
7/17 James Cagney
7/18 Red Skelton
8/03 Tony Bennett
8/06 Nathan Purdee

ART EXPERTS

4/27 Nicholas Serota
5/21 Armand Hammer
5/27 Vincent Price
6/07 Nancy Donnellan
6/11 Paul Mellon
6/22 Billy Wilder
7/03 Stavros Niarchos
7/08 Sidney Janis
7/08 Nelson Rockefeller
7/16 Sebastian Cabot
7/28 Jackie Onassis
8/10 Albert Skira
8/11 Joseph Hirshhorn
8/26 Peggy Guggenheim
9/05 Louis XIV
9/11 Daniel Wildenstein

WROTE SEA NOVELS

7/10 Frederick Marryat
8/01 Herman Melville
8/01 Richard Henry Dana
8/27 Cecil S. Forester

ADVENTURE, SUSPENSE

5/06 Gaston Leroux
5/08 Peter Benchley
5/13 Daphne Du Maurier
5/25 Robert Ludlam
5/28 Ian Fleming
6/05 Cornelius Ryan
6/18 Paul Connolly
6/22 H. Rider Haggard
6/28 Eric Ambler
7/21 Ernest Hemingway
7/24 Alexandre Dumas
7/27 Jack Higgins
8/15 Sir Walter Scott
8/27 Ira Levin
8/30 Mary Shelley
9/01 Edgar Rice Burroughs
9/15 James Fenimore Cooper

WROTE ROMANTIC TALES

4/21 Charlotte Bronte
5/05 Douglas Marland
5/21 Harold Robbins

6/06 Esther Shapiro
6/12 Henry Slesar
6/16 Erich Segal
6/21 Mary McCarthy
6/27 Richard Shapiro
7/01 Irna Phillips
7/09 Barbara Cartland
7/09 Ann Radcliffe
7/30 Emily Bronte
8/14 Danielle Steel
8/20 Jacqueline Susann
9/07 Taylor Caldwell
9/08 Grace Metalious

IN FOX TEEN SOAPS

5/16 Tori Spelling
6/04 Scott Wolf
7/14 Matthew Fox
7/15 Brian Austin Green
8/28 Jason Priestley

IN PRIME TIME SOAPS

4/18 John James
4/20 Ryan O'Neal
5/20 James Douglas
5/22 Barbara Parkins
5/23 Joan Collins
6/12 Timothy Busfield
6/14 Kim Lankford
6/15 Polly Draper

6/16 Joan Van Ark
6/18 Constance McCashin
6/23 Ted Shackleford
6/24 Michelle Lee
6/26 Pamela Bellwood
7/07 Billy Campbell
7/11 Sela Ward
7/12 Mel Harris
7/15 Ken Kercheval
7/17 Diahann Carroll
7/27 John Pleshette
7/30 Ken Olin
8/20 Peter Horton
8/28 Emma Samms
9/05 William Devane
9/08 Christopher Connelly
9/12 Linda Gray

MALE DAYTIME SOAPERS

5/01 John Beradino
5/07 Peter Reckell
5/07 Michael E. Knight
5/27 Darin Brooks
5/29 Anthony Geary
6/05 Bill Hayes
6/11 Peter Bergman
6/11 Stephen Schnetzer
6/15 Greg Vaughan
6/20 John McCook
6/27 Robert Newman
6/28 Steve Burton

7/06 Michael Park
7/15 Phil Carey
7/15 Kristoff St. John
7/27 Eric Martsolf
8/06 Grant Aleksander
8/09 Clint Ritchie
8/25 Christian J. LeBlanc
8/25 David Canary
8/25 Cameron Mathison
8/26 Jon Hensley
9/10 Jacob Young
9/13 Roger Howarth
9/15 Forrest Compton

FILM COMEDY ACTING

4/18 Rick Moranis
4/19 Dudley Moore
4/20 Harold Lloyd
4/22 Jack Nicholson
4/24 Shirley MacLaine
4/24 Barbra Streisand
5/02 Bing Crosby
5/04 Audrey Hepburn
5/07 Gabby Hayes
5/09 Glenda Jackson
5/10 Fred Astaire
5/11 Margaret Rutherford
5/12 Katharine Hepburn
5/20 Cher
5/29 Bob Hope
6/01 Marilyn Monroe

6/02 Sally Kellerman
6/04 Rosalind Russell
6/10 Hattie McDaniel
6/11 Gene Wilder
6/13 Mary Wickes
6/13 Paul Lynde
6/15 Helen Hunt
6/16 Stan Laurel
6/19 Kathleen Turner
6/19 Charles Coburn
6/20 Nicole Kidman
6/20 Olympia Dukakis
6/21 Judy Holliday
6/23 Frances McDormand
6/28 Mel Brooks
7/08 Anjelica Huston
7/08 Eugene Pallette
7/14 Terry-Thomas
7/16 Ginger Rogers
7/21 Robin Williams
7/26 Sandra Bullock
7/28 Joe E. Brown
7/29 William Powell
8/01 Dom DeLuise
8/02 Myrna Loy
8/07 Billie Burke
8/12 Cantinflas
8/13 Bert Lahr
8/17 Mae West
8/17 Monty Woolley
8/30 Fred MacMurray
9/08 Peter Sellers

9/09 Hugh Grant
9/13 Claudette Colbert

SATURDAY NIGHT LIVE

4/23 Jan Hooks
4/29 Nora Dunn
5/04 Ana Gasteyer
5/18 Tina Fey
5/21 Al Franken
5/24 Mike Myers
6/02 Dana Carvey
6/17 Will Forte
6/28 Gilda Radner
7/01 Dan Aykroyd
7/08 A. Whitney Brown
7/16 Will Ferrell
7/21 Jon Lovitz
7/22 David Spade
7/27 Maya Rudolph
8/14 Steve Martin
8/18 Andy Samberg
9/04 Damon Wayans
9/06 Jane Curtin
9/09 Adam Sandler
9/16 Molly Shannon
9/16 Amy Poehler
9/19 Jimmy Fallon
9/19 Cheri O'Teri

MISC. TV COMEDIANS

4/26 Carol Burnett
6/25 Jimmie Walker
7/12 Milton Berle
7/17 Phyllis Diller
7/18 Red Skelton
7/24 Ruth Buzzi
9/01 Lily Tomlin
9/06 Jo Anne Worley
9/08 Sid Caesar

GAME SHOW PANELISTS

5/21 Peggy Cass
5/25 Bennett Cerf
5/31 Fred Allen
6/13 Paul Lynde
7/03 Dorothy Kilgallen
7/08 Faye Emerson
7/22 Orson Bean
8/19 Ogden Nash
9/03 Kitty Carlisle

STEERED INTERVIEWS, LED DISCUSSIONS

10/23 Johnny Carson
10/31 Jane Pauley
11/03 Roseanne Barr
11/07 Lawrence O'Donnell
11/13 Jimmy Kimmel
11/13 Whoopi Goldberg

11/16 Mary Margaret McBride
11/19 Larry King
11/19 Dick Cavett
11/24 William F. Buckley
11/29 Howie Mandell
11/30 G. Gordon Liddy
12/03 Les Crane
12/04 Tyra Banks
12/09 Morton Downey Jr.
12/16 Susan Estrich
12/18 Chris Matthews
12/19 David Susskind
12/21 Phil Donahue
12/22 Diane Sawyer
12/24 Ryan Seacrest
12/26 Steve Allen
12/27 Cokie Roberts
12/30 Matt Lauer
12/30 Meredith Vieira
12/30 Sean Hannity
1/05 Charlie Rose
1/07 Katie Couric
1/12 Rush Limbaugh
1/12 Christiane Amanpour
1/12 Howard Stern
1/16 Maury Povich
1/16 Laura Schleshinger
1/20 Bill Maher
1/26 Ellen DeGeneres
1/27 Ed Schultz
1/27 Keith Olbermann
1/29 Oprah Winfrey
2/03 Joey Bishop

2/08 Ted Koppell
2/10 George Stephanopoulos
2/12 Arsenio Hall
2/13 Jerry Springer
2/14 Hugh Downs
2/25 Sally Jesse Raphael
2/28 Chris Hayes
2/29 Dinah Shore
3/01 Alan Thicke
3/09 Charlie Gibson
3/16 Jerry Lewis

STUDENT BODY PRESIDENTS

11/19 Dick Cavett
12/01 Bette Midler
12/23 Ken Hubbs
12/26 Richard Widmark
1/02 Cuba Gooding Jr.
1/13 Julia Louis-Dreyfus
1/20 Lorenzo Lamas
1/22 Bill Bixby
1/24 Oral Roberts
1/29 Oprah Winfrey
2/06 Tom Brokaw
2/15 Matt Groening
2/18 Helen Gurley Brown
2/20 Andrew Shue
3/07 Willard Scott
3/08 James Van Der Beek
3/13 Robert S. Woods
3/19 Bruce Willis

MODERN U.S. CONGRESS PERSONS

10/18 Jesse Helms
10/26 Hillary Clinton
10/26 Edward Brooke
11/14 Joe McCarthy
11/17 John Boehner
11/20 Robert Kennedy
11/20 Joe Biden
11/20 Robert Byrd
11/23 Charles Schumer
11/28 Gary Hart
12/02 Harry Reid
12/05 Strom Thurmond
12/09 Tip O'Neill
12/09 Tom Daschle
12/11 John Kerry
12/14 Margaret Chase Smith
1/29 Paul Ryan
1/30 Dick Cheney 1941
1/31 Dick Gephardt 1941
2/04 Dan Quayle
2/20 Mitch McConnell
2/22 Ted Kennedy
2/24 Joe Lieberman
3/16 Daniel P. Moynihan

PLAYED POLITICIANS

10/19 Simon Ward
11/10 Claude Rains
11/14 Brian Keith
11/30 Richard Crenna

12/09 Broderick Crawford
12/09 Beau Bridges
12/14 Patty Duke
12/14 Dan Dailey
12/31 Ben Kingsley
12/31 Anthony Hopkins
1/06 Loretta Young
1/16 Alexander Knox
1/16 Harry Carey
1/21 Geena Davis
1/29 John Forsythe
2/16 Hunt Block
2/16 William Katt
2/17 Hal Holbrook
2/18 John Travolta
2/24 Barry Bostwick
2/27 Franchot Tone
2/28 Charles Durning
3/05 James Noble
3/07 Mark Pinter
3/07 Gary Sinese

EVANGELISTS, GURUS

11/07 Billy Graham
11/19 Billy Sunday
12/03 Terry Cole-Whittaker
12/05 Little Richard
12/08 Sam Kinison
12/10 Mahara Ji
12/11 B. S. Rajneesh
12/25 Evangeline Booth

1/02 Jim Bakker
1/03 Denise Mathews
1/14 Marjoe Gortner
1/15 Dr. Fred Schwarz
1/22 George Foreman
1/24 Oral Roberts
2/05 Dwight Lyman Moody
2/16 Gilbert Tennant
3/05 Joel Osteen
3/07 Tammy Faye Bakker
3/15 Jimmy Swaggart

PLAYED EVANGELISTS

11/02 Burt Lancaster
1/31 Jean Simmons

FOLK-POP SINGERS

10/31 Tom Paxton
11/07 Joni Mitchell
11/09 Mary Travers
11/10 Dave Loggins
11/12 Neil Young
11/17 Gordon Lightfoot
11/22 Jesse Colin Young
11/28 Randy Newman
12/05 Chad Mitchell
12/07 Harry Chapin
12/19 Phil Ochs
12/30 Noel Paul Stookey
12/31 Odetta

12/31 John Denver
1/03 Stephen Stills
1/09 Joan Baez
1/10 Shawn Colvin
1/10 Jim Croce
1/12 Glenn Yarborough
1/21 Richie Havens
2/02 Graham Nash
2/03 Melanie
2/20 Buffy Sainte-Marie
3/12 James Taylor
3/17 John Sebastian

PORTRAYED TEACHERS

10/19 Lloyd Haines
10/28 Annie Potts
10/29 Richard Dreyfuss
12/19 Cicely Tyson
12/28 Maggie Smith
12/29 Jon Voight
1/31 James Franciscus
2/20 Sidney Poitier
2/24 Edward James Olmos
2/27 Howard Hesseman
3/02 Jennifer Jones
3/18 Robert Donat
3/20 Michael Redgrave
3/20 William Hurt

MISC. ROVERS, SEEKERS

11/22 Wiley Post
12/19 Richard Leakey
12/31 Simon Weisenthal
1/06 Heinrich Schliemann
1/22 Wrong Way Corrigan
1/28 Eugene Dubois
2/04 Charles Lindbergh

PLAYED NURSES, DOCS

10/20 Anna Neagle
10/26 Jaclyn Smith
10/31 Diedre Hall
11/02 Rachel Ames
11/04 Loretta Swit
11/11 Denise Alexander
11/16 Marg Helgenberger
12/01 Emily McLaughlin
12/20 Audrey Totter
12/22 Elizabeth Hubbard
12/27 Eva La Rue
12/30 Patricia Kalember
1/04 Jane Wyman
1/18 Lucille Wall
1/20 Patricia Neal
2/01 Tina Sloan
2/04 Marie Masters
2/15 Jane Seymour
2/17 Zina Bethune
2/17 Christina Pickles
2/22 Leslie Charleson

2/28 Bettye Ackerman
3/02 Jennifer Jones
3/06 Jackie Zeman
3/13 Dana Delany

PLAYED THE HANDICAPPED

12/09 John Malkovich
12/14 Patty Duke
12/23 Elizabeth Hartman
12/29 Jon Voight
12/31 Anthony Hopkins
12/31 Val Kilmer
1/03 Mel Gibson
1/03 Victoria Principal
1/04 Jane Wyman
1/06 Loretta Young
1/08 Jose Ferrer
1/22 John Hurt
1/29 Marc Singer
1/30 Vanessa Redgrave
1/31 James Franciscus
2/09 Mia Farrow
2/10 Laura Dern
2/13 Stockard Channing
2/14 Gregory Hines
2/17 Arthur Kennedy
2/19 Justine Bateman
2/20 Edward Albert
2/20 Ron Eldard
2/22 John Mills
3/06 Joanna Miles

GLOOMY OR MORBID

12/29 Maurice Rollinat
1/06 Thomas Gray
1/10 Robinson Jeffers
1/19 Edgar Allan Poe
1/21 Coach Gil Dobie
2/14 Thomas Malthus
2/18 Robert Burton
2/20 Kurt Cobain
2/22 Arthur Schopenhauer
2/29 Gioacchino Rossini

IN *DARK SHADOWS*

12/02 Jonathan Frid
1/11 Mitchell Ryan
1/26 Kathryn Leigh Scott
1/28 Joel Crothers
1/29 Anthony George
2/05 David Selby
2/26 Clarice Blackburn
2/27 Joan Bennett
3/01 Don Briscoe
3/04 Thayer David
3/14 Dennis Patrick

ALCOHOLISM IN FILMS

11/02 James Dunn
11/02 Burt Lancaster
11/19 Meg Ryan

12/11 Victor McLaglen
12/11 Donna Mills
12/13 Van Heflin
12/13 Dick Van Dyke
12/14 Lee Remick
12/21 Jane Fonda
12/28 Lew Ayres
1/03 Ray Milland
1/07 Nicolas Cage
1/08 Jose Ferrer
1/13 Robert Stack
1/14 Faye Dunaway
1/18 Cary Grant
1/23 Humphrey Bogart
1/26 Paul Newman
2/05 Jennifer Jason Leigh
2/08 Jack Lemmon
2/15 John Barrymore
2/19 Lee Marvin
2/26 Jackie Gleason
3/08 Claire Trevor
3/10 Sharon Stone

SUFFERED THROUGH MUCH STRESS

10/25 John Berryman
11/04 Gig Young
11/08 Tom Hepburn
11/11 Jonathan Winters
11/14 Jim Piersall
11/19 Dick Cavett
11/19 Ted Turner

11/29 Howie Mandel
11/30 Abbie Hoffman
12/10 Michael Boyer
12/19 Phil Ochs
12/20 Albert Dekker
12/24 Howard Hughes
12/30 Del Shannon
1/06 Lindsay Crosby
1/08 Clark Taylor
1/11 Don "Red" Barry
1/12 Harry K. Thaw
1/17 Jim Carrey
2/10 George Stephanopoulos
2/15 James Forrestal
2/16 John McEnroe
2/23 Peter Fonda
2/24 Peter Duel
3/06 Daniel Milland
10/17 Margot Kidder
10/18 Inger Stevens
10/22 Dory Previn
10/29 Winona Ryder
10/31 Jane Pauley
11/03 Roseanne Barr
11/05 Vivien Leigh
11/09 Dorothy Dandridge
11/13 Jean Seberg
11/27 Robin Givens
12/11 Christina Onassis
12/12 Connie Francis
12/12 Cathy Rigby
12/13 Mary Todd Lincoln
12/14 Patty Duke

12/23 Elizabeth Hartman
12/25 Clara Barton
1/06 Capucine
1/15 Mary Pierce
1/20 Patricia Neal
1/25 Virginia Woolf
2/06 Eva Braun
2/11 Sheryl Crow
2/19 Justine Bateman
3/02 Karen Carpenter

TV COMBAT SOLDIERS

11/05 Chris Robinson
12/09 William Reynolds
12/16 Terence Knox
1/12 Ron Harper
2/14 Vic Morrow
2/25 Christopher George
3/01 Robert Conrad

VIOLENCE, QUICK ACTION

11/03 Charles Bronson
11/17 Martin Scorcese
11/27 Bruce Lee
12/05 Walt Disney
1/07 Sammo Hung
1/17 Mack Sennett
2/21 Sam Peckinpah
3/10 Chuck Norris

DEADLY DUELERS

1/11 Alexander Hamilton
2/06 Aaron Burr

IN UNIFORM ON TV

10/23 Frank Sutton
10/25 Tracy Nelson
11/02 Paul Ford
11/03 Ken Berry
11/06 Sally Field
11/08 Joe Flynn
11/13 Madeleine Sherwood
12/15 Tim Conway
1/05 Ted Lange
1/08 Larry Storch
1/13 Richard Moll
1/23 Richard Gilliland
1/24 Ernest Borgnine
1/25 Dean Jones
1/28 John Banner
2/12 Forrest Tucker
2/18 Burt Mustin
2/20 Larry Hovis
2/21 Gary Lockwood
2/26 Jackie Gleason
2/28 Gavin MacLeod
3/01 Robert Clary
3/05 Marsha Warfield
3/06 J.C. Flippen
3/15 Joe E. Ross

THE INDIVIDUALISTS

I. VISUAL ART
- A. Painters (Representational)
- B. Celebrities Who Painted
- C. Art Experts
- D. Film Directors

II. BUILDING
- A. Architects ♒
- B. Engineers ♑
- C. Scenic Designers ♒
- D. Furniture Makers

III. BUSINESS AND WEALTH
- A. Entrepreneurs
- B. Financiers and Bankers ♐
- C. Producers (of Shows)
- D. Advertisers ♐
- E. Economists
- F. Large-Living Bon Vivants ♐

IV. RIGHT-WING BELIEFS
- A. Conservative Thinkers ♒
- B. Conservatives and Republicans in Govt. ♑
- C. Tory Prime Ministers
- D. Stars in the G.O.P.

V. ROYALTY

- A. Modern British Royalty
- B. Actors Who Played Royals
- C. The Rockefeller Dynasty
- D. The Kennedy Dynasty
- E. Beauty Pageant Queens

VI. AUTHORITY AND DOMINATION

- A. Murderous Tyrants
- B. Rulers, Conquerors, Dictators ♑
- C. Powerful Women
- D. Tough Sea Captains ♑
- E. Athletic Coaches
- F. Baseball Managers
- G. Actors who Played Strict Parents
- H. Actual Strict Parents
- I. Racehorse Trainers
- J. Wild Animal Tamers
- K. Those Alleged to Have Been Abusive ♑
- L. Sadistic Murderers
- M. Actors in Sadistic Roles ♑

VII. AGGRESSIVE QUESTIONS AND ANSWERS

- A. Lawyers
- B. Game Show Panelists
- C. Reporters
- D. Press Secretaries

VIII. TRIUMPHANT HEROES

- A. Invincible Action Heroes and Cowboy Heroes ♐
- B. Omnipotent TV Doctors ♐
- C. Omniscient Screen Lawyers ♐
- D. Adventure and Suspense Writers

E. Sea Novel Writers

IX. LOVE STORIES

A. Writers of Romantic Tales
B. Daytime Soap Actresses
C. Daytime Soap Actors
D. Prime Time Soap Actors
E. Teen Soap Actors

X. COMEDY ACTING

A. Sitcom Actors
B. Sitcom Actresses
C. Saturday Night Live Stars
D. Misc. TV Comedy Actors
E. Film Comedy Actors

XI. UPBEAT POP MUSIC

A. Drummers
B. Rock Singers ♐
C. Pop Singers ♐
D. Composers of Pop Music ♐
E. Pop Lyricists ♐

XII. RELIGION

A. Founders of Religious Organizations
B. Spiritual Leaders
C. Actors Who Played Clergy
D. Religious Celebrities
E. Writers of Hymn Verses

THE FRIENDS

I. MOVEMENT, MOBILITY

- A. Transportation Moguls and Experts
- B. Rovers and Seekers
- C. Explorers

II. VIOLENCE

- A. Military Leaders
- B. TV Soldiers
- C. Law Enforcers
- D. Actors Who Played Police
- E. Deadly Duelers
- F. Murderers and Gangsters

III. DECISIVENESS

- A. Quarterbacks
- B. Jockeys
- C. Catchers
- D. Sports Executives
- E. TV Executives

IV. POLITICIANS

- A. World Leaders ♋
- B. U.S. Leaders ♋
- C. Admired Presidents ♌
- D. Presidential Candidates ♌
- E. Student Presidents

F. Modern Congressmen
G. Actors Who Played Politicians

V. POPULARITY AND CHARISMA
A. Sports Heroes ♌
B. Evangelists
C. Actors Who Played Evangelists
D. Stand-Up Comics ♌
E. Witty Talkers
F. Nonstop Talkers ♌
G. Talk Show Hosts
H. Game Show Hosts ♌
I. Friendly Celebrities ♌

VI. HELPING AND CARING
A. Kind Helpers and Healers ♋
B. Actresses Who Played Nurses or Doctors
C. Educators ♋
D. Actors Who Played Teachers
E. Actors Who Played Benign Parents
F. Government Administrators ♋

VII. SADNESS AND DARKNESS
A. Actors Who Played the Handicapped
B. Violinists, Cellists
C. Opera Composers
D. Folk Singers
E. Gloomy or Morbid People
F. Actors in Dark Shadows
G. Those Who Experienced Defeats/Downfalls
H. Those Who Experienced Anxiety/Depression

VIII. DRUG USE

A.	Actors Who Used Drugs	♍
B.	Musicians Who Used Drugs	♊
C.	Actors in Films about Alcoholism	

IX. THE OTHER-WORLDLY

A.	Novelists	♌
B.	Abstract Artists	♌
C.	Those Who Saw Visions/Heard Voices of Beyond	♋
D.	Those Who Stretched Boundaries of Our Consciousness	♋
E.	Astronomers	

Individualists	**VS.**	**Friends**
Competitive		Collaborative
Business		Government
Accumulating		Giving
Entrenched		Mobile
Comedians to Laugh at		Comedians to Laugh with
Lone-Hero Crime Fighter		Law Enforcement Teamwork
Confrontation		Amiability
Lawyers		Politicians
Reporters		Talk-Show Hosts
Ultimate Authority		Hands-On Decisions
Monarch		Statesman
Football Coach		Quarterback
Horse Trainer		Jockey
Church Head		Missionary
Strict Parent		Benign Parent
Dispenses Knowledge		Receptive to Knowledge
Omnipotent TV Doctors		Sympathetic TV Nurses

Invincibility	Vulnerability
Actors Playing Heroes	Real Heroes
Glittery Rock Stars	Unassuming Folk Singers
Kings' and Clergymen's Robes	Uniforms
Joie de Vivre	Sadness
Peppy Music	Mournful Music
Centripetal Force	Centrifugal Force
Innermost Soul	Outermost Frontiers
Realism	Visions, Worlds Beyond
Representational Art	Abstract Art, Imagination
Narrow Focus	Wide-ranging Scope

PROVERBS FOR THE MEGASIGNS

Innovators:	Nothing ventured, nothing gained.
Preservers:	Fools rush in where angels fear to tread.
Friends:	Many hands make light work.
Individualists:	Too many cooks spoiled the broth.
Innovators:	Out of the mouths of babes and sucklings come all the wise sayings.
Preservers:	With age comes wisdom.
Friends:	Seek, and ye shall find.
Individualists:	A rolling stone gathers no moss.

Innovators	Preservers	Friends	Individualists
Intuitive	Empirical	Visionary	Practical
Attracts	Eschews	Joins	Conquers
Liberal	Traditional	Populist	Elitist
Engaging	Detached	Co-operative	Competitive
Extreme	Tempered	Spontaneous	Organized
Wants Progress	Wants Stability	Wants Approval	Wants Respect
Blossoms	Roots	Branches	Stem
Ignition Key	Brakes	Steering Wheel	Gas

RULERS AND ELEMENTS

The four planets with the most powerful influence upon human character are Mars, Jupiter, Saturn and the Moon. Let us match up these planets with the four megasigns. Jupiter is the ruler of the Innovators because it represents optimism and faith in the future. Saturn rules the Preservers because this planet symbolizes affection for the past and a desire for rules and standards. Mars is the lord of the Individualists on account of their aggressive, competitive nature. The Moon rules the Friends because they are the most empathic and socially adept.

In olden times, astrologers used to forecast the weather. Jupiter was considered warm and moist like spring. Mars was regarded as hot and dry like summer. Saturn was believed to be cool and dry like autumn. The Moon was considered cold and wet like winter. Isn't it quite a coincidence that the planet that rules the type of person born in each season is the very same planet that ruled the type of weather found in that season!

Draw a medium-sized circle with a cross inside of it, so that you have a wheel with four spokes. On the left-hand spoke, write "Spring." On the right-hand spoke, write "Fall." Along the top spoke, write "Winter." Along the bottom spoke, write "Summer." Now let's put the planets outside the circle. To the left of Spring, write "Jupiter"; to the right of Fall, write "Saturn"; above Winter, write "Moon"; and below Summer write "Mars." Now let's put in the four elements. Between Jupiter and Mars, write "fire" because what these planets have in common is warmth. Between Mars and Saturn, write "earth" because those planets have dryness in common. Between Saturn and the Moon, write "wind," for what these two have in common is coolness. Finally, between the Moon and Jupiter, write "water" because they have wetness in common. Now you can see where the elements come from. Note that they are in the correct sequence – fire, earth, air, water – as you go counterclockwise around the wheel.

PART SIX

MAXISIGNS AND SPORTS

THE THREE MAXISIGNS

We now come to the subject of athletics. There are three kinds of athletes, each of which is represented by a different "maxisign." We call these three maxisigns the Propellers, the Stalwarts and the Adjusters. Each one spans six months, resulting in quite a bit of overlapping between them.

The Propellers' dates are April 4 to Oct. 4. These athletes specialize in running or jumping. When you run, you propel yourself forward with your legs and feet. When you jump, you propel yourself up into the air with your legs and feet.

The dates for the Stalwarts are Aug. 4 to Feb. 4. These people specialize in strength, ruggedness and endurance. Their strength enables them to throw a ball hard, or hit a ball hard. Their ruggedness makes them suited for rough-and-tumble sports, and their endurance helps them achieve in sports that are tiring.

The Adjusters' dates are Dec. 3 to June 3. These athletes specialize in co-ordination, balance, grace and dexterity. Their area of expertise ranges all the way from boxing to dancing. A sport like basketball, at which the Adjusters excel, requires all four of the attributes mentioned above.

Signs of the element earth (the most physical element) are at the center of each maxisign. The center of the Propellers is in aggressive Capricorn, a cardinal sign, and all the Propellers are cardinal in terms of physical activity. The center of the Stalwarts is in immovable Taurus, a fixed sign, and all the Stalwarts partake of this fixed quality. The center of the Adjusters is in flexible Virgo, a mutable sign, and all the Adjusters share this trait. Note the counterclockwise order of the maxisigns: cardinal, fixed, mutable. Now you can see where astrology's three modes of action come from.

FLEET SPRINTERS

4/11 Stella Walsh
4/15 Evelyn Ashford
4/20 Betty Cuthbert
4/26 Fanny Blankers-Koen
4/29 Dorothy Manley
5/03 Allan Wells
5/09 Marie-Jose Perec
5/10 Marlene Ottey
5/12 Renata Stecher
5/15 Veronica Campbell
5/19 Percy Williams
5/20 Bruno Marie-Rose
5/24 Irena Kirszenstein
5/24 Audrey Brown
6/05 Tommie Smith
6/05 John Carlos
6/05 Joe DeLoach
6/06 Nelli Cooman-Fiere
6/12 Gwen Torrence
6/21 Ralph Craig
6/23 Wilma Rudolph
6/28 Elaine Thompson
6/28 Pietro Mennea
7/01 Carl Lewis
7/06 Valerie Brisco-Hooks
7/08 Harrison Dillard
7/10 Herb Mckenley
7/11 Konstantinos Kenteris
7/18 Shirley Strickland
7/18 Mack Robinson
7/23 Maurice Greene

7/28 Barbara Ferrell
7/30 Daley Thompson
8/04 Mike Marsh
8/06 Thomas Schonlebe
8/21 Usain Bolt
8/23 Elizabeth Robinson
8/29 Wyomia Tyus
9/05 Willie Gault
9/05 Graham Salmon
9/10 Jim Hines
9/12 Jesse Owens
9/13 Michael Johnson
9/13 Marjorie Jackson
9/13 Morris Kirksey
9/14 Archie Hahn
9/20 Silvio Leonard
9/28 Mel Gray
9/29 Eddie Tolan
10/01 Eva Klobukowska

SWIFT RUSHERS

4/07 Tony Dorsett
4/07 Ricky Watters
4/08 Anthony Thompson
4/10 Clarke Hinkle
4/12 Mike Garrett
4/19 Mark Van Eeghen
4/22 Freeman McNeil
5/01 Ollie Matson
5/01 Cliff Battles
5/04 Elmer Layden

5/05 Tony Canadeo
5/15 Emmitt Smith
5/16 Thurman Thomas
5/20 Leroy Kelly
5/21 Ricky Williams
5/28 Jim Thorpe
5/30 Gale Sayers
5/30 Lydell Mitchell
6/01 Alan Ameche
6/02 Lawrence McCutcheon
6/05 Marion Motley
6/08 Byron White
6/11 Ernie Nevers
6/13 Red Grange
6/17 Elroy Hirsch
7/04 Floyd Little
7/05 Johnny Rodgers
7/08 John David Crow
7/09 Nile Kinnick
7/09 O. J. Simpson
7/10 Roger Craig
7/16 Barry Sanders
7/25 Walter Payton
8/04 John Riggins
8/06 Ken Strong
8/09 John Cappelletti
8/16 Frank Gifford
8/16 Christian Okoye
8/21 Archie Griffin
8/30 Shaun Alexander
9/01 Johnny Mack Brown
9/02 Eric Dickerson
9/07 John Brockington

9/08 Anthony Davis
9/10 Jim Crowley
9/18 Billy Sims
9/19 Larry Brown
9/20 Jim Taylor
9/27 Dickie Post
9/28 Tom Harmon

SPEEDY CYCLISTS

4/15 Pedro Delgado
5/09 Fred Markham
5/12 Beryl Burton
5/15 Tomas Pettersson
5/15 Pierre Trentin
5/19 Jan Jannssen
5/21 Glen Curtiss
5/29 Huber Opperman
6/12 Felicia Ballanger
6/14 Eric Heiden
6/17 Eddy Merckx
6/26 Greg LeMond
6/27 Patrick Sercu
6/29 Sante Gaiardoni
7/16 Miguel Indurain
7/18 Leandro Faggin
7/18 Russell Mockridge
7/28 Daniel Morelon
7/29 Sergey Kopylov
8/11 Kristin Armstrong
8/12 Laurent Fignon
8/14 Herman van Springel

8/16 John Howard
8/23 Eric de Vlaeminck
9/30 Sture Pettersson

SPEEDY BASE THIEVES

4/17 Marquis Grissom
4/29 Luis Aparicio
5/02 Eddie Collins
5/03 Davey Lopes
5/15 Bill North
5/17 Cool Papa Bell
5/29 Eric Davis
5/31 Kenny Lofton
6/11 Jose Reyes
6/16 Ron LeFlore
6/18 Lou Brock
6/20 Bill Werber
7/07 Chuck Knoblauch
7/09 Willie Wilson
7/24 Barry Bonds
8/05 Carl Crawford
8/09 Deion Sanders
8/10 Chuck Carr
9/09 Frank Chance
9/09 Frankie Frisch
9/16 Tim Raines
9/19 Joe Morgan
9/22 Vince Coleman
9/25 Tony Womack
10/02 Maury Wills

DISTANCE RUNNERS

4/24 Joey Barthel
4/29 Jim Ryun
5/01 Volmari Iso-Hollo
5/05 Steve Scott
5/09 Tegla Loroupe
5/10 John Ngugi
5/15 Miruts Yifter
5/16 Joan Benoit
5/24 Liz McColgan
5/26 Zola Budd
5/31 Patrick Porter
6/03 Ibrahim Hussein
6/13 Paavo Nurmi
6/18 Bob Kempainen
6/23 Filbert Bayi
6/27 Gabriella Dorio
6/28 Belayneh Dinsamo
6/29 Rosa Mota
6/30 Billy Mills
7/01 Lynn Jennings
7/05 Tom O'Hara
7/06 Donald Ritchie
7/07 Murray Halberg
7/07 Marcel van de Wattyne
7/10 C. K. Yang
7/15 Toshihiko Seko
7/19 Juma Ikangaa
7/20 Paula Ivan
7/22 Lasse Viren
7/29 Maricica Puica
8/02 Craig Virgin

8/03 Waldemar Cierpinski
8/04 Mary Decker Slaney
8/07 Abebe Bikila
8/07 Alberto Salazar
8/12 Tatyana Samolenko
8/20 Moses Tanui
9/06 John A. Kelley
9/07 Uta Pippig
9/09 Lynn Fitzgerald
9/09 Sydney Maree
9/11 Marty Liquori
9/16 Al Howie
9/17 Doris Brown
9/19 Emil Zatopek
9/21 Ron Hill
9/21 Ilmari Salminen
9/22 Mikko Hietanen
10/01 Grete Waits
10/04 Doug Padilla

MISC. GOOD RUNNERS

5/12 Kim Fields
6/04 Dennis Weaver
6/04 Bruce Dern
6/16 Joan Van Ark
6/19 Sen. Alan Cranston
7/15 Kim Alexis
7/22 Sen. Bob Dole
7/26 Sen. Estes Kefauver
8/01 Brian Patrick Clarke
8/14 Magic Johnson

9/09 Kristy McNichol
9/22 Scott Baio

GOOD RUNNERS: FOOTBALL

5/19 Archie Manning
6/22 Bobby Douglass
6/26 Michael Vick
6/28 John Elway
8/01 Cliff Branch
8/10 Speedy Duncan
9/05 Billy Kilmer
9/09 Joe Theismann
9/28 Steve Largent

TOP RUNNERS (c. 1000 m)

4/26 Roger Moens
4/29 Robert Druppers
6/11 Kim Gallagher
6/19 Johnny Gray
8/07 Douglas Lowe
8/07 Dave Wottle
8/12 Brigitte Kraus
8/14 Inna Yevseyeva
8/22 Paul Ereng
9/05 Mel Sheppard
9/29 Sebastian Coe

FAST WALKERS

4/06 Maurizio Damilano
5/10 Ronald L. Zinn
5/31 Ronald Laird
6/02 Vladimir Golubnichiy
6/02 Kerry Ann Saxby
6/25 Alina Ivanova
7/06 Jozef Pribilinec
8/08 Ronald Weigel
8/13 Norman Read
10/03 Abdon Pamich

HURDLERS

4/21 Lyudmila Narozhilenko
4/26 Fanny Blankers-Koen
5/01 Marina Stepanova
5/16 Bob Tisdall
5/18 Rod Milburn
6/08 Willie Davenport
6/26 Babe Didrikson
7/06 Mary Peters
7/08 Harrison Dillard
7/15 Enriqueta Basilio
7/18 Shirley Strickland
7/26 Henry L. Williams
7/29 Sally Gunnell
8/01 Liliana Nastase
8/04 Greg Foster
8/18 Brianna Rollins
8/26 Roger Kingdom
8/29 Clyde Scott

8/31 Edwin Moses
9/07 Danny Harris
9/12 Glenn Davis
9/12 Jesse Owens
9/19 Nadyezda Tkachenko
9/28 Yordanka Donkova
9/29 Harald Schmid

LEAPING REBOUNDERS

4/16 Kareem Abdul-Jabbar
4/22 Spencer Hayward
4/25 Tim Duncan
4/26 Harry Gallatin
5/13 Dennis Rodman
5/19 Bill Laimbeer
5/19 Dolph Schayes
6/18 George Mikan
6/21 Derrick Coleman
6/25 DiKembe Mutombo
7/07 Lisa Leslie
7/12 Paul Silas
7/19 Teresa Edwards
7/20 Mel Daniels
7/24 Walt Bellamy
7/24 Karl Malone
7/25 Nate Thurmond
7/27 Marvin Barnes
8/05 Patrick Ewing
8/06 David Robinson
8/17 Christian Laettner
8/21 Wilt Chamberlain

8/30 Robert Parish
9/10 Bob Lanier
9/21 Artis Gilmore

LEAPING FIGURE SKATERS

4/06 Janet Lynn
4/08 Sonja Henie
4/12 Elaine Zayak
4/13 Trixi Schuba
4/20 Rosalynn Sumners
4/20 Toller Cranston
5/02 Sarah Hughes
5/09 Barbara Ann Scott
5/17 Karl Schafer
5/19 Elisabeth Schwartz
5/23 Ilia Kulik
5/28 Ekaterina Gordeeva
5/30 Caitlin Carruthers
6/04 Evan Lysacek
6/07 Gillis Grafstrom
6/10 Tara Lipinski
6/16 Aleksandr Zaitsev
6/18 Kurt Browning
6/27 Viktor Petrenko
6/28 Pierre Brunet
6/28 Maria Butyrskaya
6/29 David Jenkins
7/02 Johnny Weir
7/07 Michelle Kwan
7/12 Kristi Yamaguchi
7/16 Oleg Protopopov

7/18 Dick Button
7/18 Tenley Albright
7/21 Ludmila Smirnova
7/22 Peter Carruthers
7/23 Pierre Baugniet
7/26 Dorothy Hamill
7/27 Peggy Fleming
8/01 Jill Trenary
8/02 Linda Fratianne
8/07 Ulrich Salchow
8/07 Elizabeth Manley
8/13 Midori Ito
8/17 Robin Cousins
8/23 Nicole Bobek
8/28 Scott Hamilton
8/28 Todd Eldridge
9/07 Rudy Galindo
9/08 Jeanette Altwegg
9/09 John Curry
9/12 Irina Rodnina
9/14 Wolfgang Schwarz
9/16 Andree Joly
9/22 Tai Babilonia
9/27 Ernst Baier

LONG JUMPERS

4/07 Arnie Robinson
5/09 Ralph Boston
5/24 Irena Kirszenstein
6/30 Sheila Hudson
7/01 Carl Lewis

7/26 Galina Chistyakova
8/19 Martha Watson
8/29 Bob Beamon
9/12 Jesse Owens
9/29 Adhemar da Silva
10/03 Viktor Saneyev

SKI JUMPERS

7/08 Ulrich Wehling
7/17 Matti Nykanen
7/24 Simon Slattvik
8/03 Tina Lehtola
8/06 Wojciech Fortuna
8/17 Yukio Kasaya
8/20 Georg Thoma
8/23 Birger Ruud
8/27 Eric Bergoust
9/04 Armin Kogler

HIGH JUMPERS

4/13 Harold Osborn
4/14 Valeriy Brumel 1942
4/14 Ni Chih-chin 1942
4/19 Sara Simeoni
5/04 Ulrike Meyfarth
5/05 Heiki Henkel
6/23 Grete Bjordalsbakke
6/26 Babe Didrikson
8/04 Joni Huntley
8/29 Cindy Holmes

SKATEBOARD JUMPERS

4/15 Danny Way
5/12 Tony Hawk
9/13 Shaun White

DECATHLON JUMPERS

7/10 C. K. Yang
7/18 Dan O'Brien
7/30 Daley Thompson
8/18 Rafer Johnson

RUGGED SOCCER AND RUGBY STARS

8/18 Just Fontaine
8/31 Serge Blanco
9/11 Franz Beckenbauer
9/13 Morris Kirksey
9/14 Wolfgang Suhnhola
9/22 Ronaldo
9/29 Mike Dillon
10/15 Jorge Campos
10/19 Gunnar Nordahl
10/21 David Campesi
10/22 Lev Yashin
10/23 Pele'
10/23 Keith Eddy
10/24 Phil Bennett
10/24 Slobo Liijevsky
10/25 Michael Lynagh
10/26 Harald Nielsen

10/26 Kevin Welsh
10/27 Derek Smethurst
10/29 Henry Carlsson
10/30 Diego Maradona
10/30 Roy Turner
10/31 Simon Poidevin
10/31 Bruce Hudson 1950
11/03 Steven David 1950
11/03 Gerd Muller
11/05 Uwe Seeler
11/09 Alessandro Del Piero
11/23 John Stremlau 1953
11/25 Anthony Neary
11/27 Joe Clarke 1953
11/28 Frederick Du Preez
11/29 Kasey Keller
12/01 Franz Binder
12/02 Mike England
12/03 Cameron Gibson
12/08 Geoff Hurst
12/14 Antonio Simoes
12/17 Ferenc Bene
12/24 Eddie Pope
12/25 Kyle Rote Jr.
1/04 Arthur Berry
1/05 Jan Ellis
1/09 Didier Camberabero
1/11 Bryan Robson
1/12 Mack Sullivan
1/24 Giorgio Chinaglia
1/25 Eusebio
2/02 Kenny Cooper
2/03 Dezso Nowak

RUGGED, RESOLUTE LINEMEN

8/07 Alan Page
8/08 Bruce Matthews
8/12 Alex Wojciechowicz
8/15 Gene Upshaw
8/16 Ron Yary
8/19 Anthony Munoz
8/22 Mel Hein
8/27 Michael Dean Perry
9/06 Gordon Brown
9/10 Buck Buchanan
9/15 Merlin Olsen
9/19 Dan Hampton
9/24 Joe Greene
9/28 Turk Edwards
10/05 Bill Willis
10/11 Cal Hubbard
10/12 Truxton Hare
10/15 Joe Klecko
10/16 Chris Doleman
10/18 Forrest Gregg
10/20 Roosevelt Brown
10/20 Lee Roy Selmon
10/23 Bruiser Kinard
10/29 John DeWitt
11/02 Leon Hart
11/02 Larry Little
11/16 Harvey Martin
11/20 Mark Gastinau
11/21 Jim Ringo
11/24 Stan Jones
12/06 Andy Robustelli

12/06 George Trafton
12/08 Boomer Brown
12/09 Deacon Jones
12/13 Richard Dent
12/15 Billy Shaw
12/16 William Perry
12/18 Ox Wistert
12/19 Reggie White
12/20 Pudge Heffelfinger
12/30 Jim Marshall
1/01 George Connor
1/01 McKeever twins
1/02 Gino Marchetti
1/05 Jim Otto
1/06 Howie Long
1/15 Randy White
1/23 Jerry Kramer
1/26 Henry Jordan
1/26 Jack Youngblood

RUGGED LINEBACKERS

8/13 Chris Hanburger
8/21 Willie Lanier
8/25 Cornelius Bennett
9/01 Karl Mechlenburg
9/10 Tim Harris
9/20 Tommy Nobis
9/29 David Wilcox
10/04 Sam Huff
10/06 Les Richter
10/09 Mike Singletary

10/25 Pat Swilling
10/29 Bill George
11/01 Ted Hendricks
11/18 Seth Joyner
11/25 George Webster
12/09 Dick Butkus
12/15 Nick Buoniconti
12/23 Jack Ham
12/27 Andre Tippett
12/29 Ray Nitschke
1/01 Derrick Thomas
1/06 Charles Haley
1/18 Joe Schmidt
1/19 Junior Seau
2/04 Lawrence Taylor

STRONG GYMNASTS

8/07 Aleksandr Ditiatin
9/08 Li Ning
9/24 Hamm twins
9/29 Oleg Verniaiev
10/02 Georges Miez
10/07 Ludmila Turischeva
10/11 Sawao Kato
10/14 Nikolai Andrianov
10/17 Maria Gorokhovskaya
10/28 Miroslav Cerar
10/30 Polina Astrakhova
10/30 Nastia Liukin
11/09 Viktor Chukarin
11/12 Nadia Comaneci

11/12 Leon Stukelj
11/19 Kerri Strug
12/13 Zoltan Magyar
12/27 Larissa Latynina
12/31 Gabby Douglas
1/03 Kohei Uchimura
1/13 Vitaliy Scherbo
1/19 Svetlana Khorkina
1/24 Mary Lou Retton
1/27 Boris Shakhlin
2/04 Carly Patterson

STRONG WRESTLERS

8/09 John Smith
8/16 Rulon Gardner
9/16 Aleksandr Medved
9/16 Beloglasov twins
9/19 Aleksandr Karelin
9/28 Eemeli Vare
10/08 Valeriy Rezantsev
10/13 Carl Westergren
10/19 Wilfried Dietrich
10/21 Osamu Watanabe
10/22 John Peterson
10/22 Derrick Waldroup
10/25 Dan Gable
10/26 Mark Schultz
11/03 Edmond Barrett
11/07 Ivan Yarygin
11/11 Matt Ghaffari
11/20 Kyle Snyder

11/25 Vaino Kokkinen
12/09 Kurt Angle
12/24 Leroy Kemp
12/27 William Kerslake
1/10 Alexis Nihon Jr.
1/22 Rauno Makinen
1/31 Ivar Johansson

RUGGED RODEO RIDERS

9/01 Anne Lewis
9/20 Kermit Maynard
10/06 Jim Sharp
10/11 Ty Murray
10/23 Joe Beaver
10/28 Lewis Feild
11/05 Roy Rogers
11/12 Sunset Carson
11/13 Roy Cooper
11/21 Larry Mahan
12/07 C. Thomas Howell
12/20 Tom Ferguson
1/15 Billy Etbauer

NOTED "ROUGH RIDER"

10/27 Theodore Roosevelt

VOLLEYBALL WHACKERS

8/15 Kerri Walsh Jennings
11/03 Karch Kiraly
11/29 Steve Timmons

HOME RUN SLUGGERS

8/08 Frank Howard
8/10 Rocky Colavito
8/22 Carl Yastrzemski
8/25 Albert Belle
8/27 Jim Thome
8/30 Ted Williams
8/31 Frank Robinson
9/10 Ted Kluszewski
9/10 Roger Maris
9/17 Orlando Cepeda
9/18 Ryne Sandberg
9/19 Duke Snider
9/21 Cecil Fielder
9/27 Mike Schmidt
10/01 Mark McGwire
10/03 Dave Winfield
10/07 Chuck Klein
10/13 Eddie Mathews
10/16 Juan Gonzalez
10/20 Mickey Mantle
10/22 Jimmie Foxx
10/25 Bobby Thomson
10/27 Ralph Kiner
10/29 Jesse Barfield
10/31 Fred McGriff

11/12 Sammy Sosa
11/18 Dante Bichette
11/18 David Ortiz
11/18 Roy Sievers
11/19 Ryan Howard
11/21 Ken Griffey Jr.
11/21 Stan Musial
11/25 Joe Dimaggio
11/28 Matt Williams
11/29 Howard Johnson
12/01 George Foster
12/01 Larry Walker
12/07 Johnny Bench
12/12 Gorman Thomas
12/13 Larry Doby
12/21 Josh Gibson
12/21 Dave Kingman
12/21 Cy Williams
1/01 Hank Greenberg
1/07 Johnny Mize
1/10 Willie McCovey
1/13 Kevin Mitchell
1/16 Albert Pujols
1/18 Brady Anderson
1/31 Ernie Banks

STRONG-ARMED PITCHERS: BORN 1850 - 1940

8/07 Don Larsen
8/12 Christy Mathewson
8/18 Burleigh Grimes
8/31 Eddie Plank

9/06 Red Faber
9/09 Waite Hoyt
9/12 Spud Chandler
9/12 Mickey Lolich
9/14 Kid Nichols
9/15 Frank Linzy
9/15 Gaylord Perry
9/18 Harvey Haddix
9/19 Bob Turley
9/22 Bob Lemon
9/26 Bobby Shantz
9/29 Mike McCormick
9/30 Johnny Podres
9/30 Robin Roberts
10/09 Rube Marquand
10/13 Rube Waddell
10/14 Harry Brecheen
10/19 Three Finger Brown
10/20 Juan Marichal
10/21 Whitey Ford
10/23 Jim Bunning
10/30 Jim Perry
11/02 Johnny Vander Meer
11/03 Bob Feller
11/06 Walter Johnson
11/07 Jim Kaat
11/09 Bob Gibson
11/12 Joe Hoerner
11/17 Jim Brewer
11/20 Clark Griffith
11/22 Lew Burdette
11/23 Luis Tiant
11/26 Lefty Gomez

12/07 Dick Donovan
12/09 Hoss Radbourne
12/13 Carl Erskine
12/13 Lindy McDaniel
12/14 Sam Jones
12/25 Pud Galvin
12/26 Stu Miller
12/28 Ted Lyons
12/30 Sandy Koufax
1/04 Don McMahon
1/06 Early Wynn
1/11 Schoolboy Rowe
1/16 Dizzy Dean

STARTERS: BORN POST-1940

8/04 Roger Clemens
8/28 Ron Guidry
8/30 Cliff Lee
9/10 Randy Johnson
9/16 Orel Hershiser
9/21 Sam McDowell
10/15 Jim Palmer
10/21 Zack Grienke
10/25 Pedro Martinez
10/27 Pete Vuckovich
10/31 Dave McNally
11/01 Fernando Valenzuela
11/03 Bob Welch
11/13 Pat Hentgen
11/14 Curt Schilling
11/16 Dwight Gooden

11/17 Tom Seaver
12/13 Ferguson Jenkins
12/16 Mike Flanagan
12/22 Steve Carlton
1/01 LaMarr Hoyt
1/02 David Cone
1/12 Randy Jones
1/16 Jack McDowell
1/31 Nolan Ryan

RELIEVERS: BORN POST-1940

8/21 John Wetteland
8/25 Rollie Fingers
8/30 Tug McGraw
9/17 John Franco
9/19 Randy Myers
9/30 Kenley Jansen
10/01 Jeff Reardon
10/03 Dennis Eckersley
10/13 Trevor Hoffman
10/19 Mark Davis
10/24 Rawley Eastwick
11/14 Willie Hernandez
11/23 Jonathan Papelbon
11/28 Dave Righetti
11/29 Mariano Rivera
12/04 Lee Smith
12/06 Steve Bedrosian
12/21 Tom Henke
12/31 Rick Aguilera
1/07 Francisco Rodriguez

1/07 Jeff Montgomery
1/08 Bruce Sutter
1/09 Eric Gagne
1/15 Mike Marshall
1/24 Ron Dibble

POWERFUL THROWERS

8/23 William O. Hickok
8/27 Elizabeta Bagriantseva
9/19 Al Oerter
9/19 Dana Zatopkova
9/23 Imre Nemeth
9/23 Gabriele Reinsch
9/24 Ilona Slupianek
9/25 Clarence Houser
9/28 Avery Brundage
10/12 Truxton Hare
10/23 Miklos Nemeth
10/29 Michael Carter
10/29 John DeWitt
10/31 Michael Landon
11/10 Ramona Lu Pagel
11/11 Halina Konopacka
11/13 Olga Fikotova
11/14 Bjorn Bang Andersen
11/15 Mac Wilkins
12/23 Micheline Ostermeyer
12/29 Kate Schmidt
1/09 John Flanagan
1/12 Al Feuerbach

1/28 Parry O'Brien
1/28 Patrick O'Callaghan

WEIGHT LIFTERS

9/06 Rudolf Plukfelder
9/17 Daniel Nunez
9/30 Yoshiyuki Miyake
10/08 Arkadiy Vorobyev
10/17 Paul Anderson
10/30 Charles Atlas
11/07 Mintcho Pachov
11/23 Neum Shalamanov
11/24 Yoshinobu Miyake
12/04 Blagoi Blagoyev
12/20 Bruce Conners
12/21 Han Changmei
1/07 Vasily Alexeyev
1/12 John Davis
1/21 Katie Sandwina

POLE VAULT STRENGTH

10/17 Bob Seagren
10/26 Daniel Joe Dial
10/28 Bruce Jenner
11/17 Bob Mathias
12/04 Sergey Bubka
1/10 Bill Toomey

ROWING, CANOEING

8/24 Wolfgang Mager
9/11 Dieter Schubert
9/30 Henry R. Pearce
10/04 John B. Kelly
10/06 Rudiger Helm
10/11 James A. Gillan
11/12 Sylvi Saimo
11/15 Jutta Behrendt
11/16 Anthony Johnson
11/21 Gert Fredriksson
11/26 Ivan Patzaichin
12/02 Greg Barton
12/02 Vladimir Parfenovich
12/07 Vaclav Chalupa
12/15 Mihaly Hesz
12/26 Joachim Dreifke
12/27 Paul V. Costello
12/27 Diessner twins
12/31 Christina Hahn
1/01 Jack Beresford
1/03 Ruggero Verroca
1/05 Carmine Abbagnale
1/08 Karl-Heinz Bussert
1/12 James W. Dietz
1/14 Ludmila Pinayeva

LONG-DISTANCE SWIMMING

8/14 Debbie Meyer
8/20 Cindy Nicholas
8/28 Janet Evans

9/06 Jon Erikson
9/13 Jim McLane
10/01 Ashby Harper
10/05 Ricardo Hoffman
10/08 Thomas Gregory
10/09 Kusuo Kitamura
10/19 Marilyn Bell
10/23 Gertrude Ederle
10/24 Di Donato twins
11/06 Philip Rush
11/09 Florence Chadwick
11/23 Shane Gould
12/20 Stella Ada Taylor
1/06 Murray Rose
1/11 Petra Schneider

ARDUOUS WATER SKIING

8/04 Jennifer Calleri
8/09 Sammy Duvall
8/13 Robert Wing

PRODIGIOUS FEATS OF ENDURANCE

8/07 Russell Baze: jockey who won record 12,842 races.
8/15 Lee Chin Yong: performed 170 chin-ups nonstop.
8/24 Cal Ripken Jr.: 2,632 consecutive baseball games.
8/26 Rick Hansen: wheelchair trip of 25,000 miles in 26 months.
9/04 Lorna Johnstone: competed in Olympics at record age of 70.
9/06 Johnny Kelley: ran 61st Boston Marathon at age 84.
9/09 Lynn Fitzgerald: ran 133.5 miles in 24 hours.
9/15 Sean Maguire: walked 7,327 miles in ten months.

9/21 Teiichi Igarashi: climbed Mt. Fiji (12,000 ft.) at age 99.
10/02 George Meegen: spent 6.6 years walking 19,019 miles.
11/07 Dave Dowdle: ran 170.6 miles in 24 hours.
11/16 Tomas Pereira: walked ten years, covering 29,825 miles.
11/20 Eleanor Adams: ran 100 miles in 15.4 hours.
11/25 Mavis Hutchison: ran 3,665 miles in 69 days.
11/26 Nicholas Sanders: cycled 13,035 miles in 78 days.
11/27 Bjorn Lokken: skied 319.1 miles in 48 hours.
12/03 Duncan McLean: runner who set world age record at 92.
12/12 Randy Smith: in 906 consecutive pro basketball games.
12/22 Barbara Moore: walked 168 miles nonstop at age 63.
12/30 Jim Marshall: in 282 consecutive pro football games.
1/06 Chantal Langlace: ran 100 kilometers in 7.45 hours.
1/19 Edwin Langerwiz: jumped rope for 13.5 hours straight.
1/20 Michael Secrest: cycled 516.2 miles in 24 hours.
1/24 Plennie Wingo: for 18 months, walked backward 8,000 miles.
2/02 Max Telford: ran 5,110 miles in 106.8 days.

QUICK-REACTING, WELL-CO-ORDINATED .300 HITTERS

12/04 Harvey Kuenn
12/07 Alex Johnson
12/12 Ralph Garr
12/14 Bill Buckner
12/18 Ty Cobb
12/19 Al Kaline
12/21 Freddy Sanchez
12/22 Matty Alou
12/23 Hanley Ramirez
1/02 Edgar Martinez
1/12 Bill Madlock
1/15 Matt Holliday

1/16 Albert Pujols
1/28 Pete Runnels
1/28 Magglio Ordonez
1/31 Jackie Robinson
2/03 Fred Lynn
2/05 Hank Aaron
2/06 Babe Ruth
2/07 Carney Lansford
2/16 Billy Hamilton
2/24 Honus Wagner
2/25 Paul O'Neill
3/03 Willie Keeler
3/08 Carl Furillo
3/14 Kirby Puckett
3/19 Richie Ashburn
3/21 Tommy Davis
3/22 Billy Goodman
3/24 George Sisler
3/29 Ferris Fain
4/02 Luke Appling
4/02 Bobby Avila
4/04 Tris Speaker
4/06 Ernie Lombardi
4/14 Pete Rose
4/18 Miguel Cabrera
4/19 Joe Mauer
4/20 Don Mattingly
4/22 Mickey Vernon
4/24 Chipper Jones
4/27 Rogers Hornsby
5/06 Willie Mays
5/08 Dan Brouthers
5/09 Tony Gwynn

5/15 George Brett
5/21 Josh Hamilton
5/22 Al Simmons
5/27 Frank Thomas
5/30 Manny Ramirez

QUICK, AGILE, DEXTEROUS HOOP STARS, BORN 1880-1950

12/07 Max Zaslovsky
12/09 Cliff Hagan
12/12 Bob Pettit
12/13 Gus Johnson
12/23 Bob Kurland
01/05 Rick Mount
01/12 Burdette Haldorson
01/13 Tom Gola
01/15 Bob Davies
01/28 Barney Sedran
01/29 John Schommer
02/03 Forrest De Bernardi
02/04 Neil Johnston
02/10 Cat Thompson
02/12 Bill Russell
02/22 Julius Erving
02/22 Van Arsdale twins
02/28 Chuck Hyatt
03/07 Andy Phillip
03/10 Austin Carr
03/12 Ace Gruenig
03/14 Wes Unseld
03/22 Ed Macauley

03/28 Rick Barry

03/29 Walt Frazier

3/30 Jerry Lucas

4/05 Dutch Dehnert

4/08 John Havlicek

4/08 Jimmy Walker

4/09 Paul Arizin

4/10 Stretch Murphy

4/12 Joe Lapchick

4/15 Walt Hazzard

4/16 Kareem Abdul-Jabbar

4/17 Geoff Petrie

4/17 Kevin Porter

4/18 Nate Archibald

4/22 Spencer Haywood

4/23 Gail Goodrich

4/25 Meadowlark Lemon

5/09 Calvin Murphy

5/11 Jack Twyman

5/19 Dolph Schayes

5/25 K. C. Jones

5/25 Bill Sharman

5/28 Jerry West

5/29 Richie Guerin

5/30 Bud Foster

5/31 Honey Russell

6/03 Billy Cunningham

BASKETBALL STARS, BORN SINCE 1950

12/04 Bernard King 1956

12/07 Larry Bird 1956

12/18 Bobby Jones
12/19 Kevin McHale
12/30 LeBron James
1/03 Cheryl Miller
1/05 Alex English
1/09 Muggsy Bogues
1/12 Dominique Wilkins
1/21 Hakeem Olajuwon
2/07 Juwan Howard
2/08 Alonzo Mourning
2/16 Mark Price
2/17 Michael Jordan 1963
2/20 Charles Barkley 1963
2/24 Tom Burleson
2/26 Rolando Blackman
2/27 James Worthy
2/28 Adrian Dantley
3/01 Chris Webber
3/01 Yolanda Griffith
3/04 Kevin Johnson
3/06 Shaquille O'Neal
3/14 Stephen Curry
3/20 Mookie Blaylock
3/23 Moses Malone
3/23 Jason Kidd
3/25 Sheryl Swoopes
3/26 John Stockton
3/26 Ann Meyers
4/14 Cynthia Cooper
4/25 Tim Duncan
4/27 George Gervin
4/30 Isiah Thomas

5/04 Dawn Staley
5/29 Carmelo Anthony

PLAYED BASKETBALL

2/08 James Dean
3/18 Queen Latifah
3/28 Ken Howard

IN BASKETBALL FILM

1/21 Robby Benson
1/30 Gene Hackman
5/17 Dennis Hopper

BALLET DANCERS AND CHOREOGRAPHERS

12/21 Alicia Alonso
12/21 Paloma Herrera
12/29 Gelsey Kirkland
1/10 Galina Ulanova
1/17 Moira Shearer
1/20 Ruth St. Denis
1/24 Maria Tallchief
1/25 Jeanne Brabants
1/31 Anna Pavlova
2/12 Lysette Darsonval
2/23 Rita Poelvoorde
3/03 Hanya Holm
3/10 Tamara Karsavina
3/10 Margaret Morris
3/11 Fanny Cerrito

3/19 Marlis Alt
3/28 Karen Kain
4/15 Marie Camargo
4/20 Nadia Potts
4/23 Marie Taglioni
4/25 Melissa Hayden
4/29 Renee Jeanmaire
5/10 Judith Jamison
5/11 Martha Graham
5/18 Margot Fonteyn
12/14 Ib Anderson
12/21 Andre Eglevsky
12/24 Anver Joffre
1/01 Maurice Bejart
1/02 Jose Ferran
1/05 Alvin Ailey
1/12 Kurt Jooss
1/12 Jose Limon
1/21 Igor Moiseyev
1/27 Mikhail Baryshnikov
1/27 Frank Augustyn
2/24 John Neumeier
3/09 Fernando Bujones
3/11 Marius Petipa
3/12 Vaslav Nijinsky
3/13 Igor Youskevitch
3/15 Yorg Lanner
3/17 Rudolf Nureyev
3/25 Salvatore Vigano
4/04 Antony Tudor
4/09 Robert Helpmann
4/16 Merce Cunningham
4/18 Gaetano Vestris

4/29 Jean-Georges Noverre
5/08 Michel Fokine

STUDIED BALLET

12/11 Donna Mills
2/15 Jane Seymour
3/25 Sarah Jessica Parker
4/24 Jill Ireland
5/31 Lea Thompson

MISC. MALE DANCERS

12/14 Dan Dailey
12/23 Jose Greco
12/30 Russ Tamblyn
1/10 Ray Bolger
2/14 Gregory Hines
2/18 John Travolta
2/28 Tommy Tune
3/24 Gene Nelson
4/02 Buddy Ebsen
4/04 Arthur Murray
4/05 David Winters
4/08 Michael Bennett
5/02 Vernon Castle
5/10 Fred Astaire
5/19 Bobby Burgess
5/25 Bill Robinson

MISC. FEMALE DANCERS

12/11 Rita Moreno
12/21 Clarissa Delmar
12/24 Carol Haney
1/13 Gwen Verdon
1/16 Debbie Allen
1/23 Chita Rivera
2/08 Steffi Duna
2/09 Carmen Miranda
2/16 Vera-Ellen
2/17 Zina Bethune
2/20 Sandy Duncan
3/06 Carmen De Lavallade
3/08 Cyd Charisse
4/01 Debbie Reynolds
4/07 Irene Castle
4/08 Betty Ford
4/12 Ann Miller
4/12 Sally Rand
4/21 Eleanor Whitney
4/24 Shirley MacLaine
4/26 Bambi Linn
4/28 Ann-Margret
5/25 Renee DeMarco
5/27 Isadora Duncan
6/03 Josephine Baker

RHYTHMICALLY CO-ORDINATED SWIMMERS

12/04 Mike Barrowman
12/05 Pablo Morales
1/06 Murray Rose

1/17	David Theile
1/20	John Nabor
1/24	Jim Montgomery
2/03	Felipe Munoz
2/04	John Devitt
2/06	Charles Hickcox
2/07	Buster Crabbe
2/10	Mark Spitz
2/11	Uwe Dassler
2/17	Rowdy Gaines
2/20	Steve Lundquist
3/03	Warren Kealoha
3/03	Dimitriy Volkov
3/08	David Wilkie
3/13	Rick Carey
3/14	P. van den Hoogenband
3/14	Tim McKee
3/20	Igor Poliansky
4/02	Brian Goodell
4/21	Alex Baumann
4/23	Martin Lopez-Zubero
4/30	Don Schollander
5/12	Gunnar Larsson
5/21	Vladimir Salnikov
5/24	Adrian Moorhouse
5/26	Anthony Ervin
5/27	Bruce Furniss
5/29	John Hencken
5/31	Domenico Fioravanti
6/02	Johnny Weissmuller
6/03	Tamas Darnyi

GRACEFUL DIVERS

12/29 Phil Boggs
12/31 Vicki Draves
1/29 Greg Louganis
2/08 Irina Kalinina
3/06 Elizabeth Becker
4/10 Pete DesJardins
4/24 David Boudia
5/12 Patricia McCormick

TOP WOMEN SWIMMERS

12/06 Eleanor Holm
12/19 Claudia Kolb
1/03 Chris von Saltza
1/11 Tracy Caulkins
1/11 Petra Schneider
1/11 Yang Wenyi
1/20 Martha Norelius
2/07 Kristen Otto
2/12 Carrie Steinseifer
2/17 Amy Van Dyken
2/24 Ute Geweniger
2/26 Hendrika Mastenbroek
2/26 Keena Rothhammer
2/27 Ethelda Bleibtrey
3/05 Judy Grinham
3/06 Ann Curtis
3/17 Katie Ledecky
4/05 Maya DiRado
4/06 Rica Reinisch
4/17 Nancy Hogshead

4/18 Heiki Friedrich
4/26 Donna de Varona
5/03 Katinka Hosszu
5/06 Brooke Bennett
5/10 Missy Franklin

DEFT, AGILE FENCERS

12/18 Dario Mangiarotti
12/31 Erna Bogen
2/21 Albert Axelrod
3/06 Cyrano de Bergerac
3/14 Fiorenzo Marini
3/16 Aladar Gerevich
3/19 Bill Hoskyns
4/07 Edoardo Mangiarotti
5/06 Ellen Muller-Preiss
5/17 Ilona Elek
5/18 Ildiko Sagi-Retjo

SKILLED JUDO ARTISTS

12/21 Michael Swain
1/02 Hitoshi Saito
1/03 Angelo Parisi
1/14 Jong Gil Pak
1/20 Isao Okano
2/16 Vitali Kuznetsov
3/25 Peter Seisenbacher
4/06 Anton Geesink
5/12 Shozo Fujii
6/01 Yashiro Yamashita

QUICK, MOBILE BOXERS

12/06 Jim Braddock
12/12 Henry Armstrong
12/13 Archie Moore
12/29 Jess Willard
1/02 Pernell Whitaker
1/04 Floyd Patterson
1/04 John Ruiz
1/10 George Foreman
1/10 Felix Trinidad
1/12 Joe Frazier
1/14 Ruben Olivares
1/16 Roy Jones Jr.
1/17 Muhammad Ali
1/18 Virgil Hill
1/29 John Tate
1/30 Bruce Seldon
1/31 Jersey Joe Walcott
2/03 Emile Griffith
2/04 Oscar De La Joya
2/09 Jackie Fields
2/11 Max Baer
2/22 Abe Attell
2/22 Gus Lesnevich
2/24 Floyd Mayweather Jr.
2/24 Jimmy Ellis
3/25 Laszlo Papp
3/26 Eder Jofre
3/29 Teofilo Stevenson
3/31 Jack Johnson
3/31 Tommy Ryan
4/02 Carmen Basilio

4/03 Bonecrusher Smith
4/04 Ernie Terrell
4/07 Buster Douglas
4/13 Jose Napoles
4/15 James F. Jeffries
4/18 Johnny Kilbane
4/19 Alexis Arguello
4/26 Nino Benvenuti
4/26 Eddie Eagan
4/27 Bob Foster
5/03 Sugar Ray Robinson
5/08 Sonny Liston
5/13 Joe Louis
5/15 Mysterious Billy Smith
5/17 Sugar Ray Leonard
5/23 Marvelous Marvin Hagler
5/25 Gene Tunney
5/26 Bob Fitzsimmons
5/29 Tony Zale

PLAYED A BOXER

12/04 Jeff Bridges
12/09 Kirk Douglas
12/11 Victor McLaglen
12/29 Jon Voight
1/08 Elvis Presley
1/11 Don "Red" Barry
1/17 James Earl Jones
1/23 Bob Steele
1/26 Paul Newman
2/17 Wayne Morris

2/18 Jack Palance
3/04 John Garfield
3/16 Erik Estrada
4/01 Wallace Beery
4/03 Marlon Brando
4/07 Russell Crowe
4/09 Dennis Quaid
4/17 William Holden
4/18 Eric Roberts
4/20 Ryan O'Neal
4/21 Anthony Quinn
4/29 Daniel Day-Lewis
5/21 Mr. T
5/31 Clint Eastwood
6/02 Stacy Keach

USED TO BOX

12/25 Rod Serling
2/01 Stuart Whitman
2/26 Jackie Gleason
3/01 Robert Conrad
4/21 Tony Danza
5/04 Randy Travis
5/09 Billy Joel

EUROPEAN HOCKEY STARS

2/01 Anatoliy Firssov
2/11 Maiorov twins
2/25 Andres Hedberg
4/03 Vitaliy Davidov

5/05 Aleksandr Ragulin
5/11 Ulf Nilsson

FIELD HOCKEY STARS

1/19 Dharam Singh
3/15 Ranganandhan Francis
3/25 Leslie Claudius
6/01 Abdul Rashid

QUICK, AGILE, DEXTEROUS HOCKEY STARS

12/04 Alex Delvecchio
12/11 Pierre Pilote
12/12 Teeder Kennedy
12/13 Bob Gainey
12/13 Sergei Federov
12/19 Doug Harvey
12/26 Norm Ullman
12/28 Ray Bourque
12/28 Terry Sawchuck
12/29 Nels Stewart
1/03 Bobby Hull
1/06 Dickie Moore
1/07 Babe Pratt
1/10 Frank Mahovlich
1/14 Babe Siebert
1/17 Jacques Plante
1/18 Mark Messier
1/22 Mike Bossy
1/22 Bill Durnan
1/22 Elmer Lach

1/22 Serge Savard
1/26 Wayne Gretzky
1/29 Dominik Hasek
2/14 Bernie Geoffrion
2/15 Jaromir Jagr
2/20 Phil Esposito
2/22 Sid Abel
2/28 Eric Lindros
2/28 Joe Malone
2/29 Henri Richard
3/01 Max Bentley
3/03 Brian Leetch
3/05 Milt Schmidt
3/20 Bobby Orr
3/22 Dave Keon
3/31 Gordie Howe
4/03 Bernie Parent
4/09 Ebbie Goodfellow
4/23 Tony Esposito
4/23 Reggie Leach
4/25 Vladislav Tretiak
5/06 Martin Brodeur
5/09 Steve Yzerman
5/12 John Bucyk
5/14 Gump Worsley
5/15 Turk Broda
5/18 Jari Kurri
5/20 Stan Mikita
6/01 Paul Coffey
6/02 Larry Robinson

ALPINE SKIERS

12/03 Franz Klammer
12/11 Stein Eriksen
12/14 Hanni Wenzel
12/19 Alberto Tomba
12/25 Ossi Reichert
1/04 Barbara Cochran
1/11 Anne Heggtveit
2/01 Madeleine Berthoud
2/04 Pirmin Zurbriggen
2/11 Gretchen Fraser
2/17 Heidi Biebl
2/17 Tommy Moe
2/21 Petra Kronberger
2/28 Gustavo Thoeni
3/08 Marie-Therese Nadig
3/18 Ingemar Stenmark
3/27 Annemarie Moser-Proll
3/30 Bill Johnson
4/03 Picabo Street
4/13 Billy Kidd
4/17 Heini Hemmi
4/19 Andrea Mead-Lawrence
5/04 Kathy Kreiner
5/10 Mahre twins
5/11 Nancy Greene

NORDIC SKIERS

12/14 Siiri Rantanen
12/29 Carola Anding
1/02 Aleksandr Tikhonov

1/04 Veikko Hakulinen
1/16 Martin Stokken
1/17 Toini Gustafsson
1/24 Frank Ullrich
2/01 Franco Nones
2/03 Oddbjorn Hagen
2/04 Magnar Solberg
2/06 Sixten Jernberg
2/10 Hallgeir Brenden
2/11 Alevtina Koltschina
2/15 Ole Ellefsaeter
2/24 Johan Grottumsbraaten
2/29 Raisa Smetanina
3/12 Gunde Svan
3/16 Oddvar Braa
3/27 Thomas Wassberg
4/18 Klas Lestander
4/19 Franz-Peter Rotsch
4/26 Martha Rockwell
4/29 Galina Kulakova
5/17 Lydia Wideman
5/21 King Gustavus I

ADEPT GOLFERS

12/05 Lanny Wadkins
12/09 Tom Kite
12/09 Orville Moody
12/21 Walter Hagen
12/27 Dave Marr
12/28 Hubert Green
12/30 Tiger Woods

1/06	Cary Middlecoff
1/06	Paul Azinger
1/11	Ben Crenshaw
1/20	Lionel Hebert
1/21	Jack Nicklaus
1/26	Henry Cotton
1/28	Nick Price
1/30	Payne Stewart
1/30	Curtis Strange
2/04	Byron Nelson
2/05	Jose M. Olazabal
2/10	Greg Norman
2/14	Jay Hebert
2/22	Vijay Singh
2/22	Tommy Aaron
2/25	Tony Lema
2/27	Gene Sarazen
3/02	Ian Woosnam
3/03	Julius Boros
3/09	Andy North
3/14	Bob Charles
3/14	Bob Goalby
3/17	Bobby Jones
3/19	Gay Brewer
3/31	Tommy Bolt
4/09	Seve Ballesteros
4/14	Robert De Vicenzo
4/14	Bobby Nichols
4/25	Jerry Barber
4/28	John Daly
4/28	Hal Sutton
4/29	Johnny Miller
5/01	Frank Beard

5/04 Bob Tway
5/04 Rory McIlroy
5/09 Harry Vardon
5/10 Jimmy Demaret
5/15 Ken Venturi
5/22 Horton Smith
5/23 David Graham
5/27 Sam Snead
6/02 Craig Stadler
6/03 Hale Irwin

TOP WOMEN GOLFERS

12/21 Karrie Webb
1/06 Nancy Lopez
1/29 Donna Caponi
2/03 Carol Mann
2/13 Patty Berg
2/14 Mickey Wright
2/16 Marlene Hagge
2/18 Judy Rankin
2/22 Amy Alcott
3/10 Sandra Palmer
3/16 Hollis Stacy
3/24 Pat Bradley
4/02 Ayako Okamoto
4/04 JoAnne Carner
5/04 Betsy Rawls
5/09 Betty Jameson

DEFT BOWLERS

12/23 Dick Weber
1/18 Guppy Troup
1/28 Wendy Macpherson
3/03 Johnny Petraglia
3/25 Mike Aulby
3/31 Andy Varipapa
4/10 Mark Roth
4/11 Bob Learn Jr.
4/21 Paul Geiger
4/27 Earl Anthony
5/19 Lisa Wagner
5/28 Randy Pedersen
6/01 Rick Steelsmith

SPORTING CELEBRITIES

1/09 Fernando Lamas (swimming)
1/23 Richard Dean Anderson (hockey)
1/24 Michael Ontkean (hockey)
2/20 Ivana Trump (skiing)
2/26 Jon Hall (swimming)
2/29 Dinah Shore (golf)
3/01 Alan Thicke (hockey)
3/10 Chuck Norris (karate)
3/17 Rob Lowe (hockey)
4/12 Vince Gill (golf)
4/13 Tony Dow (diving)
5/02 Bing Crosby (golf)
5/29 Bob Hope (golf)

ANALYZING OUR FINDINGS

We added up the number of athletes under each individual sign, within each maxisign. Here are the results of that computation:

Propellers		Stalwarts		Adjusters	
Scorpio	57	Pisces	65	Cancer	86
Sagittarius	58	Aries	77	Leo	99
Capricorn	80	Taurus	108	Virgo	111
Aquarius	73	Gemini	76	Libra	97
Pisces	68	Cancer	82	Scorpio	102

Notice that, in every case, the center sign – the one that defines the nature of the whole maxisign – is more heavily populated than the rest. We know of no logical explanation, other than an ASTROlogical one, as to why the totals turned out this way.

Now let us turn our attention to the type of physical activity of each maxisign, and what individual signs correspond to that activity. In the case of the Propellers, the legs are spotlighted because these athletes excel at running and jumping. Notice that Sagittarius, Capricorn and Aquarius– the signs that rule the legs – appear in the Propellers' column.

The Stalwarts primarily showcase upper-body strength. Therefore, we find in their column Aries, Taurus, Gemini and Cancer–the signs that rule the upper body. Gemini is said to rule the arms, while Taurus is ruler of the neck and, we suspect, the shoulders as well.

The Adjusters make frequent adjustments to maintain their balance, as in basketball, dancing, fencing, skiing, hockey, etc. The signs appearing in their column rule the middle of the body, where the center of gravity would be. One of these signs is Libra, the one most closely associated with grace and balance. Mere coincidences? Hmmmm. We think not.

Note that everything revealed in the last three paragraphs is based on Earth signs. If you use Sun signs instead, none of it would hold true. Once again, the Earth sign zodiac is vindicated!

Now before we leave the subject of athletes, we have one final order of business: What do we do with tennis players? There are two indispensable components of their game. They have to be able to run fast enough (Propellers) to get to the ball, and they have to be able to hit it hard enough (Stalwarts) so that their opponent can't reach it. So are they Propellers or Stalwarts? It turns out that they are both. Their period of greatest excellence lies between the Propeller dates and the Stalwart dates. We found that we could corral the greatest amount of tennis talent if we ran the six months from May 22 to November 22. Here is our list:

TOP TENNIS PLAYERS

5/22 Novak Djokovic
5/23 John Newcombe
6/01 Justine Henin
6/03 Rafael Nadal
6/06 Bjorn Borg
6/08 Kim Clijsters
6/08 Lindsay Davenport
6/13 Don Budge
6/14 Steffi Graf
6/17 Venus Williams
7/10 Arthur Ashe
7/10 Virginia Wade
7/12 Pete Sampras
7/16 Margaret Court
7/19 Ilie Nastase
7/31 Evonne Goolagong
8/06 Helen Jacobs

8/08 Roger Federer
8/09 Rod Laver
8/16 Tony Trabert
8/17 Guillermo Vilas
8/17 Jim Courier
8/22 Mats Wilander
8/23 Nancy Richey
8/25 Althea Gibson
08/27 Carlos Moya
08/30 Andy Roddick
09/02 Jimmy Connors
09/10 Gustavo Kuerten
09/13 Goran Ivanisevic
09/13 Rafael Osuna
09/15 Ashley Cooper
09/17 Maureen Connolly
09/24 Lottie Dod
09/26 Serena Williams
09/28 Alice Marble
09/30 Martina Hingis
10/02 Jana Novatna
10/03 Neale Fraser
10/06 Helen Wills Moody
10/11 Maria Bueno
10/15 Roscoe Tanner
10/17 Ann Haydon Jones
10/18 Martina Navratilova
10/18 Michael Stich
10/26 Richard Sears
11/02 Ken Rosewall
11/03 Roy Emerson
11/22 Billie Jean King
11/22 Boris Becker

PART SEVEN

FURTHER EVIDENCE OF ASTROLOGY AT WORK IN THE WORLD

HOW ASTRONOMY VERIFIES ASTROLOGY

Astrologers have known for ages that some planets are more alike than others, in their meanings. Let us review some of these similarities, and then we will show two ways in which astronomy verifies them.

Mercury and Saturn are alike. Each rules one earthy sign and one air sign. A person who is strong in these planets is logical, sensible, scientific and good with details. Saturn is exalted in an air sign, Libra, and Mercury is exalted in an earthy sign, Virgo.

Jupiter, Neptune and the Moon are alike. Jupiter and Neptune are both associated with Pisces. If these planets are accented, a person has a strong faith in the future, an active spiritual life, and is inclined to be generous and giving. The Moon is like Neptune in that both relate to the emotions, to water, to sympathy and to a vivid imagination. Since Jupiter is exalted in Cancer, that makes it like the Moon, ruler of Cancer. Both have an association with being overweight, it is claimed.

Mars, Pluto and the Sun are alike. All are considered masculine, forceful and dominant. Mars and Pluto are associated with the same signs, Aries and Scorpio. The Sun is exalted in Aries. A person strong in these bodies, if unchecked, can be arrogant and destructive.

Venus and Uranus are almost never linked together, but they should be. Both can be quite physical in their meaning–even violent. Venus can be "angry," vehement and zealous, much like Uranus. Both are associated with air signs, and both can indicate artistic talent, though for different arts.

Now let us consider the velocity of the planets through space. This is different from their apparent movement through the sky. The Moon zips through the zodiac faster than anything else because it is so much closer to the Earth. Yet in terms of actual velocity, the Moon is a slowpoke.

Now notice how the number <u>five</u> keeps recurring. Mercury is 4.9 times faster than Saturn. Venus is 5.2 times faster than Uranus. Mars is 5.2 times faster than Pluto. Neptune is 5.3 times faster than the Moon. Jupiter is 2.4 times faster than Neptune, which is about half of five. A coincidence? We think not.

Now let's look at where the perihelions of the planets are. (The perihelion is the place where a body is closest to the Sun.) Note the correct order of the signs: Jupiter in Aries and Neptune in Taurus; Mercury in Gemini and Saturn in Cancer; Venus in Leo and Uranus in Virgo; Pluto in Scorpio, Sun in Capricorn and Mars in Pisces. The Sun of course does not have a perihelion, so we used its perigee (where it's closest to the Earth). More coincidence? We think not.

Continuing our theme of perihelions being significant, we'll consider a study of racehorses we conducted. As racing fans know, there are certain vintage years when many top-quality horses are born. Since Jupiter is in a new sign each year, we can compare different crops of horses by noting the Jupiter sign of their birth.

The first step is to make a list of the best horses and rank them from one to fifty. Assign fifty points to the top-ranked horse, forty-nine to the second horse, forty-eight to the third horse, and so on down to one point for the number fifty horse. Then add up all the points for all the horses born under the same Jupiter sign. Here are the results of the study:

5	Sagittarius	104	Gemini
33	Capricorn	87	Cancer
129	Aquarius	6	Leo
170	Pisces	128	Virgo
315	<u>Aries</u>	31	Libra
147	Taurus	120	Scorpio

The perihelion of Jupiter is in Aries, and the aphelion (point farthest away from the Sun) is in Libra. Notice how, as Jupiter moves from Sagittarius to Aries, the talent of the horses keeps increasing. Then, as Jupiter moves from Aries to Leo, the quality keeps diminishing. The peak is in Aries, just as we would expect. Moreover, the total for Libra is low, just as we might expect. But why are the numbers for Virgo and Scorpio so high? Shouldn't they be almost as low as Libra? We have a theory about this:

Horses who are close together in age tend to run against one another. We believe the Virgos and Scorpios padded their resumes and enhanced their reputations at the expense of their hapless Libra opponents. Let us examine how this has happened throughout history:

1926: Crusader (Scorpio) beat American Flag (Libra).

1938: Seabiscuit (Virgo) whipped War Admiral (Libra).

1949: Capot (Libra) defeated Coaltown (Virgo).

This seems like an exception, but it's really not because Coaltown was not the best horse in his crop. Citation was, and no one thinks that Capot could have beaten Citation.

1961-62: Kelso (Virgo) outran Carry Back (Libra) whenever the weights were fair.

1973: Secretariat (Scorpio) bested Riva Ridge (Libra).

1986: Turkoman (Scorpio) beat Precisionist (Libra).

1998: Awesome Again (Scorpio) whipped Skip Away (Libra).

2009: Zenyatta (Virgo) defeated Gio Ponti (Libra).

We rest our case.

Now that we know that perihelions are significant, perhaps astrologers should rethink how they evaluate the strength of a planet. Sagittarius has always been considered a strong position for Jupiter, but obviously this is not the case for horses. Are we so sure it is the case for people? Also, Cancer has always been considered a weak placement for Saturn – yet that is the sign of his perihelion.

Before leaving the subject of horses, we thought it would be fun to include a list of fifty steeds whose birthdays we were able to find. These are not the same fifty as we used in our Jupiter study. You will notice that there are eleven fillies and mares on the submitted list, whereas the Jupiter study was for males only. We were afraid that, if we included females, we might be mixing apples and oranges, and thereby diluting the results. If our little sample of eleven females means anything, we made a wise decision because not one of them has Jupiter in Aries. There are three votes for Capricorn, two votes for Gemini, three votes for Scorpio, one vote for Leo, one vote for Taurus and one vote for Virgo. It is interesting that eleven females are crowded into just six of the twelve signs.

Notice that twenty-nine of the fifty horses were born during the one month between March 20 and April 19. We find that remarkable. We realize that March and April are common months for equine births in the northern hemisphere. Even so, we are very confident that the proportion of foals born during that one month is nowhere near fifty-eight percent! We suspect it is something like thirty percent, and we say that as someone who pays a lot of attention to birthdays. One thing we can guarantee: no one is going to quarrel with the quality of the horses on our list.

FIFTY NOTED THOROGHBREDS

1/29 Rachel Alexandra
2/02 American Pharoah
2/07 Sysonby
2/15 Seattle Slew
2/17 Spectacular Bid
2/21 Affirmed
2/27 Ribot 1952
3/01 Swaps 1952
3/07 Real Delight
3/09 John Henry
3/11 Devil Diver
3/21 Easy Goer
3/23 Alydar
3/23 Gallant Fox
3/24 Omaha
3/24 Count Fleet
3/25 Curlin
3/25 Sunday Silence
3/25 Dahlia
3/26 Assault

3/27 Native Dancer
3/29 Man o' War
3/30 Secretariat
3/31 Tom Fool
4/01 Zenyatta
4/02 Twilight Tear
4/02 Whirlaway
4/04 Kelso
4/04 Skip Away
4/06 Dr. Fager
4/06 Bold Ruler 1954
4/06 Round Table 1954
4/08 Lady's Secret
4/11 Arrogate
4/11 Citation
4/14 Nashua
4/14 Damascus
4/17 Ruffian
4/17 All Along
4/18 Cigar
4/26 Sir Barton
4/27 Busher
4/27 Personal Ensign
4/28 Buckpasser
4/30 Forego
5/01 Equipoise
5/01 Armed
5/02 War Admiral
5/22 Gallant Bloom
5/30 Exterminator

It is interesting to compare equine birth signs from the standpoint of sign element. As we did earlier, we will be using the Jupiter sign of each horse's birth. Here is what one can observe:

Fire signs present a sharp contrast in that Aries is the very best sign a horse can be born under, while Leo and Sagittarius are the worst. Outstanding Aries horses include Sir Barton, Twenty Grand, Equipoise, Count Fleet, Nashua, Swaps, Damascus, Dr Fager, Affirmed, Alydar and John Henry.

The most gifted Leo horse was Omaha, but he was actually the worst of the Triple Crown winners – the only one who was not considered Horse of the Year. The most talented Sagittarius horse was Counterpoint, a Horse of the Year good enough to defeat another Horse of the Year. Even so, he lost more races than he won and is never mentioned anymore.

The best weight carriers are the water signs. Cancer horses include Discovery, Whisk Broom II and Assault. Pisces steeds are Exterminator, Devil Diver and Seattle Slew. Scorpios include Forego and Hermis. All of these horses won under weight between 134 and 140 pounds.

The earthy signs are the most durable, which we will define as more than sixty trips to the post. Virgos in this category are Advance Guard, Seabiscuit, Kelso and T. V. Lark. Taurus horses include Armed and Stymie. Capricorns are Roseben and Sun Beau.

In contrast to the earthy signs, air signs appear to be fragile. Many of the Libras are so delicate that it would be wise not to race them at all as juveniles. Commando ran only three times beyond the age of two. Blue Peter and Hail to Reason could not race at all beyond that age. Another promising juvenile, Devil's Bag, did not pan out at all at three. His stablemate Swale became successful, but he died right after the Belmont. Maria's Mon ran only twice beyond age two and did not win. Unbridled's Song is believed to pass on unsoundness to his sons.

Aquarius horses are delicate too, but they achieve more than the Libras. The great Sysonby made fifteen starts, rather a small number for a horse of his calibre. Blue Larkspur averaged just five starts a year. The great Native Dancer managed only three starts between August 1953 and August 1954. He was upset in the Derby by newcomer Dark Star, who got injured in the Preakness and was promptly retired. Lucky Debonair was wonderful when healthy, which was seldom. Risen Star made just eleven starts. I'll

Have Another became the first Derby-Preakness winner since 1936 to be unable to compete in the Belmont due to injury.

We need not fret about the Gemini males because the females are so good! Noteworthy fillies and mares under this sign include Imp, Maskette, Prudery, Busher, Gallorette, Gallant Bloom, Ta Wee, Shuvee, Genuine Risk, Bold 'n Determined and Songbird. Following are the birth years coming up for each of the twelve Jupiter signs:

2015 Leo	2019 Sagittarius	2023 Aries
2016 Virgo	2020 Capricorn	2024 Taurus
2017 Libra	2021 Aquarius	2025 Gemini
2018 Scorpio	2022 Pisces	2026 Cancer

ASTROLOGY AND COMPATIBILITY

A very evil person stole our research on marital compatibility, so we will have to relate to you from memory what we found to be true. There are two main things that we learned. First, soft aspects are not always to be preferred over hard aspects. In comparing the charts of a husband and wife, count the conjunction and the opposition as soft aspects, along with trines and sextiles. Count squares, semisquares and sequisquares as hard aspects, same as usual. Some combinations of planets "prefer" to be in hard aspect, while others prefer to be in soft aspect.

The second thing we learned is that there are two distinct groups of planets, which we shall call Group A and Group B. Group A consists of the Sun, Moon, Mars, Jupiter and Neptune. Group B includes Mercury, Venus, Saturn, Uranus and Pluto. Two planets in Group A "like" to be in soft aspect, and two planets from Group B also like to be in soft aspect. However, one planet from Group A and one planet from Group B prefer to be in hard aspect.

A soft aspect is like a gentle pat on the head, and a hard aspect is like a more powerful blow to the head. The planets in Group A on the one hand, and the planets in Group B on the other hand, have a strong effect on one another, so that it takes only a gentle pat to awaken or energize the pair of planets. However, one planet from Group A and one planet from Group B have a weak effect on each other, so it takes a more powerful blow to activate the combination.

Notice that all the planets in Group A rule, or are otherwise associated with, fire and water signs. This is what they have in common that holds them together as a group. Similarly, all the planets in Group B, with the exception of Pluto, correspond to earthy and air signs. Why is Pluto a happy camper in Group B? It raises questions as to whether astrologers are on the right track in so closely associating Pluto with Scorpio or Aries. If we are to link Pluto with an earthy or air sign, we think perhaps Virgo would be the best bet. Rob and Amber Mariano have beautifully harmonious charts: December 25, 1975 and August 11, 1978.

The evidence of astrology at work in the world is all around us, but people don't notice it. Consider all of the following inter-chart conjunctions, for a quite astonishing example of "kindred spirits":

CHART A			**CHART B**		
Mars:	22	Virgo	Neptune:	29	Virgo
Ascendant:	27	Virgo	Ascendant	29	Virgo
Neptune:	24	Sagittarius	Sun	13	Sagittarius
Saturn:	6	Aquarius	Venus:	0	Aquarius
Moon:	12	Aries	Mars:	15	Aries
Venus:	31	Taurus	Uranus:	27	Taurus
Jupiter	25	Gemini	Jupiter:	16	Gemini
Sun:	15	Cancer	Moon:	10	Cancer
Mercury	2	Leo	Pluto:	5	Leo

Chart A is that of wife killer Henry VIII. Chart B belongs to Richard Speck, whose systematic murder of eight nurses might have struck a nostalgic chord in Henry. Here we have two men, born centuries apart, whose characters were so much alike! Moreover, Speck was born into a violent time–just one day before the bombing of Pearl Harbor! The violent transits of that time became his natal planets, with disastrous results.

DO RESEARCH ON YOUR OWN CHART

Not every chart "works" exactly the same way. The best way to learn how your chart works is to do research on it! Unfortunately, some people are too closed-minded to try something new, while others are too lazy to do the work. Everyone should keep diaries so that they know when things happened. You can write cryptically to protect your privacy. Most people respond to some of their planets more than others, probably because of the personality traits that we inherit.

Our research on our chart reveals that, when pondering a transit, you should not rush to see which house the natal planet "rules." Instead, consider the natural meaning of the natal planet. If it's Mercury, you might do better than usual academically, or you might have a brainstorm. If Jupiter and Neptune are favored, you might be inspired to write music. Auspicious aspects to Mars or Uranus (risk takers) can help you succeed at wagering. If you like to gamble, keep a record of when you won and when you lost.

The Ascendant is always important. Favorable transits to it will brighten your day, and ominous transits will spoil it. We found that, on our happiest days, fortunate aspects outnumbered adverse aspects by a score of 33 to 15. On days that were upsetting or disappointing, adverse aspects predominated by a ratio of three to one. Transits to your emotional Moon can make you cry. If the aspects are favorable, you might still cry, but it will be over something harmless like a sad movie.

Researching your chart can also help you to understand your innermost feelings. Keep a record of the birth dates of persons you have loved. Also plot the planets of the thespians you have found most appealing. When we did this, we found that the Moon is more passionate-romantic than Venus, and that Mars is more passionate-romantic than the Sun. This agrees with Dr. Carl Jung's research on married couples. Even so, many students continue to think that the Mars-Venus combination is the all-important one because that's what they were told to believe. When will they ever learn to think for themselves? There are no oracles out there. You have to find out for yourself what's true.

When you do research on your chart, it is very important that you calculate the semisquares and the sesquisquares. Many students do not do this, usually because either they don't know how or they mistakenly think it's not important. Computing these aspects is really quite simple.

Forty-five degrees equals one sign (thirty degrees) plus one-half a sign (fifteen degrees). If Mars is in five Leo, add the forty-five degrees, and it takes you to twenty Virgo. Once you have found that point, you know right away what the other three points are because they are spaced ninety degrees apart. The other semisquare is twenty Gemini, and the two sesquisquares are twenty Pisces and twenty Sagittarius.

If Venus is in twenty-two Taurus, it is easier to subtract one and a half signs, which takes you to seven Aries. You see? It's easy!

MISCELLANEOUS FINDINGS

A study of 151 persons thought to be aggressive, who were born between Nov. 7 and Dec. 6, produced the following totals:

Nov. 7-12	20
Nov. 13-18	22
Nov. 19-24	57
Nov. 25-30	24
Dec. 1-6	28

A study of seventy actors born in June produced these totals:

June 1-10	19
June 11-20	33
June 21-30	18

A decanate is one-third of a sign. June 11-20 is the Leo decanate of Sagittarius, and we all know that Leo enjoys acting.

In a study of forty-four people who committed suicide, thirty-one were in half of the zodiac, and only thirteen were in the other half! The signs who were inclined to kill themselves were Taurus, Scorpio, Gemini, Sagittarius, Cancer and Capricorn. The signs who were disinclined to take their own lives were Leo, Aquarius, Virgo, Pisces, Libra and Aries.

Of the six highest paid baseball players (1998-2005) four of them were Towers: Randy Johnson, Mike Piazza, Albert Belle and Bernie Williams. This calls to mind our Towers' list of high-achieving athletes.

The reader might recall that our Patterns data contained many more women than did any other sign. The reason for this could be that Juno, who was believed to hold dominion over women, was considered by the ancients to co-rule Aquarius.

Solar charts have your Sun sign in the First House, with other signs following in order counterclockwise. Many astrologers don't consider the solar chart unless the birth time is unknown. This is a mistake. We can state from personal experience that Uranus transiting through the solar houses is an infallible predictor of events. Uranus has now been in ten of our solar houses, and never once has it been wrong. Most of the events signaled by Uranus were favorable.

Not everyone realizes that a stationary transit has much power. (Planets don't really stop, but they appear to, as seen from the Earth, and this is called a station.) At the beginning of each year, check to see when the stations will occur, especially those of Jupiter, Saturn and Uranus. Those three planets largely control the ups and downs of your life. Neptune and Pluto are so slow that many people can adjust to their long-lasting effects. The rest of the planets are too fast to have more than a fleeting impact.

In addition to the methods in common use, there are two very good ways to measure the strength of planets in your chart. One simple way is to count the number of squares each planet has. The more squares, the stronger the planet is. Another reliable method is to figure the orb on each of your aspects and subtract that number from eight. This gives you the power of each aspect. Then add up the power points for all aspects involving a particular planet, and that gives you the total power of that planet. Don't forget to include your semisquares and sesquisquares!

In a study of sixteen people who proved in contests that they were outstanding horse-race handicappers, eleven were born in March, June, September and December. Just three were born in February, May, August and November – and only two were born in January, April, July and October.

In a study of forty-five famous fat people, we were surprised to discover how many of them had the Moon in Virgo. With no effort at all, we quickly found thirteen of them! There also were three whose Moons were in the last third of Leo, which is right next to Virgo.

PART EIGHT

FINAL THOUGHTS

TO SUMMARIZE

At the beginning of this book, we said we would seek to discover once and for all what, if anything, was true about signs of the zodiac. We have accomplished our purpose. We have found that the Earth sign zodiac is more authentic and more reliable than either tropical Sun signs or sidereal Sun signs. We have proved this in a number of different ways:

1. When we apply Earth signs to our data on occupations, the activities that men choose are in keeping with what each sign is supposed to "mean," according to astrological literature and tradition. The sidereal zodiac also works pretty well in this regard most of the time. The tropical zodiac does not work very well at all.
2. When we studied the effect of planetary aspects on vocational choice, we found a number of cases in which the key aspected planet was the same as the planet ruling the Earth sign that was key. Neither the sidereal nor the tropical zodiac offers this type of consistency and mutual verifiability.
3. When we studied physical appearance, we found that a person's Earth sign accurately describes how that person <u>ought</u> to look, given what is taught about the meanings of signs and their planetary rulers. The sidereal zodiac seems to work fairly well for most signs. The tropical zodiac does not work at all.
4. When we studied physical prowess, we found that the birth months in which athletes excel at a particular skill correspond to the Earth signs that rule the parts of the body that are utilized in that skill. This is not the case for either the sidereal zodiac or the tropical zodiac.

In addition to the evidence cited above, we believe that the Earth sign zodiac is more logical than either of the other two. Consider these points:

1. One reason that some people are skeptical of the sidereal zodiac is that they can't fathom how constellations, so many millions of miles away from us, could have any bearing on anything that happens here on Earth. Yet the Earth sign zodiac is based on something – the changing speed of the Earth–that is happening not millions of miles away, but right under our feet.
2. In the tropical zodiac, Aries always starts on the first day of spring in the northern heliosphere – even though Australians are experiencing the first day of autumn then. If Aries is all about spring and Libra is all about autumn, you'd think that the signs ought to be reversed in the southern hemisphere. Yet we don't know of a single astrologer who does this. The Earth sign zodiac faces no such dilemma. The speed of the Earth on a given day is the same all over the globe.

Skeptics might argue that a zodiac based on the changing speed of the Earth couldn't work because we are never aware of the Earth's motion – but it doesn't have to be a conscious awareness. When you ride on a jet plane, you might be traveling 500 miles an hour, but you can't feel that. If the weather is good, your flight will be very smooth. Some passengers even sleep on planes. Yet air travel can still affect us. Some persons become airsick, and many people experience jet lag. If 500 miles per hour can matter, why not the Earth's speed of 66,000 miles a hour?

A fresh look at the twelve signs is sorely needed. People have a choice to make. They can continue to embrace and affirm the great bulk of astrological traditions, just by adopting a zodiac that verifies and vindicates those traditions. Or, they can continue to cling to a discredited zodiac that does not support what they themselves say they believe.

A fresh look at the planets also is urgently needed. Most of what is written about them is approximately correct, but often the most salient characteristics are the least emphasized. Moreover, the scope of what the planets "mean" is broader than what has been assumed in the past. Instead of cluttering a chart with a plethora of new celestial bodies about whom little is really known, we need to get back to basics and examine the old planets more objectively.

Students, you will decide what the future of astrology will be. It will be up to you to steer a sensible, practical course. Do research instead of blindly accepting whatever you are told to believe. Let's all work together to make the twenty-first century a *thinking* century. Be curious. Be observant. Be pioneers!

Printed in the United States
By Bookmasters